1 8 4 8

THE MAKIN

1848

THE MAKING OF

VINTAGE BOOKS
A Division of Random House
New York

A REVOLUTION

Georges Duveau

Translated from the French by Anne Carter
Introduction by George Rudé

Oh! Quand viendra la belle!
Voilà des mille et des cent ans
Que Jean Guêtré t'appelle
République des Paysans!

PIERRE DUPONT

Contents

Introduction / George Rudé   **ix**

February Lightning   *3*

🖺 The First Day   *5*
The Banquet of the Twelfth Arrondissement   *9*
The Gérard Plan   *20*

🖺 The Second Day   *24*

🖺 The Third Day   *33*
The Abdication: The King Leaves Paris   *38*
Regency or Republic?   *44*
The Republic   *50*

🚩 The Lyrical Illusion   53

    The Miracle of '48   60

    The Tasks of the New Government   63

    The Sixteenth and Seventeenth of March   81

    The Sixteenth of April   87

    The Twentieth of April   93

    The Twenty-third of April   95

    The Constituent National Assembly   98

    The Assembly at Work   102

🚩 "The Soldiers of Despair"   105

    The Executive Commission   108

    The New Government   111

    The Fifteenth of May   115

    The Feast of Concord   125

    Reaction   126

    Louis Bonaparte   128

    The Dissolution of the National Workshops   132

    The June Days   133

    The Real Victor in June   156

🚩 The Barricades   161

🚩 The Men of the Provisional Government   182

🚩 The Ideologies of 1848   203

    BIOGRAPHICAL DICTIONARY   231

    BIBLIOGRAPHY   242

    INDEX   245

Introduction

The year 1848 was, in France as in several other European countries, a "year of revolution." There, as elsewhere, the monarchy was overthrown and the republic proclaimed, and a new liberal constitution was enacted by the nation's representatives. But in France, perhaps more than elsewhere, the revolution was deeply marked by the impact of the streets and workers' clubs and took the form of a protracted social drama, in which the players appear in the guise not only of political leaders but of contending social classes struggling for control of the state, or simply to find a place in the sun.

This social aspect of the revolution has been stressed in different ways by all the more reputable observers and historians of the event, and is as much a feature of Marx's *Class Struggles in France* and *The Eighteenth Brumaire* as it is of Tocqueville's *Recollections* and Charles Seignobos's account in Lavisse's *Histoire de France*.[1]

And now we must add a fourth name to this distinguished group of writers: that of Georges Duveau, whose *1848* was published posthumously, in 1965, in Paris. Duveau's work has its own particular features, sharply distinguishing it from that of his predecessors. It is not a methodical history like Seignobos's, it is not a political-historical treatise like Marx's *Class Struggles*, and naturally it lacks the peculiar qualities of an eyewitness account like that of Tocqueville. It is, rather, an impressionistic reconstruction, built up of vivid episodes and colorful portrayals, shot through with shrewd insights and arresting observations, lacking the sustained analysis of Marx and the balanced narrative of Seignobos, yet presenting a more vivid picture of the conflicts and combatants of 1848, and of the actual *mechanics* of the revolution, than any other work.

A kaleidoscopic treatment such as this naturally creates its problems. The reader is plunged without warning into the midst of the dramatic events of February 22, the day before popular demonstration turned into revolution. The central characters in the events that follow—Lamartine, Ledru-Rollin, Louis Blanc, and the rest—are paraded without any formal introduction: this only comes in the last two chapters of the book. And to the student who is used to a more conventional exposition, it may appear strange that he must turn to the three closing chapters for "background"

---

[1] Karl Marx, *Class Struggles in France* (1848–50) (London, Lawrence & Wishart, 1942); *The Eighteenth Brumaire of Louis Bonaparte* (Moscow, Foreign Languages Publishing House, 1948); *The Recollections of Alexis de Tocqueville* (New York, Meridian Books, 1959); Charles Seignobos, *La Révolution de 1848—Le Second Empire* (1848–1859), Vol. VI of Ernest Lavisse, ed., *Histoire de la France contemporaine depuis la Révolution jusqu'à la paix de 1919* (Paris, Hachette, 1921). Quotations from Marx and Tocqueville are from the foregoing English-language editions.

material that he might have expected to find at the begi
ning: the tradition of the barricades, for example, and t
sources of the political and social ideas of the men of 18.

What, then, was the background—or more properly, what
were the causes—of the February Revolution? Briefly, they
may be summarized (and here there is a fair consensus among
the writers) somewhat as follows: a widespread national
discontent with the policies of Guizot; a demand for parliamentary reform, voiced by a variety of opposition groups;
the revolutionary tradition of 1789 and 1830; the government's obstinate refusal to countenance reform; the growth
of Paris; the economic crisis of 1847; and the particular
grievances of the urban workers. While each of these factors
receives some sort of attention from every serious observer or
historian of the event, the priority or emphasis given to each
has naturally varied with the writer. Marx alone makes a precise social analysis of all the parties involved, while stressing
the importance of a dual conflict of classes: that of the
nation at large against the monarchy of Louis Philippe,
which he terms a "Joint Stock Company for the exploitation
of France's national wealth"; and a growing conflict between capital and labor, exacerbated by the economic crisis
of 1846–1847. Tocqueville, while by no means sharing
Marx's hopes for a future proletarian revolution, saw the
situation in broadly similar terms. As a member of the
Chamber of Deputies, he had frequently denounced the Ministry for isolating itself from the nation, and in January 1848,
he had warned his fellow deputies that "the working classes
. . . are gradually forming opinions and ideas which are
destined not only to upset this or that law, ministry, or even
form of government, but society itself."

Duveau presents similar ideas in a somewhat different
form: in his work such an analysis of cause and effect is

implicit rather than methodically spelled out. In his final chapter, however, he emphasizes the particular importance he ascribes to the ideological preparation of these "men of 1848." This derived from a rich variety of sources: Saint-Simon's and Fourier's blueprints for a planned industrial society; Étienne Cabet's primitive-communist dream of an Icarian Utopia; Pierre Leroux's writings on socialism; Louis Blanc's *L'Organisation du travail*; Proudhon's *Qu'est-ce que la propriété?*; Buonarroti's *La Conspiration pour l'Égalité*; and the revolutionary tradition of 1789 and 1793.[2] Here he distinguishes between two main currents. On the one hand, there were the romantic or utopian systems of Saint-Simon, Fourier, Cabet, and Leroux, which offered a final solution to the ills of developing capitalist society. On the other hand, there was the popular tradition of the Rights of Man that had been proclaimed and fought for, though never fully realized, in the first great revolution. Half a century later, though society had changed, it was still possible to see the "feudal" landowner of 1789 in the guise of the banker or industrialist of 1848 and it seemed highly relevant to attempt to exorcise him with the slogans of the *sans-culottes* of the First Republic—all the more so as Buonarroti's *Conspiration pour l'Égalité*, first published in 1828, had revived the memory of Robespierre and the Mountain and attuned their policies to the needs of a later, more industrial generation. Thus Duveau, following Marx, sees the men, ideas, and institutions of 1848 in a certain sense as a replica, if not a parody, of those of 1789; yet he shows more charity and sympathy for the "utopian" thinkers and actors of the later revolution. For to Marx, during those years "only the ghost of the old revolution walked about, from Marrast, the Re-

---

[2] *The Communist Manifesto* by Marx and Engels, first published at the end of 1847, appeared too late to have any influence on the events of 1848.

publican in kid gloves, who disguised himself as the old Bailly, down to the adventurer who hides his commonplace repulsive features under the iron death mask of Napoleon." [3]

For Duveau there are two main groups of actors in this drama—the people of Paris (and he limits his canvas rather too rigidly to the capital), and the politicians and journalists who spoke in the Assembly, presided over the clubs, harangued their followers from the balcony of the Hôtel de Ville, or edited the rival opposition newspapers, La Réforme and Le National. The former are vividly represented in the persons of his three symbolic Paris tradesmen: the bonnetier (hosier) of the faubourg Saint-Denis, the ébéniste (cabinet-maker) of the faubourg Saint-Antoine, and the mécanicien (mechanic) of the new industrial suburb of La Chapelle. The characters are well chosen, for these three not only have typical and distinctive trades, but have been reared in different traditions, and each has his own particular attitude toward the revolution. The bonnetier, like the ébéniste, belongs to an old city craft and lives in a faubourg that were already in evidence in the earlier revolution. He is the most conservative, and probably the most prosperous, of the three. He reads the more moderate of the opposition newspapers, Le National or Le Siècle; he demands the vote that has been denied him under the July Monarchy; he wants France to be free and strong and to recapture some of the past glory she knew under the great Napoleon; but he has a deep respect for ordered progress and a consequent horror of social disturbance. The ébéniste, on the other hand, who hails from the old revolutionary faubourg of Saint-Antoine, cherishes the tradition of 1789 and 1793. He reads the more radical of

[3] Bailly was the first mayor of Revolutionary Paris, a moderate of 1789. Napoleon is Louis Napoleon Bonaparte, a nephew of the first Napoleon, who was elected president of the Second Republic in December 1848 and declared emperor as Napoleon III in December 1852.

the opposition newspapers, *La Réforme*, which includes among its editors both Ledru-Rollin, the radical democrat, and Louis Blanc, the socialist. He reveres the memory of Maximilien Robespierre, but it is a Robespierre seen through the eyes of Étienne Cabet, author of *Le Voyage en Icarie* and a proponent of nonviolence. There is therefore a certain ambivalence in his attitude toward reform and revolution, and he will be inclined to wait upon events. Of a different mettle altogether is the third of the three, the *mécanicien* of La Chapelle, which has recently emerged as a center of railroad workshops to the north of Paris and is already known as a socialist stronghold. Unlike the others, he is not bound to one of the traditional crafts; he is a new man, an early product of an industrial revolution that has hardly yet begun to transform the social structure and appearance of the capital. He has belonged to secret conspiratorial societies like the "Society of the Seasons" and the "Rights of Man"; he has already been schooled in the warfare of the streets, having followed Auguste Blanqui, the club leader and archexponent of direct action, in the historic but abortive workers' revolt of May 1839.

Such men were naturally inclined to follow different paths, and it needed the universality of the crisis of February 1848 to bring them together in concerted action. For in February, not only the *mécanicien* but the *bonnetier* and the *ébéniste* were all equally determined that by one means or another Guizot, the protector of the rich and "corrupt" and the declared enemy of reform, must go; and Duveau writes: "It augured ill for the monarchy that on the morning of February 22 the hosier, the cabinetmaker, and the mechanic should meet before Durand's wineshop as brothers in a common cause." Yet the alliance was short-lived. As the bloodless February Days, which toppled first Guizot and then the monarchy in a spirit of almost gay abandon, passed through the stresses of the great workers' demonstrations of March, April, and May to the bloodshed and violence of the June insurrection, the three drifted apart. Already in April, the *bonnetier*, as a member of the National Guard, was counterdemonstrating against the workers of the clubs —the "Communists"—at the Hôtel de Ville; by May, he was a convinced supporter of the "party of order"; in June, he helped General Cavaignac suppress the workers' revolt; and he rallied to Louis Napoleon, soon to become President of the Republic, shortly after. The *ébéniste*, as might be expected, followed a more uncertain course. Though basically hostile to violent action, he was swept into the June Days by the force of circumstance and loyalty to his leader, Étienne Cabet; but soon after, disillusioned with the Republic that had broken the promises made in February, he passively accepted the "strong" government of Napoleon. The *mécanicien* alone took up arms in June with a clear purpose and a strong conviction; and though refusing to commit himself to Ledru-Rollin's ill-starred coup of June 1849,[4] he was among the small number of Parisians that actively resisted Louis Napoleon's seizure of power in the coup d'état of December 1851.

But it is natural that it should have been the leaders rather than the followers in these events that have mainly commanded the attention of historians; and Duveau, though there is little system in his treatment, certainly does not neglect them. Who were they? First, there were Adolphe Thiers and Odilon Barrot, the leaders of the dynastic (Orleanist)

[4] This was the demonstration of June 13, 1849, called by Ledru-Rollin to protest against the dispatch of French troops to overthrow the Roman Republic and restore Pope Pius IX. It failed to win the support of the faubourgs and industrial districts and was quickly dispersed by General Changarnier, who commanded the Paris garrison and National Guard.

opposition in the Chamber. Like their opponent Guizot, they were overtaken by events and were momentarily swept aside by the February Revolution. Yet it was they who, in campaigning for a measure of parliamentary reform, had launched the banquets which, through a chain reaction of largely unforeseen events, led to the overthrow of Guizot and Louis Philippe's abdication. Each in turn was invited by the king, before he fled, to form a ministry in succession to the fallen Guizot, but neither was able to find support. A regency was then attempted in the name of the king's grandson, the Count of Paris; but this also failed, and a provisional government, largely hand-picked in the offices of *Le National* and *La Réforme*, was acclaimed by the people, who had invaded the Chamber, and solemnly proclaimed from the balcony of the Hôtel de Ville. This government, which held office between February 24 and May 4, was neatly balanced between the main groups and parties that had made the February Revolution; for, as Marx put it, "it could not be anything but a compromise between the different classes which together had overthrown the July throne." After a series of reshuffles, offstage bargains, and popular demonstrations, the list that eventually emerged bore the names of eleven men: six republican moderates, initially selected by *Le National*: Arago, Marie, Garnier-Pagès, Crémieux (all four opposition deputies), Dupont de l'Eure, and Armand Marrast; one liberal republican, Lamartine, attached to no party but also sponsored by *Le National*; two radical republicans, Ledru-Rollin and Ferdinand Flocon, both editors of *La Réforme*; and two socialists added to the list by popular demand, Louis Blanc and the metalworker Albert.

Some of these men—Lamartine, Ledru-Rollin, and Louis Blanc—had already established national reputations; others were party nominees, rewarded for their services as lawyers, journalists, or opposition politicians, but were little known to the wider public. Dupont de l'Eure, for example, who was now appointed a figurehead prime minister, was a relic of the past, an octogenarian who had been a deputy to the revolutionary Council of Five Hundred back in 1795. Arago, now Minister of the Navy, was an astronomer and a member of the Institute, who had championed the popular cause in a celebrated trial in 1840. Garnier-Pagès, a former stock-broker who now took the post of Mayor of Paris and later became Minister of Finance, owed his appointment more to the memory of a famous brother than to any particular merit of his own. Marie, Minister of Public Works, and Crémieux, Keeper of the Seals, were lawyers who had won a reputation as defenders of republicans brought to trial under Guizot. Marrast (Marx's "Republican in kid gloves") was the editor in chief of *Le National* and, having soon succeeded Garnier-Pagès as Mayor of Paris, would later become President of the Constituent Assembly. Albert (alias Alexandre Martin), the only worker in the government, was a veteran of the secret societies, who had acted as liaison officer between the Paris and Lyons workers in the riots of the eighteen-thirties and played a leading part in Blanqui's "Society of the Seasons." His inclusion was not much to the liking of the moderates of *Le National*; and that paper (purposely, so Duveau tells us) omitted his name from the first published list of ministers.

With the exception of Marrast and Marie, none of these men played a particularly prominent or distinguished part in the events that followed. To say the least, their reputations and activities were eclipsed by those of their more illustrious colleagues, Lamartine, Ledru-Rollin, and Louis Blanc. Blanc had emerged as the most influential socialist theorist of the day with his publication in 1839 of a pamphlet, *L'Organisa-tion du travail*, in which he proposed to reorganize industry along cooperative lines by the establishment of a network of "social workshops," to be financed by the state and where "the principle of association will be substituted for that of competition." He was one of the founders of the radical *La Réforme*, and through its columns he popularized his ideas on industrial cooperation and "the right to work." These ideas and this slogan played an important part in the February Revolution, and the Provisional Government, prodded by Blanc from within and by workers' demonstrations from without, hastily decreed the ten-hour day and "the right to work," set up "national" (though not *social*) workshops to absorb the unemployed, and appointed Blanc the chairman of a commission at the Luxembourg Palace, composed of workers and employers and empowered to draft wage agree-ments and labor codes for every industry and trade. It proved to be a short-lived experiment.

Ledru-Rollin, who took the important post of Minister of the Interior, was also an editor of *La Réforme*; but unlike Blanc, he was not a socialist and his support lay not so much in the workers' clubs as among the shopkeepers and craftsmen of the faubourgs, as symbolized by Duveau in the person of his *ébéniste*. He was a radical democrat and repub-lican of long standing, who had won popularity by his power-ful oratory, his vigorous defense of Guizot's victims, his or-ganization of "reform" banquets, and his championship of universal suffrage and social reforms. As Minister of the In-terior in the Provisional Government, he put considerable pressure on the prefects in the *départements* (though with only moderate success) to ensure the return of convinced republicans to the Constituent Assembly of 1848. In the Assembly, where the socialists formed only a small minority, he became the main spokesman for the left, which, in imitation of its forebears of 1792, called itself The Mountain.

But the outstanding figure of February 1848 was Alphonse de Lamartine, who, though appointed Minister for Foreign Affairs, was head of the government in all but name. Already in the eighteen-twenties, he had won an international reputation as France's leading romantic poet; though attached to no particular political group, he had sat for many years in the Chamber as an opposition deputy; and his *Histoire des Girondins*, published in 1847, evoked nostalgic memories of the political battles of 1793. In the February crisis, as Duveau's account so eloquently shows, he was the only man who commanded sufficient authority to harmonize and balance the rival claims of the various parties, and he played a decisive part in manipulating the rejection of the Regency, the appointment of a broadly based interim government, and the proclamation of the Republic. Marx wrote of his role at this time: "This was actually no real interest, no definite class; this was the February Revolution itself, the common uprising with its illusions, its poetry, its imagined content, and its phrases."

Yet most of these leaders (and certainly these three) proved in the event to be dismal failures. Louis Blanc was returned as a deputy to the Constituent Assembly with 120,-000 votes; but, for lack of a strong supporting socialist group, his influence in it was negligible. Ten days after the Assembly met, it was invaded by the workers in a new popular *journée*. The retaliatory measures that followed included the disbanding of the Luxembourg Commission; and five weeks later, the *ateliers nationaux* (a parody though they were of Blanc's idea of "social workshops") were closed down as being politically dangerous and a wasteful drain on public funds. The result was the June insurrection, in which Blanc played no part; but, strongly suspected of complicity, he left France and sought refuge in England. Ledru-Rollin had a longer lease of political life. After his election to the Constituent Assembly, he appeared to the moderates as "the genius of evil" (Tocqueville's phrase) for the part he had played in the electoral campaign; but on Lamartine's insistence, he became a member of the Executive Council that replaced the Provisional Government. He fell from office in June, but staged a sensational comeback in June 1849, when, returned with two million votes, he became the leader of an invigorated Mountain, now the largest group in the Assembly. But he tried to force the pace by staging an anti-government demonstration in June. The faubourgs refused to respond ("In June 1848," wrote Tocqueville, "the army had no leaders; in June 1849, the leaders had no army"); the rising was crushed in a matter of hours, and Ledru-Rollin followed Blanc to London.

Lamartine's eclipse was even more sensational. When the Constituent Assembly met in May, his republican moderates held five hundred seats in a Chamber of nine hundred and Lamartine, who had been elected with two million votes, was still the hero of the hour. According to Tocqueville, he "was now at the climax of his fame; to all those whom the Revolution had injured or alarmed, that is, the great majority of the nation, he appeared in the light of a savior." His authority was great enough to enable him to impose Ledru-Rollin as a fellow minister on a decidedly reluctant Assembly. Yet, as the tension between bourgeois and workers increased in May and came to a bloody clash in June, the time for fine phrases and political tightrope walking was past, radicals and moderates went into opposing camps, and Lamartine's influence suffered a rapid decline. In June, General Cavaignac was given dictatorial powers to crush the workers' revolt and sweep up the mess that followed; and in the presidential elections in December, Lamartine, making a final bid to recover his popularity, was crushingly defeated by Louis Napoleon, receiving 17,000 votes against the victor's 5,500,000.

Such having been their experience and their fate, it is natural that these ill-starred "men of 1848" should have been roughly treated by historians. Marx described them collectively as "republican duffers" for whom universal suffrage appeared a "a miraculous magic wand" which, they fondly hoped, would in itself assure them of a popular majority. Tocqueville thought that there had been "more wicked revolutionaries than those of 1848"; but he doubted (and here again he almost echoes Marx) "if there were ever any more stupid: they neither knew how to make use of universal suffrage nor how to do without it; they trusted themselves to the nation, and at the same time they did all that was most likely to set the nation against them." As an aristocrat of the *ancien régime*, he is appalled by the vulgarity of the Montagnard deputies, the new parliamentarians of 1848, the followers of Ledru-Rollin and Louis Blanc: "They spoke a lingo which was not, properly speaking, the French of either the ignorant or the cultivated classes, but which partook of the defects of both, for it abounded in coarse words and ambitious phrases. . . . It was evident that these people belonged neither to the tavern nor to the drawing room." A similar aristocratic prejudice exudes from his description of Auguste Blanqui, the club leader, who had "the appearance of a moldy corpse" and "seemed to have passed his life in a sewer and to have just left it"; while Blanc, when carried into the Assembly by his supporters on May 15, reminded him of "a snake having its tail pinched." Marc Caussidière, a radical democrat who had been made Prefect of Police in Paris, was "a mass of shapeless matter, in which worked a mind sufficiently subtle to know how to make the most of his coarseness and ignorance." For Ledru-Rollin he has a certain affection mingled with contempt. He discounts the moderates' picture of him as "the bloody image of the Terror," and sees in him "nothing more than a very sensual and sanguine heavy fellow, quite without principles and almost without brains, possessing no real courage of mind or heart, and even free from malice, for he naturally wished well to all the world, and was quite incapable of cutting the throat of any one of his adversaries except, perhaps, for the sake of historical reminiscences, or to accommodate his friends."

Tocqueville's picture of Lamartine is far more shattering. He allows him personal courage, a lively imagination, a commanding presence, and a gift for oratory; but precious little else. "I do not know that I have ever met [he wrote] . . . a mind so void of any thought of the public welfare as his. I have seen a crowd of men disturbing the country in order to raise themselves: that is an everyday perversity; but he is the only one who seemed always ready to turn the world upside down in order to divert himself. Neither have I ever known a mind less sincere, nor one that had a more thorough contempt for the truth. When I say he despised it, I am wrong: he did not honor it enough to heed it in any way whatever. When speaking or writing, he spoke the truth or lied, without caring which he did, occupied only with the effect he wished to produce at the moment."

Following Tocqueville (Marx gives few character sketches of 1848 other than that of Louis Napoleon), later writers have generally presented Ledru-Rollin as a good-natured but somewhat boneheaded demagogue, and Lamartine as a sort of reincarnated Girondin of 1793, romantic, vain, insincere, unused to practical affairs, and self-consciously playing a role in a historical drama. In contrast to most, Duveau is inclined to be sympathetic, even indulgent, toward the men of 1848. These are exceptions: Crémieux, for example, who only broke with Louis Philippe at the last moment to become one of the despised number of *Républicains du lendemain*; and Flocon, another turncoat, who drifted from the republican left into the moderate camp of *Le National* and became a minister under Cavaignac in June. He finds little to admire in men like Marie and Garnier-Pagès, who soon found themselves in the "party of order"; but he has a kind word for Marrast who, though sharing their political views, was rejected by the electors in 1849 and died in poverty three years later. He has of course a great deal more to say about Lamartine, Ledru-Rollin, and Blanc. Blanc was a natural target for contemporary quip, as he was minute and frail and had a shrill, displeasing voice, and the odium and ridicule inspired by the "national workshops," though they were only a pale replica of what he had intended, naturally fastened on him rather than on Marie who had organized them. To offset this unflattering image, Duveau points to his intelligence, his realism in tackling contemporary social problems, and his courage in facing attacks from both left and right in the stormy session of May 15. Of greater interest is his suggestion that Blanc's *Organisation du travail* was only utopian in the sense that it was years ahead of its time and was ill-suited to the romantic atmosphere of 1848. Blanc's practical realism and forthright style of address were naturally eclipsed, he argues, by Lamartine's poetic imagery, feeling for historical precedent, and romantic phrases, which were better attuned to the demands (if not to the needs) of their contemporaries. In fact, Duveau concludes with the paradox that Blanc was rejected not because the solutions he put forward were deficient, but for having "stated the problems of his time so clearly."

Ledru-Rollin, like Lamartine, had a style and a presence that were better calculated to evoke a response in 1848 than Blanc's. In some respects, he is the Danton of 1848 (Tocqueville suggests that Blanc aspired to be its Robespierre): large, coarse, jovial, approachable, a *bon viveur*, and possessed of a powerful set of lungs. Duveau sees in him something of a "ham" actor and of a political charlatan, overeager to win popular applause. Yet he was no careerist and showed a certain reluctance to accept ministerial office. It was only Lamartine's insistence that made him agree to join the Executive Council in May; and a year later, when he commanded a powerful party in the Assembly, he jeopardized his whole political career by staging an insurrection without adequate support. Duveau concludes that his main weakness was to have wrongly calculated the means at his disposal in both 1848 and 1849. "In 1848 he tended to overestimate his strength in the Assembly and to underestimate it in the streets. Conversely, in 1849 he underestimated his backing in parliament, while supposing that he had at his command in the faubourgs of Paris a force that he no longer possessed."

To Duveau, as to his predecessors, Lamartine appears a far more complex figure. He repeats Balzac's quip that he was "a fire raiser turned fireman" and adds that, as a poet, he deliberately played with catastrophe while, as a conservative by nature, he hastened, having done so, to piece together the society "he had helped to destroy." He echoes, too, Tocqueville's strictures on his theatrical postures, his high-sounding but empty phrases, and his egocentric concern to assure himself of a place in history. He also shows him, once the chips were down, to have been no match first for

Cavaignac and later for Louis Napoleon. Nevertheless, he writes: "I would still put in a good word for Lamartine." The plea is not entirely convincing, though he instances the historic role he played in February; for then "in his confused way he was aware that the vitality of the monarchy was exhausted, and that France could write a page in history which would transform the human condition."

So much for the actors. What of the events themselves? We have noted that Marx and Tocqueville, though their sympathies were diametrically opposed, saw the origins of the February Revolution in broadly similar terms. To both, too, its outbreak, though it was expected sooner or later, came as "a surprise attack" (to quote Marx's phrase), "a taking of the old society unawares, as the people proclaimed this unexpected stroke as a deed of world importance." To Marx, the socialist revolutionary, the essential outcome of February was the creation of a "bourgeois republic," though one "surrounded [as the consequence of the workers' intervention] by social institutions"; for "the Paris proletariat was still incapable of going beyond the bourgeois republic otherwise than in idea, in imagination." Tocqueville, however, as a champion of property and "order," saw it somewhat differently. To him it seemed that the revolution had been "made entirely outside the bourgeoisie and against it"; and he added that "socialism will always remain the essential characteristic and most redoubtable remembrance of the Revolution of February."

To Marx, then, the real victors were the middle classes, who had only made concessions to the workers under pressure from the streets. To Tocqueville the potential if not the actual victors were the workers themselves, who, if not forcibly held in check, would proceed to put their socialist theories into practice, destroy property, and bring society down in ruins. From these premises spring the particular emphasis and interpretation that each author gives to the June events that followed four months later. To both, June was the almost inevitable result of February; to both it marked a new stage in the struggle of opposing classes; and both saw the outcome as one deliberately provoked by the possessing classes and the moderates in the Constituent Assembly. Yet whereas Tocqueville believed that the workers' defeat in June merely restored the social status quo, to Marx it appeared both to consolidate the bourgeois republic, provisionally sketched out in February, and to mark a turning point in the relations between capital and labor. Returning to Paris after the April elections, Tocqueville

> saw society cut into two: those who possessed nothing united in a common greed; those who possessed something united in a common terror. There were no bonds, no sympathy between these two great sections: everywhere the idea of an inevitable and immediate struggle seemed at hand. I had always believed that it was useless to hope to settle the movement of the Revolution of February peacefully and gradually, and that it could only be stopped suddenly by a great battle in the streets of Paris. I had said this immediately after the 24th of February; and what I saw now persuaded me that this battle was not only inevitable but imminent, and that it would be well to seize the first opportunity to deliver it [emphasis mine].

And when it came, as Tocqueville had foreseen, it was something entirely new in France's recent history: "It did not aim at changing the form of government, but at altering the order of society. It was . . . a struggle of class against class, a sort of Servile War."

Marx, for his part, wrote that "the Paris proletariat was *forced* into the June insurrection. In this lay its doom." He agreed with Tocqueville that "a second battle was necessary in order to sever the republic from the socialist concessions" and that "the bourgeoisie had to refute the demands of the proletariat with arms in its hands." Holding the posts of control in the government and the Assembly, they were able to choose the ground and the moment most favorable to themselves. First, they provoked the workers to challenge the Assembly's authority (nominally over Poland) on May 15, which was followed by the arrest of their leaders and the withdrawal of many of the concessions made in February. Finally, they closed the National Workshops, thus throwing over 100,000 workers on the streets. "The workers were left no choice, they had to starve or fight"; and there followed "the first great battle . . . between the two classes that split modern society." The workers' defeat (as inevitable to Marx as it was to Tocqueville) established the bourgeois republic on firm foundations; but it did more than this; for from now on revolution (and not only in France) meant "overthrow of bourgeois society, whereas, before February, it had meant overthrow of the form of state."

Duveau has no direct answer to these questions; for primarily, these are not the problems that concern him. His presentation is pictorial and dramatic, hardly ever analytical. He is always at great pains to show *how* such and such an episode took place, *how* this or that actor in the piece behaved, but he rarely stops to answer *why*. In his book, the narrative unfolds in a series of consecutive sketches, broadly based on the chronology of events, richly interspersed with asides and nostalgic evocations, but never interrupted by the sort of methodical analysis that we have noted in the work of Marx and Tocqueville. With an eye for drama and sharp contrast, he depicts the almost inexorable progression of events from the gay, carefree days of February to the "black," bitter, bloody days of June. But precisely because he has a sense of the dramatic, he forbears to present his characters in too sharp a relief as heroes and villains. Patently, his deeper sympathies lie with the Paris *ouvriers*—the hosier, the cabinetmaker, and the mechanic—rather than with the leaders and rulers on either side. But as he parades his leading actors, he shows a certain sympathy for each in turn: even the rejected and discredited Louis Philippe has a touch of dignity as he forlornly quits the stage. Such a treatment has both its virtues and its vices. On the one hand, it makes for lively reading and brings the characters to life; but on the other, it tends to obscure the *politics* of the issues over which men fought.

Yet though it is never methodically spelled out, there emerges from Duveau's work a coherent interpretation of the February and June events, which, in some respects but not in others, accords with that presented by other means by Marx and Tocqueville. In February, he depicts at every stage the same broad alliance between the politicians and the streets—between *ouvriers* and *bourgeoisie*—to overthrow the Guizot Ministry. But he adds significant observations of his own. In the persons of his *bonnetier*, *ébéniste*, and *mécanicien* he underlines the divided loyalties among the *ouvriers* themselves, temporarily patched up by a common interest in February but ready to assert themselves afresh once the crisis was past. Moreover, he doubts if the shots fired in the boulevard des Capucines on the twenty-third had in themselves the dramatic consequences which have generally been ascribed to them. It was not this incident alone, he argues, that transformed riot into revolution; for once Louis Philippe had succumbed to the pressure of the streets by dismissing Guizot, far from saving the monarchy he had shown that he had lost control of events and was unfit to rule.

To Duveau, as to Marx and Tocqueville, the prime part in the February events was played by the Paris workers and tradesmen, the "heroes of the barricades"; but equally, he saw that once the monarchy had fallen there could have been no consolidation of the victory without the energetic part played by Lamartine and the editors of *La Réforme* and *Le National*. So the victory and its fruits were not the monopoly of one partner alone, but were common to the two. He goes even further and suggests, like Michelet in his famous picture of 1789, that not only the classes actively engaged but the nation as a whole had won a victory; and he cites as evidence the rallying to the revolution and the Provisional Government of the Church, the army, the old bureaucracy, and even many of the former royalist politicians. To Marx this harmony of classes, jointly though briefly proclaimed by all the victors, was a fraud, an illusion that blurred the realities of the struggle of classes. Tocqueville, while expressing himself in different terms, essentially shared his view. To Duveau, however, the harmony, though short-lived, was genuine enough and its reality was expressed in the early legislation adopted by the Provisional Government. But why, then, did this harmony break down in the months that followed and why did bourgeois and working-class Paris, allies in February, jump at each others' throats in June? Partly because the alliance had within itself the seed of its own disintegration; partly through stupidity (the forty-five-centime tax,[5] the organization of the National

[5] Levied to finance the social measures enacted in February, the tax was seen

Workshops); partly through the ill-will of some (men like Crémieux and Garnier-Pagès) and the weakness of others (above all, the miscalculations of Lamartine); and partly through the refusal of the provinces to follow Paris, which became evident once the Constituent Assembly met in May. So, by the middle of that month, the workers of Paris were already out on a a limb, isolated from the Assembly and from the provinces; their leaders were arrested, and the bloody clash in June, fought once more as a battle of class against class, entailed their inevitable defeat.

In Duveau's presentation, the victory of Louis Napoleon in December is just an epilogue to a drama that ends with the June events. There is no speculation, as with Marx and, to a lesser degree, with Tocqueville, about the ultimate significance of this drama. There is no suggestion, as with Tocqueville, of June's being a kind of naturally ordained retribution for the workers' presumption in February or of its being, as with Marx, an international landmark in the history of class relations. He treats it rather as the final act in a drama that could not have ended otherwise, for "does it not seem that there is a curse on the workers who, in their moments of trusting emotional abandon, are defeated by clever manipulation and who in their hour of violence are defeated by the very fear they have inspired?" Yet in another passage, he strikes a more hopeful, less fatalistic note; and as the cabinetmaker of the faubourg Saint-Antoine and the mechanic of La Chapelle return to their workshops after the June defeat, they catch the rhythm of a new popular refrain:

> *La République dure encore*
> *Malgré nos fautes et nos crimes;*

by the peasants as a device for throwing on them the burden of keeping the Paris workers in luxury and idleness.

Comme un reflet de pourpre et d'or
Son nom rayonne sur nos cimes.[6]

GEORGE RUDÉ

[6] "The Republic still lives on despite our errors and our crimes; its name shines over the hilltops, emblazoned in letters of red and gold." [But *see* translator's version.]

1848

February Lightning

There were a great many Days in 1848. The period beginning with the February barricades and ending with those in June which culminated in the dictatorship of General Cavaignac is weighed down by the pressure of events. A list of these dates in the order in which they occurred provides an essential framework to a study of the period.

The February Days: the twenty-second, twenty-third, and twenty-fourth of February witnessed the first murmurs of the revolt which was to sweep away the monarchy. Next came the Days of March 16–17. On the sixteenth, there were stirrings of discontent from the reactionary companies of the National Guard, which were succeeded on the following day by enthusiastic counterdemonstrations from the people. On the sixteenth of April there were further popular demonstrations, more violent than those of March 17 but carefully controlled and kept in check by the moderate faction of the

Provisional Government. Responsibility for the Day of April 16 can be laid ultimately at the door of the reactionary party. On May 15 the people invaded the Palais Bourbon. The government swiftly quelled the disorder, but a deep gulf had been formed between the Assembly and the people of Paris. Then came the June Days, four of bloodshed, from the twenty-third to the twenty-sixth of June, in which the bourgeois and workers of Paris were at one another's throats. The black Days of June had a much deeper social significance than the February Days and raised modern labor problems which have yet to be resolved today. Despite all appearances, it is easy to see that the wheels of the bourgeois monarchy were not running smoothly and the events of February were not entirely unpredictable. Nevertheless there was a quality of wanton mischief and good humor about February, whereas the seal of tragedy was set on June. In February Gavroche innocently thumbed his nose at the monarchy, and the throne, which he had thought more solid, crumbled. By June Gavroche was often short of bread at home; he was bitter and no longer smiling. A fierce excitement drove him back into the streets, but there was no hope shining on the horizon; the Republic was already dead in his heart.

The First Day

On Tuesday, February 22, 1848, Paris awoke uneasily. A tremor ran through the city, like that before the curtain rises in a theater. People were prepared for a comedy, packed with incident: as yet there was no thought of tragedy. It was a dull day with a leaden sky, sudden gusts of wind, and cold drizzling rain. But neither the mechanic of La Chapelle nor the hosier of the faubourg Saint-Denis nor the cabinet-maker of the faubourg Saint-Antoine wasted any time studying the barometer. In any case bad weather was traditional for Paris uprisings, with only one exception to prove the rule: September 4, 1870, which witnessed the birth of the Third Republic, was a bright, golden Sunday. But on the morning of February 22, tradesmen and workers alike had only one thought in their heads. A great reformist banquet was to be held near the Champs-Élysées on a site belonging to a certain Père Nitot, and the question was whether the police and the members of the opposition would come into open conflict at last. The Parisians, who reveled in such public demonstrations, were growing impatient at the constant postponement of the clash. "The old wizard," as Louis Philippe was still mercilessly caricatured, was far from popular, but he was known to have a good many tricks up his sleeve and no one doubted that he would manage to hold on to his throne once again. Guizot, more detested than the king, appeared by contrast the more vulnerable: both the hosier and the cabinetmaker were united in their belief that it was high time he was sent packing. During the eight years since he came to power he had governed with an arrogance that was all the more insufferable because his high-handedness at home was accompanied by an abject servility toward foreign powers. Gavroche was impatient for the sound of a few bullets whistling through the streets.

A bas Guizot! Vive la Réforme! So many dreams hung on that one word "reform." An article published in the November 1840 issue of a particularly interesting little magazine, *La Ruche populaire*, based on Saint-Simonian principles and written by the typographer Jean Baptiste Coutant, who twenty years later was to play an important part in the political life of the Second Empire, demonstrates very clearly that in the eyes of a good many workers electoral reform and social freedom went hand in hand. "If we are constantly talking [sic] about electoral reform, this is because we regard it as highly important. By this means, when we, the workers, have elected our own deputies, we shall succeed in obtaining the organization of labor, not simply from the petty viewpoint of a single branch of industry but by guaranteeing the same rewards to all branches of industry, any infringement of which will be an offense. The establishment of equal pay and equal working hours for workers of all nations will be a great step forward in the direction of equality and fraternity. . . . The electoral laws we are demanding are simply a means: our end is the *elimination of poverty and free education* for all."

In the autumn of 1843 an oddly assorted group, including men belonging to the radical left like Ledru-Rollin and Flocon, and socialists such as Louis Blanc, decided to found a newspaper that would be more violently democratic than *Le National*, which had become too much the expression of a particular clique and caste. The name of the new paper, which swiftly found a wide readership among the educated workers, was *La Réforme*.

A great many royalists also looked forward to more or less sweeping changes in the electoral system. Legitimists like La Rochejaquelein and the Abbé de Genoude, editor of the *Gazette de France*, came out in favor of universal suffrage. Orleanists, who occupied a position in the center of the legislative body and attacked Guizot bitterly while still proclaiming their loyalty to the king—these formed what was then called the "dynastic opposition"—clamored for the "enrolling of talent": they wanted an electorate composed of men of education as well as wealth. On March 8, 1847, Duvergier de Hauranne, an impressive parliamentary figure but a man of no great intelligence, put before the house a tentative but clear-cut program of reform providing for the creation of 200,000 new voters. This proposal received passionate support from the lawyer Odilon Barrot, a pompous, overbearing, but undeniably authoritative speaker. The next step was a series of reformist banquets held all over France at which radicals and royalists rubbed shoulders, not without a certain amount of friction.

Faced with the urgent need to enlarge the electoral body, to throttle the impending crisis, plug the gap in the na-

tional budget, breathe new life into Poland and Italy, and
snatch the mastery of the seas from perfidious Albion, the
best the French could do was indulge in demonstrations of
brotherly love and gape at the china-blue eyes of Odilon
Barrot or the simian features of Crémieux. Endless toasts
were drunk "to electoral and parliamentary reform," "to the
July Revolution," "to the press," "to the opposition deputies," "to improving the lot of the working classes," and
many more of the same kind. As a general rule these banquets were attended only by the middle classes, but crowded
in behind the guests, serious, respectful, and attentive, stood
the workers who genuinely believed that all this overflow of
eloquence would hasten their enfranchisement. Among
the many banquets which took place that autumn of 1847,
that at Rouen stands out because it holds a special place in
French literary history and because it contributed to the
creation of the doctrine of art for art's sake. Flaubert, who
was present among the eighteen hundred guests, was so infuriated by the tone of the banquet and the depths of sen-
tentiousness to which it descended that his retreat to his
ivory tower was largely motivated by the desire to escape
from men like Crémieux and Odilon Barrot. Presiding over
the banquet at Rouen was the lawyer Sénard, who eighteen
years later defended Flaubert in court on charges of of-
fending religion and public decency by writing *Madame
Bovary*. Sénard was flanked in the chair by twenty or so
deputies, including Odilon Barrot, Duvergier de Hauranne,
and Crémieux. Flaubert vented his spleen in a letter to
Louise Colet: "Such taste! Such cuisine! Such wine! And
such talk! Nothing has done more to give me an absolute
contempt for success, considering the price at which it is
bought. In the midst of phrases like 'the helm of State, the
abyss into which we are rushing, the honor of the flag, the

shadow of our banners, and the brotherhood of man,' and other confections of the same order, I remained cold and sickened with disgust. The finest works of the greatest authors would never have earned a quarter of this applause. Musset's Frank (*La Coupe et le Lèvres*) would never arouse such acclamations as rose from all parts of the room at the righteous bellowing of M. Odilon Barrot and the maunderings of M. Crémieux over the state of our finances After nine hours spent before cold turkey and sucking pig in the company of my locksmith, who continually slapped me on the back at all the best parts, I came home frozen to the marrow." But if Flaubert maintained a cool and critical head in the face of this display of eloquence, the workers in the Rouen textile industry, like their Parisian colleagues, were fired with enthusiasm.

⚑ *The Banquet of the Twelfth* Arrondissement

Early in 1848, the twelfth *arrondissement* of Paris decided to hold a reformist banquet. The city at that time was divided into twelve districts, or *arrondissements*, of which the twelfth, centered on the Panthéon and including the *quartiers* of Saint-Victor and Saint-Marcel, was a hive of revolution whose inhabitants were more inclined to follow the advice of Louis Blanc and *La Réforme* than to listen to Odilon Barrot. Consequently the dynastic opposition took fright at the proposals put forward by the citizens of the twelfth. The original plan was democratic in the extreme: the banquet was to be held on a Sunday, in the rue Pascal in the district of the faubourg Saint-Marcel, and tickets

were to cost three francs each. A second plan was put forward, altering the time, the date, and the cost of admission
to the banquet in order to exclude the more unruly, proletarian element: it would take place on a weekday in the
Quartier des Champs-Élysées and at six francs a head the
cost of admission would be comparatively high. Thereupon
Odilon Barrot and a deputy from Indre-et-Loire named
Taschereau—who was later to acquire a certain degree of
notoriety as a result of the publication of some documents
damaging to Blanqui—set out to look for a suitable site for
the banquet in the vicinity of Chaillot. Taschereau reached
an understanding with a gentleman by the name of Nitot
who owned a convenient site in the rue du Chemin-de-
Versailles.[1] (During the Second Republic this came to be
known as the rue du Banquet.) On the morning of February 20 Nitot agreed to let the champions of reform have the
use of his land for ten days for the sum of one thousand
francs. The demonstration was growing in scope and the
government began to show signs of alarm. After lengthy
negotiations between Guizot and the opposition in which
the intermediaries were two deputies named Vitet and
Morny, it was decided that the banquet should be banned
in theory but that members of the opposition might attend,
that a discreet watch should be kept on the entrance to the
banquet, that the proceedings should be as brief as possible
and any trouble dealt with as an ordinary disturbance of the
peace. These negotiations were unofficial, but even so they
were soon divulged by the press, and there was a good deal
of comment at the expense of the "reformists" who attacked
Guizot's government but promptly succumbed to the slightest display of firmness on the part of the minister. On Feb-

---

[1] To be precise, Nitot himself was only the tenant of the site. The actual
owner was a farmer from Passy named Pierre Leroy.

ruary 17, Doudan wrote to Prince Albert de Broglie: "The moderate leaders ask only one boon of the government, and that is to obtain a court order as to whether or not God and the Law will allow M. Ledru-Rollin to get up on the table after dinner and say more or less openly that the king is a fool, parliament a collection of scoundrels, and Danton the kindest and most humane of legislators. Now the government is perfectly willing to take them to court but not at all anxious to give them a chance to commit the necessary offense: they insist, and promise to make the offense as small as possible, just a little twopenny offense, enough to get them taken into custody! This party's ambition to get itself arrested is indeed an admirable thing, and one, I believe, which is shared by most of those who have no higher vocation, among the gentle eulogists of 1793 and 1794. For all the fundamental equality of men, it is not everyone who can aspire to the high court."

Matters were therefore as good as settled when Armand Marrast, who had succeeded Carrel as editor of *Le National*, unwittingly set light to the fuse. After a vague exchange of views with Odilon Barrot, Marrast took it upon himself to arrange the details of the demonstration which was due to take place on Tuesday, February 22. The demonstrators were to assemble at Durand's house—that is, at the opposition headquarters—in the Place de la Madeleine, and from there proceed in a body to the Champs-Élysées. Marrast laid down the order of the procession to the last detail, and appointed exactly how and where the officers and men of the various legions of the National Guard were to take up their positions. This program was published on the morning of February 21 in *Le National*, in *La Réforme*, and in *La Démocratie pacifique* (run by Victor Considérant as the mouthpiece of the Fourierist faction of the republican party). Even today, the arrogance and assurance of Marrast's article seems amazing. The opposition addresses the government on equal terms. It makes its own arrangements for keeping order in the streets. "The banquet," wrote Thureau-Dangin, "disappeared behind the huge procession of the people which was to accompany the deputies from the Place de la Madeleine to the rue du Chemin-de-Versailles. . . . Worded in the form of a police order or, more accurately, of a plan of battle, this program disposes of the public thoroughfares. The National Guards are urged to take part in the procession, in uniform if not actually armed, and to parade in legions with their officers at their head."

At ten o'clock on the morning of the twenty-first, ministers who had read their papers were gathering angrily in the cabinet room. The Minister of the Interior, Duchâtel, was particularly incensed. Duchâtel was a strange and highly characteristic figure, a mixture of conceit, flabbiness, and timidity. On one occasion, when Louis Philippe made some coarse joke concerning an affair between Guizot and the Princess of Lieven, Count Duchâtel was seen to blush. He affected an artistic disorder in his dress and his hair was often disheveled, but his features were plump and commonplace. Duchâtel had inherited a large fortune from his father, who had been registrar general under the Empire. He was fond of rare and precious things and had a mania for collecting them, but he was without real taste. He was a Malthusian and had begun his career by writing a *Traité de la charité dans ses rapports avec l'économie sociale*, which was chiefly remarkable for his suggestion that the poor should endeavor to reproduce themselves as little as possible. (This work earned him a place in the Institute.) There was one more noteworthy figure in the Council of Ministers. This was Hébert, the Keeper of the Seals. Where Duchâtel was portly, Hébert was sly-looking, and he had a trick of sucking his pen between his teeth which accentuated his resemblance to a large, ill-tempered cat. Hébert, like Duchâtel, demanded strong measures to counteract the provocative behavior of the opposition. All public meetings were to be suspended forthwith. (It is easy to imagine the outcry that would be raised by such a prohibition. With a stroke of his pen, the minister does away with the right of assembly, and so forth.) With the assistance of Vitet and Morny—for throughout the February Days these two members did not spare themselves in their zeal for the Orleanist cause—the Prefect of Police issued a proclamation which intimated in no uncertain terms that Marrast's manifesto "setting up another government beside the legal government of the country" was totally unacceptable.

In the afternoon the Chamber of Deputies met to discuss the statutes of the Bank of Bordeaux. (Parliamentary assemblies are not always remarkable for a sense of occasion.) The atmosphere was tense. Duchâtel pressed Barrot hard: "Only yesterday I was still prepared to allow matters to reach a stage where some offense could be proved and legal proceedings instituted. . . . But the manifesto which has appeared this morning amounts to the proclamation of an illegal government, speaking directly to the people, calling out the National Guard on its own authority and encouraging unlawful assemblies."

Barrot heard the lecture out sheepishly. He was the more shamefaced in that, as a monarchist, in his heart of hearts he agreed with Duchâtel. "I endorse the intention of the manifesto," he said, "but I take no responsibility for the form it has taken." That evening most of the leaders of the opposition met at Barrot's house in the rue de la Ferme-des-Mathurins. Barrot accepted his defeat in the Chamber and announced, to the considerable annoyance of his wife, that he would not attend the banquet. Odilon Barrot had married the daughter of a Carbonarist hero, Labbey de Pompières, and Madame Barrot was in the habit of enlarging on her husband's preference for words rather than deeds to anyone willing to listen to her. Yet in advocating retreat Odilon Barrot had, in a curious way, the hearty support of Armand Marrast, who admitted that he had underestimated the effect of his manifesto and that he too had decided not to attend the banquet. In all there were eighty votes cast in favor of abstention. Only seventeen diehards at the meeting insisted that the demonstration should take place whatever happened. They were strengthened by the support of Lamartine. It was nearly midnight when Lamartine heard what had passed at Barrot's house: he was told that the commissioners were discontinuing preparations for the banquet and that the Committee was abandoning the demonstration. "Very well," was Lamartine's reply, "but if the Place de la Concorde is empty and all the deputies shrink from their duty, I shall go to the banquet alone, taking my shadow behind me." Later, when he was out of the story and had taken his place among the front rank of those defeated in 1848, Lamartine reproached himself bitterly for these words, and judged himself harshly for his action on February 21. Personally, I find Lamartine the rash more sympathetic than Lamartine repentant. He is undoubtedly open to criticism. There was an element of narcissism, of the dilettante in his character, and the fondness for bringing emotional analysis into political and social life, which in Barrès was strained and somewhat unnatural, was intense and spontaneous in Lamartine. Responsibility lies heavy on his shoulders but he was, to some extent, a two-sided figure. As a poet, he contributed to the disaster, but then later on, being at heart a conservative, he tried to piece together the fragments of a society he had helped to destroy. In the spring of 1848, Balzac cruelly described Lamartine as "a fire raiser turned fireman." I would add to this that on the evening of February 21 Lamartine had a very clear idea of the crossroads lying in wait for him on the path of revolution. He knew that the people, though fundamentally law-abiding, loved nothing better than a little excitement and loved inspiring fear in others. Lamartine also knew that once frightened, the middle classes rapidly became ferocious, and that by leaving the way clear for revolution it was possible to serve the forces of reaction and hold back the course of history.

Even so, in spite of all that has been said, I would still put in a good word for Lamartine, for in his confused way he was aware that the vitality of the monarchy was exhausted and that France could write a page in history which would transform the human condition. Later, when the curtain had fallen on the bitter tragedy, a tragedy which was perhaps more bitter for Lamartine than for France itself, Lamartine was ashamed of the part he had played in shaping fate. I have been at some pains to stress Lamartine's awareness in order to refute the many historians who have portrayed him as a kind of simpleton trusting blindly in divine inspiration. But there are times when any man, however intelligent, must unwillingly come face to face with fate. On the night of February 21, Lamartine experienced one of those times when the human clay is moved by something beyond itself.

Lamartine and Odilon Barrot were not the only ones who were wakeful on the night of the twenty-first. Conferences were in progress in the offices of Le *Siècle* and La *Réforme*. Those present at the *Siècle* listened enthralled to the words of the paper's editor in chief, Perrée. Perrée was an officer of the National Guard and a member of the headquarters staff of his legion.[2] He observed that there was considerable ill-feeling against Guizot in the National Guard and that he did not believe there was any power strong enough to overcome this animosity by reason. He ended his speech with the words: "Tomorrow they will sound the retreat. Let us take up our arms and join my legion, and cry with our comrades, 'Down with the System! Long live Reform!'"

In the offices of the *Réforme* in the faubourg Montmartre, the atmosphere was more strained than in those of the *Siècle*. The men here anticipated trouble; they even thought the Republic's hour might have come, but they dared not believe it. They agreed to make their way individually, "with their hands in their pockets," to the Place de la Madeleine, and observe what happened. If the battle had really begun, then they would use it to the full to bring about the downfall of the monarchy.

The atmosphere at court that evening was relaxed. At the Tuileries—or as it was then called, the Château—Louis Philippe was rallying the old Marshal Gérard and the Prefect of Police, Delessert, because they still seemed anxious. Sallandrouze, a deputy who had made a huge fortune from the manufacture of Aubusson carpets, begged the king's ear for a moment in order to discuss the political situation. Sallandrouze was a supporter of Guizot, but he was anxious for a compromise and had tabled an amendment to this effect. Louis Philippe affected ignorance of what the wretched Sallandrouze was doing in the Chamber and asked

[2] The Parisian National Guard was made up of twelve legions each composed of citizens from one of the twelve *arrondissements*. The number of each legion corresponded to that of the district from which it was recruited, thus providing a simple guide to the social composition of each legion during the 1848 crisis. Other legions were formed among the outlying districts. Raspail, in 1848, was colonel of the third suburban legion (Sceaux and district).

him blandly how his carpets were selling. The deputy withdrew, mortified in the extreme. Toward midnight, the news came through that Odilon Barrot and his friends had abandoned the banquet. There was general delight, verging on jubilation, The queen, Marie Amélie, was radiant and even Louis Philippe permitted himself some skips of joy as he approached Duchâtel, who was being showered with compliments on all sides.

Paris went to bed, a little breathless but on the whole calm. The silence of the night was only disturbed by unusual sounds in the vicinity of Chaillot. No one had thought to tell the workmen detailed to put up the tents for the banquet that the demonstration had been canceled and they worked on by torchlight, hammering and setting up trestles far into the night.

When our little hosier of the faubourg Saint-Denis opened his copy of the *National* on the morning of February 22 and read that the banquet would not take place, and that Odilon Barrot and Armand Marrast were preaching peace, he lost his temper, blasphemed against his gods, and wondered whether the members of the opposition were not as great cowards as the "pritchardists" and the "satisfaits." Only the day before he had been moved to the heart by Armand Marrast's appeal, and his bosom had swelled with pride at the thought of dressing up in his National Guard uniform and marching behind Odilon Barrot and Duvergier de Hauranne. And now, today, there was nothing to do but sell a few yards of cloth and stand quietly behind his counter looking out at the rain. Politicians like Marrast imagine people to be much more pliable than they are; they find it difficult to realize that the hatred which they pour, drop by drop, into the hearts of peaceful citizens can have such serious effects. At that moment the hosier hated Guizot with all his heart. For weeks the whole fabric of his daily life had been conditioned by anger, indignation, and a fierce, tumultuous patriotism. He devoured the *National* with his coffee every morning, and especially the reports of the trial taking place in Toulouse. What was that monster Brother Léotade up to now? What new tricks had the clerical party thought up to pervert the course of justice? In the evening, he went to the Théâtre Historique to see Alexandre Dumas's play *Le Chevalier de Maison-Rouge.* In the play he could hear the song of the Girondins, *Mourir pour la patrie,* encored again and again to wild applause. Insensibly, the hosier was moving closer to the cabinetmaker of the faubourg Saint-Antoine and the mechanic of La Chapelle. It was a temporary and, one might almost say, accidental rapprochement, and it is this which makes the tragedy of 1848. The hosier, the cabinetmaker, and the mechanic were all three different types of men. The first read the *National* and the *Siècle,* looked forward to political changes, and wanted to live in a greater, more glorious France, but was afraid of any kind of social upheaval. The cabinetmaker read the *Réforme* and genuinely believed, in a confused way, in revolution. Robespierre was his god, but a god about whom he knew very little, who had demanded bloody holocausts indeed, but who was nevertheless revered by Cabet. The communist leader, Étienne Cabet, was an extremely mild, peaceable man who had attracted the attention of the public by two works, a four-volume history of the French Revolution—this book, written at top speed, was a lengthy apologia for Robespierre calculated to touch the hearts of the workers—and *Le Voyage en Icarie.* Icaria is an ideal city and until it can be built on earth, Cabet is content to describe it. There is nothing particularly unusual about the contrast between the utopian idyll of Icaria and the guillotine of 1793. The men who set up the guillotine and fed the Reign of Terror in the eighteenth century were sentimentalists at heart, with Virgilian leanings toward the beauties of nature. Even so, it is still true that Cabet's book is full of contradictions, and that these contradictions were echoed in the opinions of the cabinetmaker. The mechanic of La Chapelle had more first-hand experience than the cabinetmaker: he had belonged to the secret societies, he had seen street fighting before with his comrades of the "Seasons" or the "Rights of Man," and had already dabbled in revolution, and he was not afraid of violence. It augured ill for the monarchy that on the morning of February 22 the hosier, the cabinetmaker, and the mechanic should meet before Durand's wineshop as brothers in a common cause.

By nine o'clock in the morning there was already a good deal of excitement in the vicinity of the Madeleine. Soon afterward a procession of students which had formed up near the Panthéon emerged into the Place de la Concorde singing the *Marseillaise*. Later still, a few of the demonstrators even invaded the Palais Bourbon, although they were swiftly ejected and driven back into the Place de la Concorde. The Chamber was not sitting at the time and the incident seemed of little importance. Toward midday there was a more serious attack on the Ministry for Foreign Affairs. It should be recalled that at this time the ministry was situated in a building on the boulevard des Capucines. (To be quite accurate, in between the rue des Capucines and the site occupied today by the rue Daunou. It was not until the Second Empire that the ministry was removed to its present position on the Quai d' Orsay.)

At two o'clock the deputies assembled to discuss the question of the Bank of Bordeaux. With a theatrical gesture, Odilon Barrot laid before the House a demand for the minister's impeachment. It had been signed by only fifty-three deputies. Two of these signatures, those of Abbatucci and of Drouyn de Lhuys, deserve special mention because Abbatucci and Drouyn de Lhuys were among the most devoted servants of the Second Empire. A great many opposition deputies had refused to follow Odilon Barrot, believing that their leader was acting mistakenly. At this time Thiers was convinced that Guizot had the situation well in hand and that the murmurs of revolt could even strengthen the minister's position because there were plenty of "dynastics" who still preferred Guizot to rebellion.

Guizot read the charge laid down by Odilon Barrot with an expression of contempt. He faced Barrot with an arrogance that was all the greater because he sensed that the Chamber was becoming increasingly docile. Even so, his arrogance concealed a measure of anxiety; unlike the king, he was beginning to fear the unrest in the streets.

🚩 The Gérard Plan

The excitement did not abate as the afternoon wore on. In the Champs-Élysées huts and chairs had been set on fire and the dark smoke rising into the air caused further anxiety. In the rue Bourg-l'Abbé and the rue Mauconseil minor clashes occurred between the demonstrators and the Municipal Guard. At five o'clock the government decided to set in motion the security arrangements known as the "Gérard Plan" or alternatively as the "Order of December 25."

In December 1840, old Marshal Gérard had drawn up a plan in which the operations to be carried out jointly by the army and the National Guard in the case of an insurrection had been laid down methodically to the last detail. All through the eighteen-forties, officers dressed in civilian clothes had made frequent excursions into the poorer quarters of the city in order to familiarize themselves with the scene of possible future operations. At the time of the July Revolution of 1830, the government had possessed only twelve thousand ill-armed and poorly supplied troops. In 1848 they had at their disposal three times this number and the troops were not short of bread or of weapons. Besides which the Municipal Guard—comprising 3,200 men under their commander Lardenois—was an extremely efficient body of troops. Consequently it seemed that Louis Philippe and his ministers had every reason to be sanguine. Yet in spite of this, they were defeated.

The reasons for this were threefold. First, the Gérard Plan involved the use of the National Guard and, as the words of the editor of the *Siècle*, Perrée, have already shown, the National Guard was not to be relied on. In the second place, both Louis Philippe and his advisers were extremely reluctant to resort to any kind of military action because they could not bear the thought of bloodshed. Third, the troops lacked a competent commander. Louis Philippe and Guizot had made the mistake of heaping honors on certain families without taking proper care of the actual worth of the men to whom they entrusted heavy responsibilities. Nepotism played an important part in the collapse of the monarchy, and it was nepotism which had placed General

Tiburce Sébastiani in command of the army units concentrated in Paris. Sébastiani was a man without either intelligence or ability, and he owed his position purely to the fact that he was the brother of the Marshal Sébastiani who was at that time Minister for Foreign Affairs. (The Marshal was one of the pillars of the bourgeois monarchy and in 1847 had had the misfortune to lose his daughter in the most tragic circumstances: the Duchess of Choiseul-Praslin was beaten to death by her husband.) At the head of the National Guard was another mediocre individual, General Jaqueminot, an old parliamentarian, one of the *satisfaits* who had risen to a position of eminence through the influence of his son-in-law: Jaqueminot's daughter was married to the Minister of the Interior, Duchâtel. Still more unfortunately Jaqueminot was a sick man, and during the February Days he was too ill even to rise from his bed. In addition, relations between Tiburce Sébastiani and Jaqueminot were far from friendly and it was a mistake to rely on the authority of the Duke of Nemours to settle such disputes which might arise between the two commanders in chief. Meanwhile, however, on the evening of the twenty-second, the atmosphere at the Château was still cheerful.

"The people of Paris know what they are about," declared Louis Philippe confidently. "They won't swap the throne for a banquet."

Not everyone shared his optimism, and at the very moment the king was announcing his confidence the Parisian deputies, Carnot, Vavin, and Taillandier, who were men of very different political views, were demanding an interview with the Prefect for the Seine, Rambuteau.

Rambuteau heard them out politely but sadly. He understood their anxiety but could say nothing to reassure them. He was as much in the dark as they were. Evidently neither the court, nor the government, nor any of the various authorities responsible for maintaining order in the city had seen fit to communicate their decisions to the unfortunate Rambuteau, or give him any instructions, a fact at which he evinced considerable annoyance.

The Second Day

WEDNESDAY, FEBRUARY 23 A second day of tension. By now a large part of the city was in a state of uproar. The revolutionary outbreak was chiefly confined to an area within the following bounds: the rue Montmartre in the west, the line of the Grands Boulevards running from the Madeleine to the Bastille in the north and east, and the Seine in the south. (For this first plan of the Revolution of 1848, I have relied on the memoirs of Caussidière, who was the next Prefect of Police for the city of Paris.) This covers a considerable area, but even so the insurrection could have been brought under control very quickly if the National Guard had remained loyal to the System. The defection of the National Guard was one of the decisive events of the day. Jaqueminot had told the king, "Out of three hundred and eighty-four companies, I have possibly six or seven that are unreliable." "More than that, surely," had been

Louis Philippe's reply, "say seventeen or eighteen!" Both Jaqueminot and the king had been very wide of the mark, and their mistake is all the more difficult to explain because as early as 1840 the king had abandoned his traditional practice of reviewing the corps for fear of rioting and abusive language.

The legions assembled between ten and eleven o'clock on Wednesday morning. Their mood, in general, was frankly ugly.

Only one legion, the first—the Champs-Élysées and the Place Vendôme—supported the government and hissed the left-wing deputies.

The second legion—Chaussée-d'Antin and Palais-Royal —took up a position in front of the Pavillon de Marsan with shouts of "*Vive la Réforme!*"

The third—faubourg Poissonnière, faubourg Montmartre, and Saint-Eustache—which was supposed to be guarding the Bank of France, crossed swords with General Friant's cuirassiers. It was commanded by a wealthy stockbroker who, happening to encounter Maxime Du Camp, had some extremely typical remarks to make on the subject:

"I have just been protecting the people against the cuirassiers' attempts to cut them down. This government is making us the laughingstock of Europe. I intend to march my men through the city as an example to the bourgeoisie, and if necessary I'm quite prepared to arrest Guizot and escort him to Vincennes."

The fourth legion—faubourg Saint-Honoré, Louvre, Banque de France—drew up a petition similar to that presented by Odilon Barrot, demanding the minister's impeachment.

The Fifth—faubourg Saint-Denis, faubourg Saint-Martin, Bonne-Nouvelle; the Sixth—Porte Saint-Denis, Saint-Mar-

tin-des-Champs, les Lombards, le Temple; and the seventh—Saint-Avoye, Mont-de-Piété, Marché Saint-Jean—all
followed the example of the second legion by raising an almost unanimous cry of "Vive la Réforme!" Feeling in the
seventh legion ran particularly high and there was a demand
that the Prefect for the Seine, Rambuteau, should call on
the king to dismiss Guizot.

The tenth legion—la Monnaie, Saint-Thomas-d'Aquine,
les Invalides, and the faubourg Saint-Germain—was divided,
part remaining loyal to the government while the rest, the
more numerous or at least the more vociferous, cried, "Vive
la Réforme!" Their colonel, deeply disillusioned, marched
off and left them, dramatically tearing off his insignia as he
did so.

The effect on the regular troops of this attitude adopted
by the National Guard was to weaken them considerably.
In the event, the army, which throughout the early stages of
the insurrection had maintained a high standard of discipline and had been prepared for vigorous action, lost its
nerve when it realized that it was liable to be struck in the
back by the National Guard. The brunt of the whole affair
fell on the wretched men of the Municipal Guard, who were
extremely unpopular in working-class districts. Without
lavishing undue praise on this police force, I do believe that
the Municipal Guard of 1848 has been dealt with very un-
kindly by history. The Swiss Guards have become the center
of a respectful and admiring legend for their heroic defense
of the Tuileries on August 10, 1792. Plenty of people with
no love for the royalist cause have dwelt sentimentally on
their courage and desperate tenacity. But no one has spoken
a single kindly word on behalf of the poor devils of the
"cipaux" and the remarkable courage they displayed in waving the monarchist banner firmly aloft to the bitter end. Not

a hand was raised to help them as they fell: the National Guard looked on jeering and the military with embarrassment, but neither made any attempt to save them from the mob.[1]

Rambuteau is unlikely to have passed on to the king the seventh legion's imperative demand for Guizot's dismissal, but even so the Tuileries was very soon aware of it and, surprisingly, gave way. The first suggestion that a government which was seriously compromising the monarchy itself should be asked to resign came from Queen Marie Amélie. Louis Philippe yielded to her arguments. "I have seen enough bloodshed," he said, again and again. "All my life I have hated this evil men call war."

Count Duchâtel arrived at the Tuileries in the early afternoon. He was a worried man. "It is the twentieth of June all over again," he said. On June 20, 1792, the mob had broken into the Tuileries and threatened Louis XVI to the point of making him wear the Phrygian cap on his head. Duchâtel went on to recall the tenth of August, which has already been alluded to. "From the twentieth of June to the tenth of August was a short step, and we live in an age when things move more quickly than they did sixty years ago. Events, like travelers, move by steam." Even so, Duchâtel was somewhat taken aback when he found himself invited to tender his resignation on the spot and that the king had already made up his mind to dismiss the prime minister, Guizot. Duchâtel returned to the Chamber, which was then in session, feeling both angry and bewildered. Guizot, too, heard the news

[1] There is no evidence to suggest that the rioters invariably reacted with such ferocity to the Municipal Guards. There were plenty of workers fighting on the side of the insurrectionists who treated Municipal Guards with great humanity and even hid them for several days until the revolutionary fervor had had time to cool down. Daniel Stern (*Histoire de la Révolution de 1848*, Paris, 1862, Vol. II, p. 260, n. 1) records a number of such incidents.

brought by Duchâtel with amazement, and the two ministers who had been so abruptly dismissed returned together to the Tuileries. Louis Philippe informed Guizot of his intention to ask Molé to form a government. Molé was a court man, he had been made a minister at a very early age during the First Empire and he knew his way about the world of politics, but he had no personal influence with the people. In the corridors of power he was in his element, but he could not control a crowd. He came to the Tuileries at about four o'clock and accepted the heavy responsibilities thrust on him by Louis Philippe, but asked for time to form a new cabinet. In fact, he acted as leisurely as though the ship of state were utterly becalmed. Having dined first, Molé then went to call on Thiers in the Place Saint-Georges. He found him in high good humor, since at that time Thiers actually believed he had the situation in hand. At half past four Guizot had returned to the Chamber and announced his resignation.

The general reaction was one of anger against the king, and it is a fact that by yielding to the pressure of the mob Louis Philippe had acted unconstitutionally. A number of deputies realized only too well that a crack had formed in the System which was bound to grow wider. One elderly deputy, a former registrar general named Calmon from the province of Lot, leaned across to his neighbor, Muret de Bord, and remarked with a smile that he thought the Citizeness Muret de Bord would do well to prepare for a removal. "You will not be popular with the Republic," he said. Muret was a textile manufacturer from Châteauroux, one of the *satisfaits* who had distinguished himself in parliament by his silence and general acquiescence.

The opposition expressed its delight in a manner that was foolish as well as unseemly.

Naturally, this last statement deserves some qualification. Dynastics like Thiers or Odilon Barrot appeared to have good reason to believe that they had won without putting the monarchy seriously in jeopardy, and it is true that the atmosphere in the capital at the end of that afternoon was a good deal less tense. Cheerful crowds were everywhere and there was a feeling of general rejoicing in the air. Many historians have seen this relaxation as an indication that Paris was returning to normal and that Guizot's dismissal had saved the monarchy. They may be right, although it is my own personal belief that by giving way to public pressure in parting from his minister, Louis Philippe gave the impression that he was no longer in control of events, that the System was steadily running down and the days of the Juste-Milieu were over.

Whatever the truth, the troubles were by no means at an end. An incident occurred in the boulevard des Capucines whose tragic outcome is only too well known. A procession was making its way down the street coming from the faubourg Saint-Antoine toward the Madeleine. Daniel Stern observes that some of the demonstrators were carrying torches and waving the red flag and adds that this was the first time the red flag had made its appearance on the scene in 1848. In the boulevard des Capucines, the marching column came face to face with a detachment of the fourteenth regiment of the line standing guard outside the Ministry for Foreign Affairs. "There was a shot. The soldiers, believing themselves in danger, fired in their turn. More than fifty people fell. Forty were later taken up dead. . ." [2] Naturally there were enquiries as to who had been respon-

---

[2] Fifty-two according to Elias Regnault, who had been Ledru-Rollin's secretary before becoming the historian of 1848. Garnier-Pagès claims that there were thirty-five killed and forty-seven wounded.

sible for the first shot which had led to the massacre, and for a long time it was believed—on the authority of Lamartine himself—that it had been fired by a certain Charles Lagrange, a veteran conspirator and member of the secret societies who had been active in Lyons in 1834 and was a typical figure of 1848. Lamartine's theory was the more likely because Lagrange was well known as an unruly trouble-maker. "One of those men," wrote Victor Hugo, "who are never taken seriously but who sometimes make it necessary to take them tragically." Lagrange, indeed, could well have been among those extremists who were by no means pleased to see things returning to normal on the evening of February 23, and who wanted the "coup de torchon" at all costs. It took the grim barrier of a great many corpses lying between the government and the people before the fiery image of Revolution rose once more into the winter sky, the inky sky of that February.

Lagrange denied firing the shot and his tone has a touching ring of sincerity. He was a chivalric figure, devoid of meanness or trickery, with something of the manner of an actor of the old school, though one more fitted to enact the melodrama than to originate the plot. Moreover, Maxime Du Camp, in his fascinating memoirs of 1848, also claims to possess the key to the mystery. According to Du Camp the fatal shot was fired by a Corsican sergeant named Giacomini in the belief that his commanding officer—Lieutenant Colonel Courant—who was closely surrounded by the demonstrators, was in danger. If this is the case, he must have fired against the orders of the lieutenant colonel himself, who was begging his men to keep calm.

Some of the workers hoisted a few of the bodies onto a cart and the impromptu hearse was driven around the streets of Paris. On reaching the rue Pelletier, where the *National* had its offices, it was the subject of a lengthy oration by Garnier-Pagès. The reaction it produced in the faubourg Saint-Denis and the faubourg Saint-Martin can easily be imagined. (Once again the pavings were torn up and the barricades erected.) For three hours the cortege rolled on until at last the bodies were set down in the *mairie* of the fourth *arrondissement*, not far from the Châtelet.

Another incident, less well known, also occurred in the boulevard des Capucines. A few minutes after the firing a stagecoach turned into the boulevard coming from the rue Neuve-des-Augustins. The contents were flung out and it too was filled with corpses. Driven by a worker whose name, Soccas, as well as his actions makes him sound like a character out of Balzac, the vehicle set off along the rue Royale, where a detachment of dragoons made a halfhearted attempt to arrest its progress. Soccas whipped up the horses and thundered past at a gallop, bawling at the top of his voice, "Respect for the dead!" The dragoons and the National Guards of the second legion remained paralyzed with shock and horror, staring after Soccas and his load.

It was ten o'clock before Louis Philippe heard the news of the bloodshed in the boulevard des Capucines. At midnight, Count Molé formally declared that he was unable to form a government. The king made two decisions: Thiers was to head the new government and Bugeaud to take command of all the armed forces, superseding both Tiburce Sébastiani and Jaqueminot. Looking back, in the light of history, Thiers appears as a ruthless politician who would act swiftly to put down a rising rather than come to terms with it. He was largely to blame for the massacre of the peaceful inhabitants of the rue Transnonain in 1834, and in 1871 he drowned the Commune in blood. Even so, although Louis Philippe was mistaken in his estimation of the popularity enjoyed by this resourceful individual in February 1848, Thiers could pass in the last resort for a man of the left, a man of the "Movement." At all events, Louis Philippe, who loathed Thiers, called on him to form a government with the object of propitiating the people and consolidating the position of the throne. Bugeaud, on the other hand, was called in simply as a strong-arm man. Although he himself denied it, Bugeaud's own part in the affair of the rue Transnonain had been no very creditable one, and if he was no more guilty than Thiers in the long run, he was frankly hated by the people of Paris.

In surrounding himself with men like Thiers and Bugeaud, Louis Philippe was committing an act of folly. Everything that he gained by putting forward the name of Thiers was lost by the very fact that the people would inevitably jib at Bugeaud. Bugeaud neatly canceled out Thiers.

The Third Day

🎺 THURSDAY, FEBRUARY 24 The third Day of
revolution began at half past one in the morning when
Bugeaud held a council of war at the Tuileries. At dinner-
time the previous day, Bugeaud had been stalking through
the Château, having offered his sword to the monarchy in
its hour of need and having had his services rejected. Louis
Philippe had small fancy for Bugeaud's overbearing personality. Then at last, force of circumstances had brought the
old veteran from Africa the summons to take command of
the troops concentrated in Paris. His first words were "No
princes!" and they struck an echo in the heart of the king,
for Bugeaud had fretted openly at the presence of the Duke
of Aumale in Algeria.

Bugeaud's second in command at the Tuileries was a
young officer named Trochu who, twenty-two years later,

was himself to become the head of the government as a result of a day of revolution.

When he summoned the officers of his headquarters staff Bugeaud was at the top of his form, sparkling with Gascon high spirits. He recalled complacently that he had never been defeated in battle and added that he had no intention of "losing his virginity" on the morrow. He reminded them of his tactics at the siege of Saragossa and announced that he was hoping for the cooperation of the National Guard; "but if it fights shy of us, gentlemen, then we shall win on our own." Finally he explained his plan of operations, which was to sweep Paris clean with four separate columns of troops.

The first of these was under the command of General Tiburce Sébastiani. As a professional soldier, the unfortunate Sébastiani was still anxious to play some part at a time which was decisive for the monarchy, and after his humiliating demotion he had requested, with a good deal of dignity, to be allowed to hold at least a subordinate command. Sébastiani's column was to approach the Bank of France by way of the Hôtel de Ville, a mission involving few difficulties. The column set out at five A.M. and by seven had reached the Place de Grève with a total of twelve dead and twice that number wounded.

The second column—of approximately two thousand men—was entrusted to General Bedeau, who happened to be in Paris at the time. This was to make for the Bastille by way of the Bourse and the Grands Boulevards. There will be more to say later of the misfortunes attending Bedeau's contingent, which played an important part in the day's events. The third column was to advance under cover of the other two and prevent the barricades from re-forming at points where Sébastiani's and Bedeau's troops had forced a passage. A fourth body of troops was to make for the Panthéon.

At half past two in the morning Thiers arrived at the Tuileries. He agreed to form a government but his conversation with the king took a sharp turn. Thiers insisted on having Odilon Barrot as one of his chief ministers. Louis Philippe winced. He winced still more when Thiers demanded the immediate dissolution of parliament. "No," was his answer. "No dissolution." Thiers conceded the point and left the Tuileries to look for politicians to make up the new cabinet. On his way he was frequently obstructed by the barricades and was forced to take an extremely roundabout route. At four o'clock in the morning he returned to the Tuileries accompanied by Rémusat, who was furious at Bugeaud's appointment. Then the two men set out again into the night for further political discussions. Thiers came back to the Tuileries again at eight in the morning, realizing that events were beyond his control, and somewhat hesitantly suggested that Odilon Barrot should assume the responsibilities of office.

This is the moment to return to Bedeau's column in the boulevard Bonne-Nouvelle. The troops had been brought up short by an exceptionally well-defended barricade. Bedeau was reluctant to give the order to attack and attempted to talk to the insurgents and convince them of the king's good intentions. He told them of Odilon Barrot's return to power. Tocqueville, who was present at this scene and had no fondness for Bedeau, says, "I have never seen a general wax so eloquent." Bedeau's eloquence was unavailing as far as raising the barricade to allow the soldiers to pass was concerned. However an officer of the National Guard, a local businessman of some consequence named Fauvelle-Delabarre, came forward confidently to meet the general. The merchant vouched for the goodwill felt by those manning the barricades and said that he was sure there was some misunderstanding. He expressed a wish to go and discuss the matter with Bugeaud at the Tuileries. Then he would return to the boulevard Bonne-Nouvelle and explain exactly what Bugeaud and the king meant to do. Everything would be all right.

Not surprisingly, he managed to convince Bedeau. What is more surprising is that he also succeeded in getting around Bugeaud. Bugeaud was visibly disconcerted by the turn events had taken, since he guessed that the princes would not forgive him for bloodshed, and he therefore fell in with the suggestions put forward by the merchant from the boulevard Bonne-Nouvelle. A long time afterward, during the Second Republic, Bugeaud happened to meet this merchant socially and was extremely rude to him, accusing him in no uncertain terms of having brought about their downfall in February. "*C'est vous, Monsieur, qui en février nous avez foutus dedans.*"

It is true that Fauvelle-Delabarre played a far from negligible part in the course of events, but this should not be exaggerated. In his modest way he was an even greater talker than Bedeau, and he had a clear field with Bugeaud, the princes, and the king. During the exile at Claremont, when the conversation turned on the way Bugeaud had given the order to withdraw, and the question of responsibility arose —whether it was Bugeaud or Bedeau who had given the untimely order which dug the grave of the monarchy—old Louis Philippe shrugged and said, "The order was in the air."

While Fauvelle-Delabarre was arguing with Bugeaud, Bedeau was having a good deal of trouble maintaining some semblance of order among his inactive troops in the boulevard Bonne-Nouvelle. He was not unduly worried, for at one point during his comings and goings he had caught sight of Odilon Barrot gesticulating among the crowd of demonstrators, and Barrot's very animation had struck him as a good omen. By the time Fauvelle-Delabarre returned to the barricade, the troops were beginning to disintegrate in the face of pressure from the people—a pressure that was at the same time friendly and menacing. When they heard that their orders were to withdraw they offered no further resistance to the rioters. Most of the soldiers mutinied and others shamelessly handed over their weapons to the demonstrators. The troops fell back on the Tuileries in a sad state of disorder, powerless rage, and confusion, their officers marching with bowed heads. The army did not forget this retreat, and a great deal of the vindictiveness displayed against the people in June, by officers and men, can be put down to motives of revenge.[1] Bedeau's column, or what was left of it, had dug itself in, in the vicinity of the Tuileries by about eight in the morning. At the same time, in the Place de l'Hôtel de Ville, Sébastiani's column was ceasing hostilities. It stood by impassively while violent clashes occurred between the demonstrators and the Municipal Guard. At eleven o'clock a captain of the National Guard, followed by a number of students from the École Polytechnique,[2] took the Hôtel de Ville without a blow being

[1] This is only a generalization. The regular troops had no mercy on the insurgents in June, as we shall see, but even so, many units showed more stoical resignation than real enthusiasm. The attitude of the regular troops pales in comparison with the eagerness of the National Guard and the garde mobile. Everything in this field is relative, but there is no doubt that the army as a whole was keener in June than in February.

[2] There were clearly a number of students from the École Polytechnique (the military academy of artillery and engineering) among the insurgents of 1848, but in general they form a less important part of the over-all picture in February 1848 than in July 1830. Public feeling gives an impression of

struck. General Sébastiani and the Prefect for the Seine bowed before the inevitable and the soldiers returned to barracks.

The mob, surprised at this easy victory, grew bolder and began to flow from the Hôtel de Ville toward the Château. The shooting was closer to the Tuileries. Both demonstrators and Municipal Guards were firing, and in the confusion one deputy of ministerial standing named Jollivet lost his life. Paradoxically, he was shot by bullets fired by his own side. There was a dramatic moment at the Palais Royal where two companies of the fourteenth regiment of the line had dug themselves in at a position known as the Château d'Eau. (This seems an odd name for it today, but it was called after a fountain which has since been demolished.) The soldiers put up a stubborn defense which proved useless when their assailants set fire to the building.

✐ The Abdication: The King Leaves Paris

The court was in a state of panic and Thiers was incapable of making heartening speeches. All he could say, over and over again, was, "The tide is rising, the tide is rising." He did, however, produce one plan—the same as that he actually carried out in May 1871. He proposed that the king should leave Paris and return to conquer the city at the head of an army of sixty thousand men. Duvergier de Hauranne's reaction to the plan was vehement: "When you have left

comparative lack of enthusiasm on the part of the Polytechnicians. Raspail's paper, *L'Ami du Peuple*, contains numerous references to the "babies of the Polytechnic" who stayed at home with their nurses and shunned the barricades.

Paris, you won't get back." Thiers was annoyed and not long afterward he took advantage of the general confusion to quietly disappear. Those who met Thiers in the street that day were struck by the childish nervousness of his manner. Thiers could be a bully to those who opposed him, but at the prospect of any violence being done to himself he literally collapsed. When Louis Napoleon Bonaparte had him arrested, on December 2, 1851, he behaved with a physical cowardice which shocked even the hardened police superintendent.

At half past ten, Louis Philippe sat down to dine as usual. He was worried and especially surprised not to have seen Barrot. He ate heartily, and when the meal was over he decided to make one last effort to regain control of the situation. There were still a great many troops surrounding the Tuileries, both regular soldiers and National Guards, and the king intended to review them to rally their spirits. He set out on horseback, wearing the uniform of a general, and escorted by two of his sons, Nemours and Montpensier,[3] and also by Bugeaud and Lamoricière. The first and tenth legions gave Louis Philippe a warm welcome, but the fourth uttered hostile cries of "*Vive la Réforme!*" The king promptly lost his nerve and turned away, muttering, "You'll have your reform!"

At midday Émile de Girardin, editor of *La Presse*, arrived at the Tuileries. Girardin is a well-known figure, the father of modern journalism and a man with a genius for publicity, but the shrewd expression on his pale, flabby countenance betrayed more cynical self-importance than real intelligence. At this moment, in the twilight of the monarchy, Girardin

[3] The king's two remaining sons, Aumale and Joinville, were not in Paris. Aumale was governor of Algeria and Joinville was spending the winter with his brother, as the Princess of Joinville was an invalid and the Algerian climate was good for her health.

lost no opportunity of putting himself forward. He played his part in the general chorus of condemnation raised against those accused of "corruption." The spectacle of this cynical schemer presuming to teach Guizot a lesson in morality is not a pretty sight. In the summer of 1847, Girardin was called to account for certain libelous accusations he had published very prominently in *La Presse*. With his back to the wall, he lost his nerve and became hopelessly confused, but the minister unexpectedly failed to follow up his advantage. Victor Hugo, drawing attention to the fact and asking why the minister and Girardin had not ended up in court over the matter, received the answer: "Because Girardin does not feel strong enough and the minister does not feel sufficiently blameless."

Girardin tried unsuccessfully to organize a progressive party in parliament, and on February 14 he solemnly handed in his resignation on the grounds that there was no place in the Chamber for anyone who seriously wanted to get things done. "The majority," he said, "is intolerant, and the minority irresponsible." Ten days later Girardin casually asked the king to abdicate.

Utterly resigned to the situation, Louis Philippe agreed.

"But, Monsieur de Girardin, under what conditions do you suggest I should abdicate?"

"You will abdicate," Girardin went on, "in favor of your grandson, the Count of Paris, and since the people of Paris would not take Nemours, you will entrust the regency to the Duchess of Orleans."

"Very well. I abdicate. I renounce the throne in favor of my grandson."

And slowly, in a large, careful hand, the king wrote out his act of abdication. In it, he said nothing on the subject of the regency. He was not fond of the Princess Hélène. He argued that France came under Salic law, which excluded women. He said that parliament would have to sort it out. Whatever the king might say, it seemed that the Princess Hélène would now be called upon to play a major part in affairs and a number of courtiers regarded her as regent from that moment. The old Queen Marie Amélie observed maliciously, "Well, you're happy now, Hélène."

The cruel words struck home and the Duchess of Orleans flung herself at the queen's feet exclaiming, "Oh, mother!"

Nevertheless some attempt at decision was being made. First the king and queen made ready to leave. Their departure was beginning to look more and more like flight.

The lawyer Crémieux bustled around the king, friendly and officious. At midday he was still leaning toward maintaining the monarchy and supporting the Count of Paris, but by nightfall he had become a minister of the Republic.

It was Crémieux who urged Louis Philippe to dress as an ordinary citizen and provided him with a frock coat and bowler hat. Montpensier, in fact, clung to Crémieux as a savior, begging the lawyer not to desert the royal family at this crucial moment. In the end, Louis Philippe reached Honfleur and Trouville without much trouble and took ship from Le Havre for England, where he died in 1850, a broken man. The problem of the king's safety had been dealt with comparatively quickly. For those who still believed in the possibility of a monarchy, however, there was another problem, namely, how to re-establish order. As a last resort it was decided to put Lamoricière, whom we last saw on horseback beside Louis Philippe and Bugeaud, in command of the National Guard. He was dressed somewhat oddly for riding, because he had just returned on leave from Africa and, seeing that matters were taking a serious turn, had gone directly to the Château as he was, in nankeen breeches and without his uniform. Someone gave him a National Guard uniform, which he put on over his civilian clothes and, thus equipped, began dashing all over Paris haranguing the demonstrators, telling them of the king's abdication and urging the citizens to acclaim the little Count of Paris as their new sovereign and Odilon Barrot as head of the government. Naturally the mob paid no attention to Lamoricière, but they were highly amused by the big fellow struggling equally with his own eloquence and the voluminous folds of his various military and civilian garments.

Several aged marshals who had been pillars of the regime came to be with the king at the time of his abdication. Among them were Soult and Gérard. Soult, Duke of Dalmatia, was seventy-nine and Gérard seventy-five. Gérard was crippled with age and infirmity, but even so he was begged to show his devotion to the monarchy once again by playing a similar role to that of Lamoricière. Gérard, dressed up to the nines and put on a horse, cut an even more ridiculous figure than Lamoricière, for although his dress was somewhat less bizarre, he carried an olive branch in his hand to show that he was a messenger of peace, and his quavering voice was drowned by the jeers of the people.

Odilon Barrot's carriage was another grotesque spectacle. We left Barrot on Tuesday, laying his demand for the impeachment of Guizot before the house. On Tuesday and Wednesday, Barrot had smelled the sweet smell of success. His house stood in the rue de la Ferme-des-Mathurins, a street connecting the boulevard de la Madeleine with the northern end of the rue Tronchet. On Tuesday evening some enthusiastic citizens had rechristened the street and given it the new name of the "rue du Père-du-Peuple." By Thursday, however, Barrot realized that his popularity had waned considerably. Bedeau made a mistake when, as I mentioned earlier, he took comfort from the sight of Barrot addressing the crowd with animated gestures. The Father of the People gesticulated all the more wildly as it became clear that it was useless. There was nothing friendly about the exchanges going on between Barrot and the crowd, and what Bedeau had taken for satisfaction and even applause was no more than angry protests, and Barrot had been mobbed in the faubourg Saint-Denis. Friends who had gone after him urged him to go back to the Tuileries and consult with the king as to what could be done to retrieve the situation, but Barrot told them he was tired and would go home to rest and reassure his wife. It was a pathetic excuse. Madame Odilon Barrot had the blood of heroes in her veins and would never have expected her husband to shirk any danger; quite the reverse, in fact. But to try to be fair to Barrot, although plenty of evidence deals severely with him, there are other witnesses, Tocqueville among them, who are kinder, and record that Barrot spent only a few moments at home and then, after his brief call in the rue de la Ferme-des-Mathurins, went straight to the Ministry of the Interior, which at that time was situated at 101 rue de Grenelle.

Barrot had some difficulty in forcing his way through to the rue de Grenelle. A number of demonstrators swarmed onto his carriage. They must have acquired their arms and accouterments by plundering a theatrical costumier's, and it was this that made me earlier describe as grotesque the spectacle of the pompous Odilon Barrot, who never possessed much sense of humor, struggling with a gang of toughs dressed up in period armor and waving crossbows. But Odilon Barrot had other things to worry him besides these weird, flamboyant characters. Garnier-Pagès and

Pagnerre had also got into the carriage and were urging the Father of the People to join the *National* party and declare for the Republic.

🏴 Regency or Republic?

It is not certain to what extent the February rising which began with the cry of "*Vive la Réforme!*" and ended with shouts of "*Vive la République!*" was a spontaneous movement. Historians in general are inclined to regard it as such, quoting in support of their theory statements made in old age by one of the republican leaders of 1848, the lawyer Marie, who was one of the most prominent men in the *National* party. Marie's evidence says that until eleven o'clock on February 24 there had never been any intention of overthrowing the monarchy. The rising was unplanned and developed along its own lines. Moreover, added Marie, "I knew everything that was afoot. No clear-cut, calculated plan by any particular group could have been hidden from me." Evidence of this kind does not constitute absolute proof; the first thing that should be noted is his tendency to exaggerate the part played by the *National* and to present the founders of the Second Republic as responsible citizens who were in no way to be blamed for the turn of events but who in a chaotic situation were prepared to take on a crushing burden of responsibility. Why does Marie put the decisive moment at eleven o'clock on Thursday? The answer to that is because it was a little after this that the conference took place in the offices of the *National* which led to the proposal for setting up a provisional government. The moderates at the *National* even insisted that the dynastics should form part of this government. Thus it was that Pagnerre and Garnier-Pagès came to be clutching Odilon Barrot's sleeve and asking him to become a member of the new coalition.

However, as the meeting went on and the rioting spread hourly, the *National* men decided in self-defense that it was advisable to negotiate with the left rather than the right, and to reach some compromise with the staff of the *Réforme* instead of with the dynastic opposition led by Odilon Barrot. Through the intervention of Martin de Strasbourg, the *National* and the *Réforme* came to an understanding. The *National* was to have a majority in the new government, but all the same a number of ministries were to go to the editors of the *Réforme*.

Orthodox Orleanist historians have frequently ground their teeth at the memory of this coalition, and claimed that the February Revolution was brought about by a newspaper with a circulation of under three thousand. This is something of an oversimplification. Even before the gentlemen on the *National* had decided on the setting up of a provisional government, the committee of the *Réforme*, which also had extremely close ties with the old headquarters of the secret societies, had been campaigning vigorously for the establishment of a republic. Marie had no means of knowing what was being planned by the followers of Flocon or Caussidière, since the men of the *Réforme* loathed and distrusted those belonging to the *National* and were in no mood to confide in them. Even while the first barricades were going up, Marrast and Ledru-Rollin were exchanging angry notes and were on the point of fighting a duel. We have already seen that at the headquarters of the *Réforme*, although displaying some reservations about the development of the situation, they had been prepared for any eventuality since Monday evening. Lagrange, describing the February insurgents, says, "We were only a handful of men." That is as may be, but they were a handful which acted on the night of February 23 with remarkable discipline and unanimity. Our hosier in the National Guard may have been content with paralyzing any attempt at action by the regular army, but our mechanic and even our cabinetmaker joined the army of insurrectionists referred to by Lagrange. Lamartine, too, describes the strong impression made on him by the workers who left their factories on Thursday morning to stand about in small, silent groups along the streets leading to Clichy, La Villette, and the Ourcq Canal. Their leaders were one or two comrades, better dressed than the rest in cloth jackets or heavy caped coats. In this complacent description of the workers, Lamartine sees them as former members of societies like the "Rights of Man" and the "Families." Their ideals were a mixture of Jacobin and Babouvist, and they had absorbed Babeuf's teaching via Buonarroti. As for their jobs, many of them worked as foremen in factories, and there were also a large number of printing workers. Craftsmen such as carpenters and cabinetmakers also made up a substantial element of the insurrectionist army, and leading the carpenters was Raspail himself.

The twenty-fourth of February was like a tragedy in three acts. The first act—the king's abdication—we have already seen, and this took place at the end of the morning in the palace of the Tuileries. The second act was set in the Palais Bourbon in the afternoon, and the third in the evening at the Hôtel de Ville.

The Chamber of Deputies was due to meet at three o'clock. Much against his will the president, Sauzet, agreed to put forward the session. Sauzet seems to have been panic-stricken. He was a lawyer and a magistrate and in periods of comparative calm had shown himself capable of delivering some telling speeches, but at the first sign of danger Sauzet lost his head. Two factors contributing to augment his distress were the information that the Princess Hélène had promptly applied to the deputies for protection and the further knowledge that in the Palais Bourbon the deputies would be at the mercy of the insurgents.

Princess Hélène had left the Tuileries, accompanied by her son and the doctor responsible for the care of the young prince. The ten-year-old Count of Paris was actually very ill, but though feverish and shivering he managed to follow his mother's example and put on a good face for parliament and to the mob. Their exit from the Tuileries was a wretched affair: the troops of the line did not even present arms to the princess. At the Chamber of Deputies she found her brother-in-law, Nemours, who offered her his protection. He too displayed considerable courage, but of a somewhat passive kind. Nemours stood bolt upright behind Hélène and acted throughout like an automaton, showing a complete lack of initiative. A few deputies raised a cheer for the princess and her son, more from sentiment than conviction, but on Lamartine's suggestion, it was soon agreed that the princess and the Count of Paris had better not be present during parliamentary sessions, and the pair left the chamber. At last, when all was lost beyond recall, they reached the Invalides.

Marie opened the debate. Marie, the lawyer, has been neatly summed up for us by a journalist named Auguste Lireux in three words: "neat, eloquent, and cold." Marie made a long speech and although even he seemed none too sure of where it was leading, this scarcely mattered since no one was listening to him. No, this is not altogether true, for one person, Crémieux, was enraptured by Marie and kept calling for silence.

Marie was followed by Barrot, who urged all the deputies to rally to the princess's standard and acclaim the Count of Paris as king. It was a timely speech and aroused a good deal of enthusiasm, but Barrot's lack of stamina soon put an end to it. Next to be heard were the caustic accents of La Rochejaquelein. As a legitimist he allowed himself some sarcastic comments on the collapse of a monarchy which had been born on the barricades, as a result of treason to the rightful rulers, and now perished in its turn on the barricades. La Rochejaquelein bowed before the hand of fate.

As though to point the eloquence of the deputy from the Vendée, the image of fate which La Rochejaquelein had portrayed with such scornful emphasis took shape in the form of the mob which poured in increasing numbers and ever more threatening mood into the Chamber. Ledru-Rollin raised his voice in a vain attempt to call for silence. Then came Lamartine's turn to speak, and such was his popularity that he obtained comparative quiet. The crowd, though still restless, listened to him with passionate attention.

Lamartine began his speech with a well-turned plea for the Duchess of Orleans and the Count of Paris. "We have just beheld one of the most touching sights in all the annals of mankind: a noble princess leaving an empty palace and coming to appeal, on behalf of herself and her innocent son, to the representatives of the people." At these words monarchists such as Barrot and Dupin took fresh heart for an instant, but Lamartine had gone over to the republican side. He had wavered all morning, but before the session began he had spent some time closeted in a small antechamber in the palace with a delegation from Le National. This delegation was made up of Jules Bastide, Armand Marrast, Hetzel, the editor, and the actor Bocage. (Bocage hailed originally from Rouen and was a typical figure of 1848. He had been brought up to the textile industry and had later moved crowds by his performances in the tragedies of Alexandre Dumas at the Porte Saint-Martin. He played in *Antony* and in *La Tour de Nesle*. During the Second Republic he became government commissioner for the Odéon.) "Come on, Lamartine," they said to him, "join us—we cannot form a provisional government without you . . . " Lamartine had agreed and he therefore concluded his speech with an appeal to the citizens to rally to the Provisional Government.

"Let this government be set up at once, let it be set up in the name of the public peace, in the name of all the blood which has been shed, in the name of the people who may be starving because of the glorious deeds they have performed in the last three days."

Lamartine reached his peroration, and it was just as well, because the uproar was growing in violence and intensity. Some even leveled their weapons at the poet, but he ignored them and preserved an imperturbable calm. One of the insurgents actually snatched the hat off the wretched Sauzet's head, crying, "Get out, president of the corrupt!" Lamartine joned Ledru-Rollin, and the two men decided to make their way to the Hôtel de Ville and proceed, with perhaps a little less confusion, to form a government.

⚑ *The Republic*

A vast crowd had gathered by torchlight outside the Hôtel de Ville. Lamartine and Ledru-Rollin had trouble forcing their way through. Lamartine was brave and proud, his seriousness lightened by a rare smile; Ledru-Rollin, stout, perspiring, and short of breath. At one point, when Ledru-Rollin complained to Lamartine that he was being suffocated, he got the answer: "We are climbing Calvary, my friend." Ledru-Rollin remembered that evening of the twenty-fourth of February during one of the stormiest sessions of the Constituent Assembly, during the Second Republic, and said, "I knew then that I was climbing Calvary."

As they arrived at the Hôtel de Ville, Lamartine and Ledru-Rollin met Martin de Strasbourg on his way from the *National* offices and he told them the latest news about the negotiations in progress between the two great opposition newspapers. These negotiations were going on all over the Hôtel de Ville, despite the fact that all the republican leaders were under extreme pressure from the mob of the people. Already there had been some sharp exchanges between François Arago and Louis Blanc. Finally some kind of agreement was reached on a list to be read to the people, who were growing impatient. The new ministers were to show themselves at the windows to receive the plaudits of the crowd. Some incidents occurred at this stage which throw an interesting light on their individual temperaments. Lamartine was given a list and asked to read it out. He disclaimed hurriedly, saying that he would be embarrassed because his name was on the list. One was also offered to Crémieux, but he declared bitterly, "How can you expect me to read it when my name does not figure on it?" The government was to be led by a veteran republican, Dupont de l'Eure, who had been a member of the Council of Elders under the Directorate. A tremor of excitement ran through the crowd because Dupont was already a legendary figure, but it was an excitement tinged with sadness.

"All the same, he's very old."

Then, as though for reassurance, the crowd added, "But the rest are young, and they can take care of our well-being for thirty years."

The names of Louis Blanc, Flocon, and the worker, Albert, were received with endless acclamation. The men of the *National* roused much more temperate applause. When the name of Garnier-Pagès was read out, one worker shouted, "He's not the good one. The good one was his brother and he's dead."

There was a sting of truth in the words. Garnier-Pagès was a mediocrity who owed his fame to the things his brother had done in the past. The man known as Garnier-Pagès the elder had stood beside Godefroy Cavaignac as one of the most ardent leaders of the republican party. Garnier-Pagès and Cavaignac were both in their graves but the people had not forgotten them.

The *National* men had no intention of proclaiming a republic without reservations. They had their way. The final text of the proclamation drawn up to be presented to the nation ran: "While the Provisional Government, acting in the name of the French people, prefers the republican form, neither the people of Paris nor the Provisional Government lays any claim to set their opinions above those of the sovereign people, who shall be consulted on the final form of the people's government." Daniel Stern states that in the original version the word "prefers" was covered by an ink blot. Louis Blanc wrote these words in the margin: "Be heart and soul for the republican government." But on the night of February 24 the members of the Provisional Government would not have dared read out to the crowd the words set down here, though they were the result of a laborious compromise. The people were crying out impatiently for the Republic.

Angry voices were raised: "They're not going to serve us the same trick as they did in 1830."

Lamartine went out onto the balcony and cried resolutely, "The Republic has been proclaimed."

His words were received with prolonged, hysterical applause. "The Republic is proclaimed!" Now everyone had heard the magic words, and a few workers immediately inscribed them on large banners and clambering up the face of the Hôtel de Ville, attached the banners to the building. One man lost his footing and crashed to the ground. The crowd surged around the body, wondering in sudden terror if this were an evil sign.

The Lyrical Illusion

La France s'est reconquise. On va enfin con-
stituer une société de justice dont tous les
membres seront libres et égaux. Le Travail
sera délivré de l'arrogante et effroyable exploitation des manieurs d'argent. Puis, qui sait,
la contagion aidant, si bientôt l'Europe entière
ne va pas se transformer en une fédération de
peuples libres?

GUSTAVE LEFRANÇAIS

Our hosier from the rue Saint-Denis opened his copy of
Le National on Friday morning, February 25, remembering
dizzily, and also with a good deal of amazement as well as
some anxiety, the events of the previous day. He wondered
what he would find there concerning the decisions taken
during the night at the Hôtel de Ville.

"The members of the government are: Dupont de
l'Eure, Lamartine, Crémieux, Arago (member of the Institute), Ledru-Rollin, Garnier-Pagès, and Marie. The secretaries are Armand Marrast, Louis Blanc, and Ferdinand
Flocon."

The various ministries were distributed in the following
order: President of the Council: Dupont; Minister for Foreign Affairs: Lamartine; Minister of the Interior: Ledru-
Rollin; Minister of War: General Bedeau;[1] Minister of

[1] Bedeau declined the War Ministry, which then went to Baron Subervie,

Finance: Michel Goudchaux (Goudchaux was a Jewish banker who had risen to fame as a result of the publication of a series of articles in *Le National* advocating state control of building and running the railroads); the Navy: Arago; Agriculture and Trade: Bethmont. (Bethmont was a lawyer of straightforward moderate views. He was of humble origin and was fond of reminding people that his father had been a baker. In 1844 he defended the typographer Pascal, director of the paper *L'Atelier*, in the assize court.) Minister of Public Works: Marie; Education: Hippolyte Sarnot; Governor General of Algeria: General Eugène Cavaignac. (I referred at the end of the preceding chapter to the memory of Godefroy Cavaignac. Like Garnier-Pagès, Cavaignac owed his rise to fame to the immense prestige his brother's memory enjoyed in the republican party.[2] But the general evinced scant appreciation for this exceptionally flattering appointment and the Provisional Government never forgave him for it.) The Mayor of Paris was Marie and supreme command of the National Guard went to Courtais. (The Vicomte de Courtais was of Bourbon origin, although he showed every willingness to drop his prefix. A retired cavalry captain, he had represented L'Allier in parliament during the July Monarchy. He took his seat among the radical republicans.)

There are two striking observations to be made on this list. The first is the omission of one name: that of the worker

who had formerly been a general serving under the Empire and was seventy-six in 1848.

[2] The name of Cavaignac was a noble one in the annals of republicanism. Jean Baptiste Cavaignac, a native of Gourdon, had represented the Haute-Garonne in the Convention and was furthermore among the Thermidorians. He was sentenced to exile at the Restoration and died in Brussels in 1829. His elder son, Godefroy (1801–1845), took part in the insurrection of April 1834. The younger, Eugène (1802–1857) went into the army and served in Algeria. During the bourgeois monarchy he had kept his republican feelings very much to himself.

Albert, whose name appeared only in the issue of February 26. Alexandre Martin, known as Albert, was a worker from the button factory of Bapterosse and a veteran of the secret societies. He had played a leading part in the society known as "The Seasons." During the eighteen-thirties he had acted as a link between the workers of Paris and those of Lyons. When it was agreed at the Hôtel de Ville that one member of the working class should be appointed to the government as a symbol, Albert had been the general choice, one which was warmly supported by Louis Blanc. (According to Lamartine, Albert was Louis Blanc's faithful hound, standing "silently behind his master.") Even after the decision concerning Albert had been ratified, there is no doubt that the gentlemen from the *National* were distinctly averse to accepting a workingman as one of their colleagues. Hence the omission of his name from Armand Marrast's paper. Later, when people in the provinces read the name "Albert, worker" on the official list published in the *Moniteur*, they thought it must be a mistake. It was thought to be some kind of curious joke on the part of the Parisians. Moreover the wretched Albert's name contained a misprint and appeared in the *Moniteur* as Aubert. People refused to believe that the new member of the government really was a worker and Albert had to ask his employer, Bapterosse, for a reference to prove it. Fate seems to have been against him and even today it is not easy to conjure up a picture of the man himself. Indeed, a good many historians have confused him with Corbon, the man behind the paper *L'Atelier*, and Albert has often been wrongly associated with the followers of Buchez. It is not only the moderates who have had some hard things to say about Albert. Sébastien Commissaire, an army NCO who was social-democrat representative for the Rhône during the Second Republic, wrote that "Albert made no contribution to the Provisional Government and did not initiate a single serious measure. He was so insignificant and left so little trace of his presence that he could be said, however unintentionally, to have killed, perhaps for years, all chance of working-class candidates in the government of the country."

It should be said, however, that aristocrats such as Lamartine and members of the upper middle class were occasionally moved and touched by the air of melodrama, of the romantic hero, which clung to Albert. He was the common man, inarticulate, wild, and mournful. But a great many of the workers who took part in the events of 1848 regarded this romantic, aesthetic and, in their eyes, pointless interest their comrade aroused simply as a source of irritation.

In the second place, the government outlined in this list was sharply divided into two categories. At the head appeared the names of the seven members of the cabinet. With the single exception of Ledru-Rollin, these were all men of the *National* (Lamartine having more or less joined the *National* party). They were followed by the three secretaries who, with the exception of Marrast, were all members of the editorial board of *La Réforme*. The *National* meant to make it clear that the radicals and socialists of the *Réforme* were the poor relations. Louis Blanc took umbrage at this hierarchy in the government and the three secretaries were rapidly put on an equal footing with their fellow members of the government. This brought the total number up to eleven members.[3]

It will be seen that there were certain members of the government who were not ministers, and certain ministers who

[3] The ten whose names appeared on the list printed in *Le National*, with the addition of Albert.

were not in the government. This made some kind of hierarchy inevitable. The eleven wielded much more power than ordinary ministers like Bethmont, Goudchaux, or Carnot. Flottard, a former Carbonarist leader, acted as secretary to the Provisional Government.

Étienne Arago, formerly director of the Vaudeville, took over the job of Postmaster General. Arago had a talent for versifying and he wrote these lines on his appointment:

> Conduit par le peuple vainqueur
> Aux postes secouant mes guêtres,
> Je fus acclamé Directeur
> Et grâce à ce poste flatteur,
> Je fus deux fois . . . homme de lettres.[4]

The Arago family wielded considerable influence during the Second Republic, and Raspail in particular found this extremely irritating. The astronomer François Arago was in control of the arsenal and his brother Étienne of the postal services, while at the same time François's son, Emmanuel, was sent to Lyons as commissioner for the Provisional Government. Shortly afterward Emmanuel Arago turned diplomat and represented the Republic at the court of Prussia.

Lagrange was appointed governor of the Hôtel de Ville and Marc Caussidière, known as Marcus, was installed in the prefecture of police. Caussidière, like Albert and Lagrange, was a former member of the secret societies, but whereas Albert was somber and Lagrange melodramatic, Caussidière was a cheerful extravert, although this does not mean that he had not had his times of trial. (His brother perished in the Lyons rising, after being first hideously mutilated.)

---

[4] Roughly: "The conquering people bundled me into the Post Office and hailed me as Director, and by this honorable post (or office) made me twice over a man of letters."

Caussidière traveled all over France on a twofold mission, both as a liquor salesman and as an agent for the *Réforme*, for which he collected two thousand subscribers. He was a big, swarthy, high-complexioned man and after his appointment as Prefect of Police developed a habit of prowling about the city dressed in a curious uniform which included a helmet, a pair of pistols stuck in his belt, and an enormous cross belt carrying a saber. "But then," he wrote in his memoirs, "I knew that a prefect of police ought to look the part." For all his unconventional appearance, he was clever, sensitive, and generous, and went to a good deal of trouble to make sure that his predecessor at the prefecture of police, Delessert, suffered no personal harm.

Using every means that came to hand, Caussidière re-established order under extremely difficult conditions. He is quoted as saying, "I made order out of chaos." In this he was assisted by his lieutenant, Sobrier, a former comrade of the "Seasons," whom he installed in one of the public buildings in the rue de Rivoli.[5] Caussidière and Sobrier created a "People's Guard" made up of former political detainees. They wore a blue uniform with red facings and bands and hats like those of the Consular Guard, with floating red cockades. The middle classes viewed these guardians of the peace and their formidable appearance with some alarm. Their terror was increased by the fact that Caussidière, an admirer of the Montagnards, had actually called one company of his new corps the "Compagnie Saint-Just."[6] The

[5] Sobrier, in the rue de Rivoli, was something more than simply a policeman. He also ran a newspaper, *La Commune de Paris*, whose ideals were very similar to those of *La Réforme* but more violently expressed. Moderate republicans protested vigorously at the publication of a paper of such extreme views from an official address which, as it were, gave it the stamp of official approval.

[6] The People's Guard was made up of four companies: the Montagnarde, the Compagnie Saint-Just, the Compagnie de Février, and the Compagnie Morriset (so called after a veteran fighter of the secret societies).

bourgeois had no need for alarm. As guardians of law and order, Caussidière's and Sobrier's men behaved with propriety and intelligence. Even so, sinister stories began to accumulate around the Prefect of Police. He was accused of having set up a kind of *Vehmgericht* in order to strike at his enemies. Delahodde, who spied on the republican secret societies for Louis Philippe's police, was taken before Caussidière's secret tribunal, but nothing much was done to him and the spy had reason to be grateful to the republican Prefect of Police for letting him off with his life. At a time when political reaction was setting in, in the country, Delahodde's pamphlets attacking Caussidière made a considerable mark.

Caussidière's Montagnards were a source of some anxiety even in government circles during the early days of the Second Republic. However, Garnier-Pagès, who disliked them as much as he disliked Caussidière himself, made it his business to pay them a visit and his manner was friendly, jovial, and blatantly demagogic.

"My son," he told them, "my own son is a grocer's boy in the rue de la Verrerie. Your mayor's son is a grocer's boy! We are all workers. My son works in a grocer's shop!"

Pinning little faith on the ability of the Montagnards to safeguard the capital, the men in the Hôtel de Ville agreed on the formation of twenty-four battalions of *gardes mobiles*. Each battalion was to be made up of one thousand men. The *garde mobile* was composed of young volunteers who contracted for a year's service at a salary of one and a half francs per day. They were easily recognizable by their green epaulets.[7]

---

[7] The strength of the *garde mobile* never actually rose much above 15,000 men.

✎ The Miracle of '48

It was only natural that the February Days should have been followed by a certain amount of civil disturbance. A château belonging to the banker Rothschild was set on fire, but he appeased the people's anger by a donation of 25,000 francs to the fund in aid of those wounded in the February riots. A wind of indiscipline was blowing even through the ranks of the Empire and the veterans of the Invalides, and on one occasion the governor of the Invalides, General Petit, suffered some inconvenience. (General Petit has been immortalized as the symbol of the imperial army in the famous lithograph of Napoleon's farewell to the Old Guard at Fontainebleau.)

On March 29 an angry crowd poured down the rue Montmartre and broke the presses on which Girardin's paper was printed, because Girardin had been waging a fierce and quite unjustified war on the Provisional Government. In the summer of 1848 he also clashed with Cavaignac, and he was finally among those responsible for installing Louis Napoleon Bonaparte as President of the Republic.

A number of incidents also occurred in the provinces. Angry murmurs were directed against certain industrialists, and the Croutelle textile works in the faubourg Fléchambaut in Rheims was burned to the ground. There were outbreaks of violence against religious houses where the monks and nuns were accused of working for cut rates and consequently undermining the claims of the workers. On March 26 the Bon Pasteur Institute at Lyons, which provided work for fallen women, was broken into and similar scenes took place at Saint-Étienne on April 13 in the convents of La

Reine, La Refuge, and La Sainte-Famille. Yet on the whole the country was quiet. The explosion which occurred in 1848 was nowhere near as violent as that of 1789. There are even grounds for thinking, as Lamartine believed, that the persistent efforts of communists like Cabet to teach the militants to do without violence had not been altogether vain.

This is the moment to mention the matter of the red flag, over which feelings ran high. It was Lamartine's eloquence which extinguished this spark. "The red flag," he said, "has been dragged in blood around the Champ de Mars. . . . The tricolor flag has gone around the world carrying freedom in its folds." Goudchaux, the Finance Minister, begged the government to give up the red flag. "If France adopts it for her emblem, the stock exchange, which is already in the throes of an appalling crisis, will collapse altogether." However, the members of the government were not anxious to inflict such a humiliating defeat on the artisans of the red flag, and there was an abortive attempt to introduce a red rosette on the flagstaff which was to be the badge of the highest authority. (The members of the government wore it more for show than from real enthusiasm.) Daniel Stern regretted that the red flag had not been adopted openly since this would, she said, have removed any odious stigma which might have attached to it later, and would have won the support of the working-class masses for the government.

Despite all the friction, the declaration of the Republic brought with it an extraordinary sense of freedom, joy, and plenty. In this chapter I want to stress the depth and intensity of this feeling, although I fear I am not doing so very well. The curious atmosphere of Paris during the last days of February and the beginning of March can be experienced with remarkable clarity and precision in Flaubert's novel *L'Éducation sentimentale*. Maxime Du Camp has also dwelt on this almost miraculous sense of joy in his book on 1848, and Du Camp cannot be accused of any fondness for the Second Republic. Paris resembled a woman in love, rapturous yet quiescent. The city felt utterly secure, for was she not cradled in the strong arms of the people? But this sense of security, generally so narrow and prosaic, was accompanied by a dreamlike trust. The future seemed limitless. The schoolmaster Lefrançais, who was to become a member of the Commune of 1871, was twenty-two in 1848 and he wrote: "The fine plans that were made for the future! France was herself again. At last a society was going to be created that would be based on justice in which every member would be truly free and equal. Labor would be freed from the arrogant and dreadful exploitation of financiers. Then, who knows whether with the spread of contagion, the whole of Europe might not soon have been transformed into a federation of free peoples. Then would have been the time of the Universal Republic. After all, it needed only the vigor and uprightness of the Provisional Government which had just been set up in the Hôtel de Ville."

From all sides adherents flocked to the new government. The Church of France declared for the Republic. In his house in the rue Fortunée, Balzac, who loathed the new regime, shook with indignation when, on March 28, he heard the parish priest of Saint-Philippe-du-Roule preaching in the open air in the Place Beauvau and giving his blessing to a liberty tree. Not only priests but monarchists as well were crying "*Vive la République!*" Raspail, in his paper *L'Ami du Peuple*, emphasized the importance of the aristocracy's support for the Republic. He never doubted that once La Rochejaquelein had come out in favor of the Republic he would bring other legitimists in his train.

On March 3, General Changarnier wrote a letter to the Provisional Government from Algeria expressing his "ardent wish to devote all his strength to the safety of the Republic." With unabashed bravado he requested that his "will and habit of victory" should be put to good use. (Changarnier omitted to say that before writing this republican letter he had offered the Prince of Joinville and the Duke of Aumale the assistance of the army in Africa to escort them back to Paris.) Even Bugeaud placed himself at the disposal of the government, which however declined his proffered services. In this period of general rejoicing of all people in France, those least carried away and a prey to the most anxiety were the members of the government and in particular the republicans belonging to the victorious faction, the men connected with the *National*. Sainte-Beuve later remarked, "My own imaginings in February were by no means as black as those I saw in some of yesterday's republicans, who appeared surprised and even terrified by their own success."

✄ The Tasks of the New Government

The Provisional Government was faced with three main tasks. First it had to improve the lot of the working classes and to straighten out the economic and financial situation.

Secondly, it had to obtain recognition of the new republic from other nations and to find a way of creating a stable balance of power in Europe.

Thirdly, it had to deal with the question of universal suffrage and give the country a chance to decide its own future. In fact, it had to provide food, peace, and freedom for all.

The government's immediate consideration was to provide substantial satisfaction for the workers.

1. On March 2, 1848, a law was passed abolishing sweated labor. This was directed at the notorious practice of subcontracting. The subcontractor undertook to carry out a particular job for his employer for a fixed price and then ensured an exorbitant profit for himself by taking on labor to do the actual work, either directly or indirectly under his control, at the lowest possible rate. The subcontractor was loathed by the workers because his dictatorship was all the more cruel in that it was concealed under an appearance of blunt good-fellowship. There were a great many workers in the eighteen-forties who wanted trade unions set up in factories. L'Atelier's advice to the workers was typical of the spirit of 1848: "You may form small societies of six, eight, or ten members as the case may be. Each society shall choose its most trustworthy member to act as its intermediary with the contractor. He will take the place of the old subcontractor or jobber, but then it will be to the advantage of all his associates, since the profits will be divided among them according to the amount of work done by each." (Issue of September 1840) I stress the importance of this passage because, to my way of thinking, it contains the germ of the solution which must one day be found to all labor problems. The small unions envisaged by L'Atelier should be able to develop within the framework of huge factories equipped with all modern technological developments. Perhaps in this way we may be able to reconcile the dignity of labor with efficient workmanship. In the eighteen-

forties, however, the advice of the workers who directed *L'Atelier* was followed only in rare instances, and the efforts of the Provisional Government to do away with the practice of subcontracting were an almost total failure.

2. Another law, passed on March 2, 1848, fixed the working day at ten hours in Paris and eleven elsewhere. The commissioners sent into the provinces by the Provisional Government often made valiant attempts to put this law into practice. Two lawyers, Frédéric Deschamps of Rouen and Émile Ollivier of Marseilles, deserve a special word of praise in this connection. Deschamps decided on March 10 to enforce the eleven-hour working day in factories in Normandy. On April 6, Ollivier, more radical still, declared a ten-hour working day in the province of Bouches-du-Rhône. Both men made enemies of the industrialists, and Deschamps and Ollivier very quickly learned the cost of attacking the employers. Deschamps retired from public life at the end of April and not long afterward Ollivier was dispatched to the Haute-Marne in disgrace. The act reducing the length of the working day was scarcely more effective than that abolishing the practice of subcontracting. On September 9, 1848, the Constituent Assembly decreed that actual working hours in factories and workshops should not exceed twelve. But there was no guarantee that even this new law, severe as it was, would be observed. The workers continued to work inordinately long hours, just as they had done under the monarchy.

3. On February 25 a much more important act was passed, one which was to have a far-reaching effect on French social and political history. "The Provisional Government of the French Republic pledges itself to guarantee a living wage for the workers. It pledges itself to guarantee every man the right to work." Proudhon wrote this characteristic com-

ment: "What are you called, Revolution of 1848? My name is the Right to Work." For once Proudhon was in agreement with Louis Blanc, who drew up the law of February 25. At the time he took up his appointment, the government in the Hôtel de Ville was being besieged by delegations of the people. They came with threats as well as encouragement. A worker by the name of Marche, the leader of one of these delegations, distinguished himself by announcing, "The people offers the Republic three months of poverty."

It was to some extent due to the insistence of Marche that Louis Blanc made his official proclamation of the right to work. But how was the new act to be enforced? On February 28, Marie, the Minister of Public Works, in turn issued a decree authorizing the setting up of National Workshops. It is a fact that the nation had been paralyzed by economic troubles for the past fifteen months and after the events of February these had simply increased. The curve of unemployment was mounting. Marie's act was scarcely published before there was a rush on the offices taking on workers for the new sites. (Two enrollment offices, one in the meat market and the other in the rue de Bondy, were besieged almost to overflowing.) Marie was desperate when the head of his department introduced him to a young engineer from the École Centrale named Émile Thomas, who cherished ambitions on a Napoleonic scale. Thomas wanted to see the workers "organized into units created along the lines of army units, with eleven men to a section, four sections to a brigade, four brigades to a company, and three companies to a unit" (La Gorce, *Histoire de la Seconde République*). Marie was beside himself with delight and Garnier-Pagès was even more dazzled by the idea. Garnier-Pagès regarded Émile Thomas as one of the great thinkers of the age and exclaimed that "a Statesman had emerged." Émile Thomas was made director of the National Workshops. By the end of March, 21,000 workers had been enrolled. By the end of April the figure was 94,000. Between the fifth and the middle of May, the National Workshops cost over seven million francs.

The middle classes objected to the thought that their money was being wasted on ne'er-do-wells in this way. The workers enrolled in the National Workshops spent most of their time playing billiards and making speeches in praise of the social-democrat Republic. Here and there a few were to be found carting one or two barrowloads of sand on the Champ de Mars or the heights of Belleville. They did a bit of digging and then went back to their games or talk. A good deal of feeling was growing up against the National Workshops and their creation shook the faith which had been placed in the Provisional Government. It was felt that only incompetents could have envisaged assembling so many idle hands in the capital in its present unsettled state. This anger was directed increasingly against Louis Blanc. Blanc, in his book *L'Organisation du travail*, had advocated the setting up of social workshops which were, in fact, simply co-operatives. Production would be controlled by workers' associations without the help of the bosses. Insofar as they were successful at all, they spread. These small groups became a kind of microcosm of the city of the future, cutting out the profit of the middleman. The cooperatives envisaged by Louis Blanc bore no relation to the National Workshops, which were simply ordinary charity institutions, but, especially in times of crisis, people's reasoning is not dictated by cold-blooded observation and the very similarity of the two names, National Workshops and Social Workshops, was enough for Louis Blanc.

Louis Blanc was the more unfortunate in that the National Workshops for which he was so bitterly criticized became associated in the minds of Marie, Armand Marrast, and Lamartine, and in the minds of all those who constituted what might be called the "reactionary" element in the government, with a kind of extra Praetorian guard. Lamartine and Marie were wondering anxiously whether the *garde mobile*, which seemed to include a good many young thugs, would stand firm in defense of the establishment in the event of an uprising. The prospect of possessing, in the shape of the National Workshops, an army of workers capable of checking any move by the extremist elements in the capital sent a thrill of relief through Lamartine, Marrast, and Marie. The workers of the National Workshops were not required to work; they were only required to maintain a more or less undercover connection with the representatives of the *National* party. Émile Thomas himself was surprised at the ease with which he was allowed to indulge in the ruinous expense of the National Workshops. "Don't worry about money," Marie told him. "If necessary we'll make you a grant from the secret funds." All question of political Machiavellianism aside, I repeat that it showed remarkable naivety even on the part of the moderates in the government to authorize the creation of the National Workshops in their final form. A large section of the population objected strongly to the sight of all these idle hands and put the blame not only on socialists of Louis Blanc's persuasion but even on those so-called "honest republicans" like Marie or Marrast. In the affair of the National Workshops, the *National* men were not only striking a telling blow against their opponents on the *Réforme*, they were also digging the ground from under their own feet. They were destroying themselves politically by initiating a reaction whose effects would be sufficiently far-reaching to bring about their own downfall.

4. Finally, on February 28, a Government Commission for Labor was set up to take the place, both literally and metaphorically, of the Chamber of Peers: hence its title of the Luxembourg Commission. Louis Blanc would have liked to have a ministry, but his requests for the creation of a Ministry of Labor and Progress were unsuccessful and he had to be satisfied with the chairmanship of the Luxembourg Commission.[8] This was a kind of parliament representing the world of labor. Workers and employers in every line of business appointed delegates to the Luxembourg, and a great many workers who had played more or less prominent parts in combinations or mutual-aid societies met again there. It was they who forced through the acts concerning subcontracting and length of working hours, by threatening the government that if these were not passed immediately they would boycott the Luxembourg.

As well as the actual delegates, the Commission also contained socialist writers and even economists in the liberal tradition such as Le Play, Dupont-White, Wolowski, Victor Considérant, and Constantin Pecqueur. Proudhon was asked but declined to join the Luxembourg and waged a fierce campaign against the Commission. Vidal, a socialist theoretician who two years previously had published a major work on the redistribution of wealth (*La Répartition des richesses*), acted as secretary to the Luxembourg. As a result

[8] Albert acted as vice chairman, and also presided over a commission known as the "*Récompenses nationales.*" Delegates to the Luxembourg were accused of dipping into the funds of the *Récompenses nationales*, and this not only on their own account but also on behalf of their families and other more or less unworthy persons.

of the Commission's debates, Vidal in collaboration with Pecqueur published a long account in the *Moniteur* (April 27, and May 2, 3, and 6, 1848) touching on the setting up of workshops or agricultural colonies, the reorganization of the insurance system and the Bank of France, and other matters. It was an interesting series of articles, but purely theoretical.

In practice the Commission was powerless. Admittedly Louis Blanc arbitrated successfully in a number of disputes between workers and employers and he also contributed to getting the workers' associations under way, but most of these lost their original impetus when the wave of reaction swept over the country. Louis Napoleon's coup d'état on December 2, 1851, dealt them a mortal blow. However, I should like to stress the incidence of political evolution in the development of the workers' associations. Some of these associations expired of their own accord as a result of the incompetence or inadequacy of their members, but others which seemed reasonably viable were doomed because they bore the stamp of a republic which was itself doomed. The state of the economy should also be taken into account. In this connection, the story of the great iron foundries of Jean François Cail is a case in point.

During the economic crisis and social disturbances of 1848, the workers and employers came before the Luxembourg to settle their differences. The outcome was a decision to turn the Cail works into a workers' cooperative. Business deteriorated gradually until in 1850 the firm of Jean François Cail et Cie came into being in the normal way with a capital of seven million francs. But we should not be too hasty in assuming that when the Cail workers in the rue de Chabrol or the Quai de Billy took over management of the firm they proved unequal to the task. In 1848 the industry was facing a slump. By 1850 conditions had improved. The Cail company's return to normal coincided with a return to prosperity. It cannot be said to have created that prosperity.

The impotence of the Luxembourg Commission had one effect on the development of working-class thought which, in my opinion, has generally been treated with insufficient emphasis by historians. It helped to turn a substantial minority of the proletariat back to the path of violence. Workers in the eighteen-forties were not in the habit of reading methodically through the works of the great social theorists. They simply had a vague idea that there were wise men engaged in seeking a remedy for their troubles and they believed that these remedies had in fact been found. Proudhon and Pierre Leroux have described how, after the February Days, they were called on by workers anxious to "closet" them together as quickly as possible. The workers' reasoning was simple: they intended to get together Proudhon, Leroux, the Fourierist Victor Considérant, and the communist Cabet and put them all together in one room under a strong guard, in the belief that they were bound to reach an agreement in the end and produce some positive plan for the social revolution.

Unfortunately all the wretched workers could see at the Luxembourg was endless discussion, and they were beginning to lose faith in the theorists who preached patience and nonviolence but produced no practicable solutions. Consequently the workers fell back on vague revolutionary ideas derived from Babeuf and the Jacobins, in which neither the wealthy nor the aristocratic were to be spared. One kind of vague utopian faith was being replaced by another equally vague faith in strong, direct action. The shade of Blanqui was beginning to rise again from the ruins of the National Workshops and the Luxembourg Commission. Auguste Blanqui was typical of the kind of man who believes that, with a few determined comrades not afraid of violence, it is possible to turn the whole structure of society upside down in a moment.

FINANCE The Provisional Government was called upon to deal with a financial situation that was grave in the extreme. To us, who have been hardened by our own experience of all the financial manipulations which have taken place in the world during the last thirty years, it may seem that the panic which occurred in 1848 had very little to justify it. Nevertheless, it was the wealthy middle class itself which, by its utter lack of faith in the credit of the new government, precipitated disaster by demanding that the Bank of France redeem notes with gold. The bank's gold reserves dropped by over 50 per cent in a fortnight. On March 15 alone, the bank paid out ten million francs in gold.

On the other hand, financial stability was regarded not only by conservatives but even by the majority of revolutionary theoreticians as the keystone of the economy. Goudchaux, who had been landed with responsibility for finance on February 24, announced with a confidence that was to say the least indiscreet that back interest on 5 per cent bonds would be paid in advance. Achille Fould, a banker like Goudchaux himself and, like him, of Jewish descent, who was to become Minister of Finance in October 1849 and was among the staunchest supporters of the Second Empire, said openly that Goudchaux was acting idiotically. On the contrary, he prophesied inflation and advised suspending payment of interest altogether. A journalist named Delamarre, who as editor of *La Patrie* also became one of the pillars of the Empire, suggested that Goudchaux ought to assemble all the wealthiest capitalists and compel them to underwrite a loan of thirty million frances.

When things had returned to normal, Achille Fould and Delamarre both naturally insisted that their intentions had been misinterpreted and that they had never contemplated any infringement of orthodox financial practice. On March 6 Goudchaux resigned and Garnier-Pagès took over the Finance Ministry, while his place at the *mairie* was taken by Armand Marrast. Garnier-Pagès instituted a number of sensible measures including the circulation of hundred-franc notes, merging the departmental banks with the Bank of France, and setting up discount banks. He was obliged to make notes compulsory legal tender. A fund was set up to receive patriotic gifts to the nation, and a great many workers offered the government one or more days' wages. On this generous roll of honor the workers of Puteaux deserve a special mention. But all these were no more than palliative measures. The deficit in the budget was getting bigger and already there was a flourishing market in gold. The depreciation in the value of notes in relation to gold was around 15 per cent.

Georges Lefebvre is right in thinking that Garnier-Pagès acted far too hesitantly in his dealings with the Bank of France, which should have cooperated far more fully with the state. As yet the Bank's monopoly extended only to Paris and it printed only large-denomination notes. When he authorized the issue of hundred-franc notes, which extended this monopoly, Garnier-Pagès could at the same time have asked for a substantial advance. The result would have been inflation, "but," continues Lefebvre, "this would have been a slight inconvenience compared with the political advantages. And even in a country in the throes of an economic crisis, inflation would have been a useful means of creating the purchasing power to raise prices and encourage enterprise." [9]

Garnier-Pagès found his solution in the notorious "forty-five-centime tax," which raised all direct taxation by an additional forty-five centimes to the franc. Garnier-Pagès could hardly have done better if he had wanted to bring about a complete split between the peasantry and the new regime. For a great many peasants, the Republic became identified with the forty-five-centime tax and was thenceforth symbolized by a stupefying and extortionate sheaf of contributions.

PEACE   The second problem was peace and what Lamartine, now occupying Guizot's seat in the boulevard des Capucines, was to do about it. He had to pursue a very tactful policy with regard to the major powers because the February Revolution had proved contagious. In Germany, Austria, Poland, Hungary, and Italy there was growing unrest, and Louis Philippe, at Claremont, was saying, "Europe is giving me splendid obsequies." If France displayed open hostility to all those governments and princes who attempted to maintain the Holy Alliance against the people, she would be embarking on a course fraught with danger. Any move on the part of France toward upsetting the balance of power established in 1815 risked bringing about a revival of the coalition between England and Russia against her. But on the other hand, to opt for peace also had its perils. French inactivity could be fatal to any action undertaken by the people in the shape of a rising against their old oppressors, the established monarchs. If the Republic was

[9] From a lecture given by Georges Lefebvre at the Sorbonne, February 24, 1946. Reprinted in the first issue of the new series of the review La Révolution de 1848. Caussidière (Mémoires, Vol. I, p. 233) has some interesting things to say about the financial measures put forward by the editorial body of La Réforme.

too cautious it could paralyze the emancipation of Europe, and once the kings had defeated their own subjects they might, thanks to French passivity, turn against France. The Republic ran an even greater risk of subjugation if she failed to help all those everywhere who were fighting for their freedom. In 1850–1851, when the Republic seemed to be on its last legs, a great many Frenchmen who had loved and supported it but had at the same time openly longed for peace, beat their breasts and admitted that they had been wrong. There is a fine passage in Flaubert's *L'Éducation sentimentale* in which the two chief characters draw up a reckoning and an indictment of their own youth and at the same time of the 1848 revolution. The conversation between the two men ends with the words, "We should have set fire to the four corners of Europe." The same sentence can be found, word for word, in 1850 in *L'Atelier*, a paper which, as I have already observed, was run by moderate workers.

Lamartine, at least on the surface, opted for peace. On March 4 he sent out a circular to French diplomatic representatives. It was obviously the result of deep cogitation and it was couched in noble and utterly contradictory terms. Lamartine began by saying that as far as Republican France was concerned, the treaties of 1815 had ceased to be valid. As Guizot's successor, Lamartine was concerned to avoid any impression that he was merely a reincarnation of Guizot—an impression which he nevertheless managed to give to the population of the capital at large—and consequently he had to deliver an unequivocal condemnation of the treaties of 1815 which had put an end to the great hopes of the Revolution and the Empire. But this declaration of principle once put into words, Lamartine was ready to be accommodating. He did his best to reassure the chancelleries, stating that there was no need to fear aggression from France and that the status quo was still perfectly acceptable. France would ensure that there was no trouble on her frontiers, and would keep a close watch on the development of affairs in Italy. The note contained a warning to Austria, but even the tone used toward Vienna was more firm than actually threatening. After the Revolution a great many Poles had invaded Paris and were pressing the government to do something toward liberating their country. Lamartine had taken no trouble to disguise his impatience with them, and this attitude itself seemed like a substantial guarantee of peace. His aristocratic connections, his reputation as a poet, and his diplomatic experience made him the only minister in the government capable of maintaining continued friendly relations with the diplomatic world. With the help of the French authorities, a small free corps had been formed to start a revolution in Belgium, and a small engagement had taken place, more stupid than bloody, at a place called "Risquons-tout" on the Franco-Belgian frontier. After the February Days, the Belgian press as a whole had attacked France viciously. King Leopold I took it into his head that the Second Republic would follow the example of the First in attempting to annex Belgium, and he appealed to every court in Europe for help against France. There was also an incident involving a German legion which marched from Strasbourg with French backing and was dispersed and disarmed in the region of Baden. Lamartine exerted himself to the utmost to show that these were small, insignificant incidents. He sent personal messages of reassurance to the princes. Lamartine had played a decisive part in the 1848 revolution in order to create a climate for peace.

This is not necessarily to say that he had not dreamed of reshaping the map of Europe. Lamartine followed events in Germany very closely: he thought that the King of Prussia,

Frederick William IV, might become a liberal sovereign. For a few weeks it looked as though Prussia would give the province of Posen a charter which would be the beginning of a new life for Poland, but of this notion people were quickly disabused. Lamartine had in mind a close alliance between France and Germany which could free Europe from the haunting specter of Russia and create the kind of security which would be favorable to gradual progress in easy stages. But Frederick William IV swiftly tired of his leanings toward liberalism. The Frankfurt parliament, with its aims of making Germany into a unified, democratic state, irritated the King of Prussia and he turned increasingly toward St. Petersburg and Vienna. Lamartine's cherished plans had been no more than phantoms.

LIBERTY   As soon as the Provisional Government took office it proclaimed the freedom of the press, the abolition of the stamp tax, and the people's right of free assembly and of presenting petitions. Immediately clubs and newspapers proliferated, and this is one of the most characteristic aspects of 1848. The government also abolished slavery and the death penalty for political offenses.

But introducing a people to freedom is no easy matter. On February 24, the men who took over the Hôtel de Ville made a solemn declaration that they had undertaken the burden of power only as a temporary measure and that the people were to be completely free to choose whatever form of government they wished. But this granted, there were a good many ways of consulting the people, and only a people with a certain degree of political education is in a position to express a coherent opinion. Education, however, implied influencing and this surely constituted an infringement of the very freedom which had been the keystone of the new edifice.

Ledru-Rollin replaced the prefects of the monarchy by republican commissioners who were sent to every part of the country with apparently unlimited powers. I say *apparently*, because these commissioners did not in fact undertake any radical changes. The examples of Ollivier and Deschamps have already given an indication of the powerful forces they were up against. Ledru-Rollin had every reason to fear that the aristocracy and the middle classes would immediately get the masses on their side and turn the opinion they were called on to express to their own advantage. The commissioners' task was more than simply an administrative one. They had also to act as educators and propagandists, and teach the populace, which was totally uninformed on political matters, what the Republic stood for. Immediately a howl of anger went up from the ranks of other parties. "Your commissioners are dictators," they told Ledru-Rollin. Undoubtedly the choice of commissioners was sometimes unfortunate, and Ledru-Rollin frequently made the mistake of recalling the first commissioners he had appointed to a particular *département*. The arrival of a successor in a city which had already suffered a greater or lesser degree of social upheaval only led to a further useless proliferation of hostile clans. Republicans who shared the same political views were divided when some favored the first commissioner and others the second—and in some cases there was even a third. Commissioners in a number of cities —Latrade at Bordeaux, Leclanché at Amiens, Napoléon Chancel at Valence, and Sauriac at Montauban—were forced to retire in the face of the hostility of the local populace. Nevertheless, whatever ill has been said of Ledru-Rollin's commissioners, many of them carried out their tasks with success, and a large number were elected to the Constituent Assembly by the *départements* to which they had been appointed. This is proof that they had won the hearts of those they administered.

The business of fixing a date for the elections provoked serious civil disturbances. At the beginning of this study, I drew up a list of the Days of 1848. Two of these Days, the seventeenth of March and the sixteenth of April, were marked by demonstrations in which the people of Paris made it clear that they were worried at the prospect of sudden elections. The mechanic of La Chapelle or the cabinetmaker of the faubourg Saint-Antoine was conscious of playing an intelligent part in history when he prepared to drop a voting paper with the name of Ledru-Rollin, Louis Blanc, Albert, or Caussidière into the ballot box. But when he thought that his vote might be canceled out by that of a peasant in the Vendée who did what his priest told him, or a farmer in Normandy following his master's orders, or even of a miner from Anzin who put his mark by the name of his loathed but all-powerful boss, then the mechanic of La Chapelle was a worried man. I have already observed more than once that Buonarrotti's book *La Conspiration pour l'Égalité, dite de Babeuf* was his bible. What Buonarrotti actually said was that "moral reforms should come before the enjoyment of liberty." Buonarrotti applauded the members of the Convention because they delayed the putting into practice of the Constitution of 1793. "They knew that before the People could be given sovereign power, there must first be a general love of virtue." In other words, the problem of the elections was the same as the problem of political education which we have already encountered in discussing Ledru-Rollin's commissioners. There is no doubt that if Ledru-Rollin had waited for his commissioners to spread the reign of virtue throughout the land before giving the citizens the right to vote, the Provisional Government would have been able to remain in office for a long time.

The government's state of indecision can easily be imagined, with Lamartine clamoring for the elections to be held as soon as possible and Louis Blanc wanting them put off for as long as possible. Ledru-Rollin wavered between Lamartine and Louis Blanc. The first date suggested was April 9, but this was postponed to April 23 in order to give an impression that some concessions were being made to the demonstrators of March 17. The demonstration of April 16, which was partly aimed at producing a further postponement, did not this time alter the government's decision. The elections were held on the twenty-third. Looking at the matter from the point of view of the government's own interests, it is my belief that this final solution was a ghastly mistake. *The elections should have been held either before or after this date.* If the government had gone to the country immediately after the February Days, when the nation's enthusiasm was still at white heat and while their political opponents were still suffering from shock, they would have gained an overwhelming majority. It may be objected that this would have been a surprise ballot, but it would at least have made it possible for a vigorous government to undertake large-scale measures. Had the elections been held later, on the other hand, republican ideals would certainly have taken root in a number of *départements* and the government could have won a great many more votes. (In many *départements*—the Dordogne is a typical example—there was a stronger republican vote in the elections for the Legislative Assembly on May 13, 1849, than in those for the Constituent Assembly on April 23, 1848.) Civic education would have borne fruit. But to hold the elections two months after the Provisional Government had been set up was displaying an extraordinary lack of political acumen: enthusiasm for the new government had naturally subsided a little and the supporters of the other parties had recovered from their initial shock and were in a position to wage a campaign against the Republic which was all the more effective in that it was aimed, as the mechanic of La Chapelle was well aware, at a downtrodden and uneducated population, at illiterates who would believe any slanders that were uttered by those above them and at poor people whose material well-being was in the hands of these very people.

✍ The Sixteenth and Seventeenth of March

On March 14 the government decided to do away with the elite companies of the National Guard. Equality being one of the principles of the February Revolution, entry into the National Guard would no longer be open only to influential members of the middle class and small traders. Every citizen could be a voter and a member of the National Guard. The government believed that if this were so, the equipment and organization of the various corps of the great civic militia should in no way reflect the hierarchies of social life. Such a measure touched the hosier of the faubourg Saint-Denis on the raw. Parading about in uniform—and a particularly glittering uniform at that—in the company of men like Odilon Barrot and Duvergier de Hauranne and showing that one was tired of Guizot's insolence was all very well, but when it came to mixing with the common people and defending the laws of the Republic dressed in the same uniform as the mechanic from La Chapelle or the cabinetmaker from the faubourg Saint-Antoine, then our hosier protested. The result was that the unanimity which had existed in the Place de la Madeleine on February 22 broke up three weeks later. On March 15 the hosier demonstrated his disapproval of the new government. There was no lack of grievances against the men ensconced in the Hôtel de Ville. They had devalued the currency, they were maintaining an army of layabouts in the Champ de Mars, and they were allowing the *partageux* (or socialists) to speechify in the Luxembourg. It is worth noting here just how sensitive people can be to pinpricks and how they can take matters of etiquette and social precedence deeply to heart. When the hosier indulged in his first demonstration against the government it was not dictated by the political crisis or by financial considerations or by any genuine ideological grievances. He was protesting because his fur hat had been taken away from him.

On March 16 several thousand National Guards demonstrated in the streets in order to protest against the disbanding of the elite companies. At the Pont au Change they came up against hostile bands of mechanics, typographers, and cabinetmakers. They too were angry, roused to fury by such a dreadfully anti-egalitarian demonstration.

"Down with the fur hats!" they shouted.

"Down with Ledru-Rollin!" retorted the National Guards.

This cry is worth remembering, for it was the first time the reactionary element had raised its voice. Even so, when our hosier reached the Hôtel de Ville he was soon made to feel ashamed of himself because the moderates in the government trounced him thoroughly.

"You are out of your minds," Armand Marrast told the

demonstrators. "Sensible men like you ought never to take the law into your own hands to make your demands heard. If you behave like this it will encourage the people to rebellion."

François Arago had this to say: "Tomorrow we shall have a counterdemonstration from the working classes on our hands, and where will that get us?"

In fact, the next morning, March 17, did bring an answering demonstration against the *bonnets à poil*. The people's unity was surprising. More than 100,000 men had been gathered together and marched in a body from the Place de la Concorde to the Hôtel de Ville. The people showed their strength in a disciplined manner, with no angry shouting. The workers' attitude to the government was one of loyalty mixed with concern. They feared some action on the part of the monarchists and were also disturbed by the high spirits shown by notoriously antirepublican officers in the army. They wanted the regular army sent away from Paris and the elections both for parliament and for the officers of the National Guard to be postponed.

Louis Blanc was among the instigators of this popular demonstration, although at the same time, as a member of the government, he had no wish to see the demonstration turning into an insurrection. In the Hôtel de Ville there was a certain amount of vacillation. Cabet and Sobrier were satisfied that the people had shown firmness and deliberation. (Their feelings were the same as those which inspired the majority of the demonstrators.) The extremist elements, on the other hand, men who were increasingly following the dictates of Blanqui—and our mechanic from La Chapelle spent practically every evening at Blanqui's club in the Conservatoire de Musique—wanted the Provisional Government called on to take more vigorous steps against the *bonnets à poil* and against all those who were sabotaging the Republic. The mechanic, in fact, was beginning to lose faith in Louis Blanc, and when he encountered him in the Hôtel de Ville on March 17 he said to him privately, in a tone more of sorrow than of anger, "So you too have turned traitor?"

Sobrier uttered soothing noises: "The delegates have complete confidence in the government . . ."

"Not in all of them," objected Blanqui's supporters.

At that moment all eyes were turned on Lamartine. He looked extremely worried and this was not easy to understand, because he had foreseen a large republican element in the government. Unlike Garnier-Pagès, he had not attempted to dissociate himself from Ledru-Rollin. This is not the place to discuss whether Lamartine's chosen policy was a sensible one in itself or whether it stood any great chance of success, but we must make an effort to understand it and see if it holds together. Certainly it relied heavily on the people and especially on the progressive elements in the population of Paris. The kind of grand national republican synthesis described by the author of the *Histoire des Girondins* retained a frankly popular character: for appearance' sake it was bound to revolve around the working-class masses. A quietly impressive demonstration like that which took place on March 17 seemed a typical illustration of the kind of republic Lamartine had dreamed of and created. But men are full of contradictions, and although Lamartine had cut himself off from the right wing and was increasingly losing touch with the hosier and, all in all, was much closer to Ledru-Rollin than to Garnier-Pagès, he felt a genuine panic terror at the prospect of a popular rising. He lost control of himself. After the February Revolution he had been in the habit of saying, "The Republic is a surprise which we have turned into a miracle." The word "surprise" is itself surprising coming from the poet, since if anyone was entitled to regard himself as the author of the appearance presented by France in 1848, that person was Lamartine. It was largely Lamartine himself who had foisted this surprise on the country. The word "miracle" also rang somewhat false in the mouth of a statesman, because at the time he uttered it, Lamartine no longer believed in it and he was filled with gloomy forebodings.

Lamartine loved the people and was actually one of the few individuals in 1848 who faced up to them boldly and with undisputed physical courage. Unlike Garnier-Pagès or Marrast, Lamartine did not lose his nerve. In the first weeks of the revolution, he was the prop and stay of the government. Armed mobs might stand before him, waving their weapons and uttering the most terrible threats: he faced them without flinching. Whenever the time came to enter the lion's den, Lamartine, in marked contrast to his colleagues, answered, "Ready." But unconsciously he may have grown tired of this role of lion tamer. He had plunged into the first battles with a mixture of confidence and amateurishness, but it was not long before he began to regard the poor, wretched proletariat as a serious enemy, and directed his efforts more to charming than to convincing it. Lamartine believed that at any moment the frail chariot of the Republic could be tipped into the mire of dictatorship. He acquired a horror of the masses, seeing the anarchic and malignant crowds, in a constant state of fermentation, as the unconscious instrument of counterrevolution. Not without some reason, Lamartine was haunted by the thought of violence, and these processions of the people, however well ordered, seemed to him a melancholy foretaste of an era of impending dictatorship. "The Eighteenth Brumaire of the people," he said on March 17, "bears the name of Eighteenth Brumaire of despotism." It could be argued that with somewhat greater confidence and method Lamartine might have rendered the masses he feared rather less anarchic and malignant and that he was miscast in his role of snake charmer or lion tamer. When he began his political career, Lamartine saw himself principally as a schoolmaster. It is a pity he did not stick to the role. Because in the last resort he was afraid of the people, he helped to foster in them the very terror which led to political disintegration and the "Eighteenth Brumaire." By conniving with Marie and Marrast against Louis Blanc and by his dreams of turning the brigades of the National Workshops into a kind of Praetorian guard explicitly designed to safeguard the Provisional Government, he was preparing the way for the social upheavals which brought Louis Napoleon Bonaparte to power.

Lamartine may have shown too much presumption on February 24, but after the victory he emerged as simultaneously too timid and too Machiavellian. On March 17 we find him announcing in the Hôtel de Ville: "This is our twentieth of June. When will our tenth of August come?" They were the very words uttered by Duchâtel in the presence of Louis Philippe in the Tuileries on February 24. So are men imprisoned by history, or rather by their historical imagery. But although Lamartine may have made private comparisons with the past which paralyzed his ability to act, he retained his masterly command of words. The charmer could still make himself heard on March 17:

"We are without guards, weapons, or material support; we have no power beyond that of our moral rightness, and we shall defend this last barrier of our independence to the death."

The Sixteenth of April

Old General de Courtais, who commanded the National Guard and took an obvious pleasure in his role of people's general, did not regard the grievances of the *bonnets à poil* at all seriously. Unlike Lamartine, Marrast, and Marie, he reveled in great popular demonstrations. In an effort to make his headquarters more democratic, he had decided that his staff should include fourteen officers from the working class to be elected by their comrades. The election was to take place on Sunday, April 16, on the Champ de Mars. The Luxembourg delegates together with the militant members of the clubs, friends of Raspail and Blanqui, meant to make it a great day for republicanism. Among the groups of Blanqui's followers the atmosphere was stormy. Taschereau, in *La Revue rétrospective*, had recently published some documents damaging to Blanqui, who in a moment of weakness had turned police informer. Taschereau published some depositions made by Blanqui at the Ministry of the Interior in October 1839. Personally, I am not prepared to commit myself as to the authenticity of Taschereau's document. Maurice Dommanget, who devoted fifteen years to a painstaking study of Blanqui, was reluctantly convinced, at the time he began his study, that Taschereau had been telling the truth. Now, on the other hand, Dommanget has gone over to the theory that he was not. Whatever the truth, Blanqui, in April 1848, was like a man struck by a sledgehammer. His reply was feeble and slow in coming. Raspail, in his paper *L'Ami du Peuple*, which was widely read by Parisians, took Blanqui's part but with more enthusiasm than deep conviction. Raspail's article actually appeared on

April 16. I give all these details to re-create the atmosphere of a day which was one of the turning points of 1848.

"The day that little M. Taschereau, a man belonging to Louis Philippe and his party, flung in the public face the document just described," wrote Raspail, "all my ideas were turned upside down." Why had Blanqui's reply been so long in coming? Raspail went on. It was because Blanqui was suffering from exhaustion. "But this reply seemed to me, and still seems, crushing . . ." All in all, the demonstration of April 16 did not appear in the rosy colors which had attracted the kindly imagination of General de Courtais.

To the moderate element in the government, and to the men of the *National* on the evening of April 14, it even appeared particularly black. A cabinet meeting had just ended that evening when Louis Blanc and Albert announced with apparent carelessness that the people would be demonstrating in the streets on the next Sunday but one. "You are talking about that ceremony of Courtais's?" someone asked. "Not exactly," Louis Blanc answered with some excitement. "There will be a double demonstration. After the elections have been held in the morning in the Champ de Mars, the workers will proceed to the Hôtel de Ville in the afternoon. Their aim will be twofold: they will take their donations to the government [it will be remembered that a fund had been set up to receive donations from the citizens], and they will also present their demands." Despite himself, Louis Blanc's voice held a note of harshness on the last words. The elections were to take place in nine days, and it looked as though they would signal the end of the social republic he had dreamed of building. The members of the government parted coldly.

In the camp of Ledru-Rollin and Caussidière there was considerable apprehension in case Blanqui should be preparing a *Putsch* for the sixteenth. There was anxiety, too, among Lamartine's followers and in the moderate camp of the *National*, who felt that Ledru-Rollin was betraying them in order to ally himself with Louis Blanc and Blanqui.

Lamartine and Marie were more worried than ever on the evening of the fourteenth, after the cabinet meeting, when they looked with amazement at the latest issue—number 16—of the *Bulletin de la République*, which was edited from the offices of the Ministry of the Interior. One article in this *Bulletin* was devoted to the thorny subject of the elections. It contained passages which were loaded with menace: "Unless the elections bring about the triumph of *social truth*, if they are no more than an expression of the interests of one class, wrenched from the loyal and trusting people, then the elections which should be the salvation of the Republic will be its destruction, of that there can be no doubt. Then there will be only one road to salvation for the people who set up the barricades, and that will be to demonstrate their wishes for a second time and put off the decisions taken by a false NATIONAL REPRESENTATION."

It was later discovered that the author of this article was George Sand, and that at the time the editor, Elias Regnault, had been called to the bedside of his sick mother and was unaware of the inflammatory prose being handed out to the country by George Sand. The fact remains that the reactionary members of the government were terrified. That night Lamartine drew up his will.

On April 16, the demonstration which had been arranged on the Champ de Mars took place without undue excitement. It is true that a few sinister rumors were being passed around among the groups of men to the effect that Ledru-Rollin and Louis Blanc had been assassinated.

Ledru-Rollin had not been assassinated, but he was in the

throes of a painful crisis of conscience. A move toward Blanqui would be a move in the direction of chaos and uncertainty. A move toward Lamartine meant the risk of moving too far to the right and of playing into the hands of the reactionaries. Ledru-Rollin ran that risk, telling himself that by this display of loyalty to the majority in the government he was preserving the unity of the authorities and so preserving the Republic.

At half past ten Ledru-Rollin was in Lamartine's office at the Hôtel de Ville, offering him his complete and unreserved cooperation. Lamartine welcomed Ledru-Rollin with open arms: at last he could breathe freely. The two men decided to give way on the matter of the National Guard in order to safeguard the regime. A second visit, from Changarnier this time, finally succeeded in calming Lamartine's fears. General Changarnier had been appointed by the Republic to the post of minister plenipotentiary to the court of Prussia. Changarnier had returned from Africa and, before taking up his new post in Berlin, he went to the Foreign Office in the boulevard des Capucines to receive his instructions. There he met Madame de Lamartine, who painted a vivid picture of her husband's terrified condition and begged him to go at once to the Hôtel de Ville. And a few minutes later Changarnier emerged once more onto the stage of history—a melancholy return for the republicans. He outlined a plan of operations to General Duvivier, commander of the *garde mobile*. The workers were to be allowed to hold their procession in the afternoon, but the route was to be lined with hostile National Guards and the procession divided into several sections with the demonstrators interspersed with battalions of the *mobiles*. Lamartine was delighted. The claws of the proletarian lion were being drawn at last.

We shall, of course, never know whether the little Blanquist party was really resolved on direct action. What can be said for certain is that the huge working-class crowd which straggled from the Champ de Mars to the Hôtel de Ville was not an army of conspirators, or anything of the kind. Whatever their anxieties, and these were undoubtedly serious—I have already drawn attention to the apprehensions aroused by the forthcoming elections—as far as the people were concerned the day was still something of a holiday: in the morning they cheered the new officers of the National Guard and in the afternoon they gave a little money to the government and asked it to act with republican vigilance. In all this there was no suggestion of an ulterior motive. And then suddenly there was this call to arms and National Guards everywhere shouting "Down with the communists!" Then there were the soldiers of the *garde mobile* channeling the surging people. The worker felt hurt, as though he were being treated like a criminal. There was not even, as there had been on March 17, the satisfaction of hearing the siren songs of the government in his ears. The people's delegates were given a chilly welcome at the Hôtel de Ville by Marrast's assistant, Edmond Adam. (Adam did not rise to fame until after 1871, when he had married the woman who was the Egeria of the Third Republic.) Still, hurt and bewildered as they were, the cabinetmaker of the faubourg Saint-Antoine and the mechanic of La Chapelle went on shouting at the tops of their voices, "Long live the Provisional Government!"

Ledru-Rollin listened to them sentimentally, which was natural, but also with a degree of complacent pride, which was silly. Louis Blanc and Albert may have been appalled to hear the drums rolling and have regarded their colleague in the Ministry of the Interior as a traitor, but Ledru-Rollin, convinced that his vigilance had saved the Provisional Government without seriously affecting the goodwill of the people, Ledru-Rollin was feeling like a conqueror.

Yet at this very moment his power was on the wane and Garnier-Pagès, who was as jealous as a man as he was incompetent as a politician, was getting sick of the incense with which the people were still filling Ledru-Rollin's nostrils. Hearing the burst of acclamation in honor of Louis Blanc and Ledru-Rollin, he slipped in between his two colleagues and took Ledru-Rollin's arm. The latter shook him off.

"Look here, old man, won't you even give me your arm?"

"If you gave me a helping hand more often in parliament," Ledru-Rollin retorted, "you might have a right to take my arm in public."

Who, then, was the real victor on the sixteenth of April? Not Ledru-Rollin or Garnier-Pagès or Lamartine, but the hosier of the faubourg Saint-Denis. After his demonstration on March 17, he had been sent home with a flea in his ear. Today people had remembered him, had clung to him to preserve the regime, and he could shout "Down with the communists!" to his heart's content. He had a hold over the Provisional Government and the future was in his hands. The shop counter had carried the day over the factory bench, and from April 16 onward a great wave of social reaction began to spread over the country. "All devoted republicans," wrote Caussidière, "are lumped together under the name of communists."

A young man from Périgord named Lachambeaudie, whose talent, though still a trifle quavering and anemic, was beginning to have a certain success at Popincourt or Vaugirard, composed a not altogether unmoving song entitled *Ne criez pas à bas les communistes*. But Lachambeaudie's folderols could scarcely be heard above the din made by the defenders of the regime.

🔖 *The Twentieth of April*

On the following Thursday, however, those who had lost the day on Sunday felt they had their revenge. The Feast of Fraternity was held on April 20 and was a resounding success for those whom Caussidière had described as "devoted republicans." The members of the government assembled beneath the Arc de Triomphe and watched the army and the National Guard march past. Colors were presented to legions and regiments.

"It was a curious ceremony," wrote Pierre de La Gorce, "at which magistrates rubbed shoulders on the platform with political prisoners, generals with men who had been wounded in February, and representatives of the Church with representatives of the clubs." Pierre de La Gorce was an Orleanist by nature, and when he wrote his *Histoire de la Seconde République*, he did not realize that the spirit of the twentieth of April was exactly the same as the spirit of the February Revolution. On the twentieth of April, Caussidière was radiant, and looked with contempt at Armand Marrast sitting on the government platform looking bored and cynical.

At ten o'clock that night the last columns filed past the Arc de Triomphe. Raspail, like Caussidière, was bursting with enthusiasm: "At all events, all the reactionaries' paeans of victory have gone up in smoke very quickly: MM. the SATISFAITS, PRITCHARDISTS, GUIZOTINS, and the PENSIONERS of the civil list who turned to their own advantage the demonstration, or should I say the mystification, of April 16, and immediately afterwards paid such moving tributes to MM. de Lamartine, Marrast, and even, I believe, to M. Pagnerre, all these reactionary gentlemen, I say, were less satisfied on the twenty-first." (*L'Ami du Peuple*, April 23.) Fifteen years later, in 1863, the remembrance of April 20, 1848, still had power to inspire the typographer Corbon, who was vice president of the Constituent Assembly, to some moving paragraphs:

"What made this festival so remarkably impressive was not only the formidable deployment of strength which the great revolutionary city was able to show to the representatives of Europe, who were deeply affected by it. It was, above all, the spirit of brotherhood which made itself felt all that day between the various different sections of the populace. . . .

"The Provisional Government had had the excellent idea of sending the legions from the wealthy districts to the Bastille to form up in the morning, while those from working-class areas went to the Madeleine, with the result that these legions were bound to pass one another. . . . I saw with my own eyes the encounter between the eighth and second legions, that is the legion from the faubourg Saint-Antoine and that from the Chaussée d'Antin, the poorest and the richest. Never shall I forget the fervent enthusiasm with which they greeted one another. Faces on both sides were radiant with joy and confidence. . . . This warmth of feeling did not abate throughout the day despite the rain which fell incessantly yet could not cool their hearts. It was the general cry which gave this festival its name, the Feast of Fraternity, and it was well named. . . .

"Moreover, it was not altogether the fault of the people that the noble sentiments which were so clearly to be seen on that day were so soon to disappear. . . ."

☙ *The Twenty-Third of April*

EASTER SUNDAY, APRIL 23   This year France celebrated Easter as a civil as well as a religious festival. It was
not without some hesitation that the government had settled on April 23 as the date for the elections. Universal
suffrage was about to be exercised for the first time, and
even those like Ledru-Rollin who had been its warmest defenders wondered anxiously how the new citizens would use
their rights. The day was not expected to pass without some
serious disturbances, and it was felt that such incidents oc-
curring on Easter Sunday would be particularly unfortunate. But the Church had been more optimistic than the
government and was not at all shocked at the sight of the
country engaged in political activity and glorifying the Res-
urrection of Christ at the same time. There was a moving
parallel to be drawn between Christ rising from the tomb
and the people, like a modern Lazarus, called by the resur-
rection which had taken place in February to raise its voice
for the first time in public affairs. The Church was still, as it
were, the backcloth for the new regime and a great many of
the clergy were by no means displeased that it should be so.
The clergy, and the highest Church dignitaries such as
Monsignor Affre in particular, had felt little love for the
July Monarchy and the regime of the "Bancocrats." Louis
Philippe was a notorious unbeliever, and the mixture of
greed and Voltairean philosophy which characterized the
bourgeois royalty contained little to commend it to the
Church, whereas the February Revolution was overflowing
with religious zeal. The people flocked to the banner of a
proletarian, *sans-culotte* Jesus of Nazareth.

In the provinces, processions of electors formed up on April 23 under the direction of the parish priests. The Provisional Government had very sensibly decided that voting should take place in the regional capitals. They feared, with good reason, that in the communes local influences might interfere too much with the expression of the true will of the electorate. The influence of local notabilities would be felt much more within the small framework of the commune than in the canton as a whole. Because of this the election scenes of 1848 are reminiscent of those made familiar in modern times by recruiting boards. The roads were packed with long processions with drums and trumpets at their heads. The electors assembled in the church square as they came out of mass, led by the mayor and the parish priest. Then, with banners waving, they set out for the regional capital. At every crossroads they encountered processions on their way from other communes in the neighborhood, and all greeted one another enthusiastically. The proportion of those who actually voted was extremely high: 84 per cent. Not under the Second Empire, the Third Republic, or even in modern times has it ever reached this figure again.

No serious incidents occurred during the actual polling, but when it came to scrutinizing the votes it was a different matter. Workers in the porcelain industry of Limoges had welcomed socialist ideals and even before the outbreak of the February Revolution they had formed a powerful "société populaire." In spite of all they could do, however, the société populaire's candidates failed to get elected because the peasants from the Haute-Vienne voted conservative. The working-class urban population was furious and there were violent clashes. The historian should however note that although the underlying motives for the disturbances in Limoges in April 1848 were socialist, they were closely connected with the strong feelings which had grown up under the *ancien régime* against the grain monopolists. There were a number of people in prison in Limoges in 1848 who had taken part in the Buzançais riots of the previous year. In 1847 a flour shortage had precipitated some murderous incidents in the little Berrichon town of Buzançais, and Limoges was still haunted by the shadow of Buzançais when, on April 28, 1848, a mob of citizens armed with clubs made their way to the house of a mill owner named Lanouaille who was accused of having acquired a monopoly of corn and chestnuts in 1847. For a short while, Limoges was in the hands of a revolutionary committee. But the incidents which took place in the regional capital of the Haute-Vienne were nothing compared with those in Rouen, where Ledru-Rollin's commissioner for the region of Seine-Inférieure, Frédéric Deschamps, was standing as a candidate for the Constituent Assembly. He, and the other candidates of his party, failed to get in. When news of his defeat reached the workers of Rouen on April 27, they flew to arms. "Deschamps, who was responsible for maintaining the peace, went to the rue Saint-Hilaire and the rue du Ruissel, where the barricades had already been erected, and vainly urged his friends to remain calm. The situation was put to rights, in a somewhat brutal fashion, by the *procureur général*, Sénard, a *National* man and in fact Deschamps's opponent, and on April 28 the troops of General Gérard occupied the two suburbs of Martainville and Saint-Sever, where the insurgents had dug themselves in after some fierce fighting in which artillery was actually used against the workers."[10]

10 See the introduction to my own book: *La Vie ouvrière en France sous le Seconde Empire.*

✒ The Constituent National Assembly

Politically speaking, the elections to the Constituent National Assembly were indecisive. (The results of those for the Legislative Assembly in the following year were much more clear-cut.) The ballot was carried out according to a departmental list. A great many Orleanists had been much too farsighted to compete, but others had entered the lists and, in order to make themselves less conspicuous, remained very lukewarm in their attitude toward the Republic. These were known as "tomorrow's republicans," and frequently they were to be found bracketed with the *National* men, who regarded themselves as "yesterday's republicans." All things considered, this alliance is perfectly understandable. The lawyer or doctor who was an old subscriber to the *National*, and who was also extremely cautious on the social plane, asked nothing better than to ally himself with the lawyer, doctor, or industrialist who was a reader of the *Constitutionnel* or the *Journal des Débats*, since by so doing he could enjoy the benefit of a great many right-wing and right-of-center votes. Conversely, the subscriber to the *Constitutionnel* or the *Débats* was not ill-pleased to appear on the same platform as a *National* man, primarily because this certified him as a republican and could gain him a substantial increase in the number of votes cast for him. In several *départements*, the commissioner appointed by Ledru-Rollin ran side by side with men who, a few weeks earlier, would have been only too happy to throw the said commissioner in the river.

This being so, it is not easy to define the political features of the new Assembly very precisely. It was composed of nine hundred representatives, and the moderate republicans held about five hundred seats, but I must say again that these so-called "republicans" in no sense formed a coherent party. The progressive republicans held only eighty seats. The Orleanists who were more or less for the government, the "republicans of tomorrow," numbered two hundred or so and the legitimists another hundred. The consternation which must have been felt by the mechanic from La Chapelle can easily be imagined.

The eleven members of the Provisional Government were elected without trouble in the Seine district, which had thirty-four seats. Lamartine obtained 260,000 votes, Dupont de l'Eure, 245,000: François Arago, 243,000; Garnier-Pagès, 241,000; Armand Marrast, 230,000; Marie, 225,000; Crémieux, 210,000; Albert, 133,000; Ledru-Rollin, 131,000; Flocon, 121,00; Louis Blanc, 120,000. The *National* party was ahead of the *Réforme* by more than 100,000 votes, and the comparative failure of Louis Blanc, who was the last member of the government to be elected, is significant. General Duvivier, commander of the *garde mobile*, had 182,000 votes. Corbon was elected nineteenth with 135,000, coming before Caussidière, who was twentieth with 133,000. Corbon and Caussidière stood for the two different aspects of 1848: Corbon the religious, fervent, sentimental, and slightly humbug; Caussidière the brilliant, romantic Montagnard. (Caussidière was like a character out of Dumas.) There were undoubtedly a few people who had voted for both Corbon and Caussidière, but on the whole the 130,000-odd votes cast for each man came from very different social and religious sections of the community. Lamartine, with his 260,000 votes, came top of the poll in the Seine, and Lamennais, with 105,000, bottom. It is also worth remarking that the political theorists and social reformers suffered a severe setback in the Seine. Raspail obtained only 52,000 votes, Pierre Leroux 47,000, Victor Considérant 29,000, [11] Vidal 25,000, and Cabet 21,000.

Ledru-Rollin had urged his commissioners to encourage working-class candidates. With the same object, the Minister of Education, Carnot, sent out a circular to schoolteachers which was to cost him his post. It urged schoolteachers to make it clear to the new citizens that wealth or education were not necessary qualifications for membership in the Constituent Assembly. Carnot had used the word education unadvisedly. The minister had meant it in the traditional sense of cultivation and a greater or lesser refinement of manners. In his view an intelligent peasant or a working man capable of some constructive thought would be just as useful in the Assembly as lawyers, doctors, or industrialists.

Carnot's circular created a furor among the moderate and conservative elements, who were horrified—or pretended to be—that a minister entrusted with the charge of educating the nation should make it his first task to invite the people to choose common, ignorant bullies to represent them. Schoolteachers may have followed their minister's advice but if so it had little effect on their fellow citizens. In the event, the Constituent Assembly was composed largely of those very notables whom Ledru-Rollin and Carnot distrusted. A bare thirty-four representatives came from the working class. No historian, as yet, has written a detailed account of the working-class representatives in 1848. It would be a chapter full of surprises, because the workers who did become representatives of the people revealed no strong class prejudices. They set out to please the moderates and even to win the goodwill of the more reactionary

[11] Considérant was elected for the *département* of the Loiret.

representatives. Once inside the Palais Bourbon, the very worker who had affected such a tough and uncompromising attitude in the streets —it was unwise to tread on the lion's paws—became a little dictator, full of assurances that the lion of the people knew of course that progress could only come about by easy stages, that the demands of the public peace must be met and so forth. All in all, it was the representatives of the workers who treated Louis Blanc with the greatest severity and allied themselves with members of the right wing in discrediting the actions of the Provisional Government and going on to make General Cavaignac a dictator.

The Assembly had set up a number of committees (or, as we should call them today, commissions) among its members, including a Labor Committee presided over by Corbon. Corbon immediately took a stand against Louis Blanc and the Luxembourg delegates. Another representative from the Seine, the clockmaker Peupin, spoke even more violently than Corbon against Louis Blanc. Peupin was a good and on occasion a brilliant speaker. On May 10 he delivered an eloquent diatribe attacking Louis Blanc. Louis Blanc, chairman of the Government Commission for Labor, was flung down from his pedestal by a genuine worker. The right wing jumped for joy. The textile worker Joseph Benoît, who was social-democrat representative for the Rhône in 1848 and in 1849, has some harsh things to say about Corbon in his admirable but still regrettably unpublished memoirs. "Corbon," wrote Benoît, "was heart and soul for the reactionary royalist element in the Assembly, and the majority of the workers shared his views." Corbon's biased attitude in the Labor Committee shocked even conservatives like Vogué. Let me repeat that a great many working-class representatives acquiesced in Cavaignac's appointment as dictator during the June Days, and the day they did so they lightheartedly laid the Republic in its grave.

It is not easy to pass judgment on the Constituent Assembly. It accomplished nothing remarkable and yet it was not made up of unremarkable men. The flower of the nation were among its members, including Victor Hugo, Montalembert, Lamennais, Proudhon, and Lacordaire. At the end of his life Thiers used to say that it was addressing this chamber which had given him his greatest thrills as an orator, and this is no mean praise from the lips of a statesman of such rich parliamentary experience. But the Assembly was uneducated politically, although it was not without a certain idealism of spirit. At one time it believed that it was going to make the nation happy without too much difficulty. Then the troubles began to multiply, there was grumbling in the streets, and outbursts of savage fury, and the Assembly took fright; it displayed stupid spite and in the end turned violent. It was easily swayed and one speech was enough to make it change its mind.

The Assembly at Work

The Assembly began work on May 4, 1848. The representatives were distinguished by the red and gold rosettes they wore in their buttonholes. The Provisional Government had decreed that they were to wear a costume based on that worn by their great forebears of the Convention, but the government's decree never took effect. The only one to obey it was Marc Caussidière, who turned up at the Palais Bourbon dressed in a white waistcoat with broad lapels and looking like a reincarnation of a Montagnard. One veteran of the secret societies, Démosthène Ollivier, a representative of the Bouches-du-Rhône, demanded that each member of the Constituent Assembly should be asked to swear fealty, individually, to the Republic. Crémieux cordially opposed Ollivier's proposal, reminding his hearers that so many oaths had been sworn and violated in the course of French political history that the new republic would do better not to encumber itself with a formality associated with such depressing memories.

Crémieux could speak with authority, since he himself had displayed equal zeal on February 24 for the monarchy and for the Republic.

As Crémieux finished his speech, the Assembly rose to its feet with cries of "Vive la République!" The cry was repeated seventeen times. It was four o'clock and General de Courtais came into the debating chamber. "The citizen representatives," he said, "will now assemble in the porch of the Palais Bourbon, facing the Place de la Concorde, and proclaim the Republic in the presence of the people." Naturally the citizen representatives responded favorably to this suggestion, and formed up into a solemn yet joyous procession. Caussidière happened to find himself standing next to Lacordaire, and the white waistcoat of the Montagnard and the Dominican's white habit made a conspicuous light patch. The two men smiled at one another and linked arms in a brotherly fashion.

The people, wild with excitement, took a long time to file past the members of the Constituent Assembly. The warm spring breeze stirred the colors of the army and the

National Guard. "There were tears in every eye," wrote Daniel Stern, "hand sought hand and clasped complete strangers' in an inexpressible sense of joy and confidence."

The scene is typical of the lyrical illusion which dominated this period. When we look back on the full story of the great hopes of 1848, three pictures spring to mind: the Hôtel de Ville on February 24, the Arc de Triomphe on April 20, and the Palais Bourbon on May 4.

"The Soldiers of Despair"

To anyone who wants to understand both the spirit and the failure of 1848 the actual leadership of the Assembly can be highly informative. The two doctors Buchez and Recurt—president and vice president respectively—were old conspirators, honored veterans of the republican societies. It would be doing them an injustice to say that their fervor and enthusiasm had diminished. They were not skeptics or cynics like Marrast. But the apparent political success of 1848 concealed from them the social problem. This is all the more surprising because they were not simply academic politicians and had themselves made a considerable contribution toward solving social questions. They had come into direct contact with the people. Recurt had devoted himself with tireless energy to caring for the poor in the faubourg Saint-Antoine, and Buchez had founded the association of workers in the jewelry trade. Buchez and

Recurt suggest that politicians age quickly and that they often come to power only when it is too late. By 1848, Buchez and Recurt had grown cautious and because universal suffrage had been made law they believed that by obeying its dictates they were necessarily serving the Republic. This often led them to join with the monarchists and reactionaries to stab the workers of Paris in the back without compunction.

Buchez occupies an important place in the history of social theory. He had been one of the founders of the Charbonnerie in the eighteen-twenties and had then become a disciple of Saint-Simon. Ultimately he became converted to Catholicism, although this did not prevent him from remaining an ardent defender of the Convention. He was one of those who set up Jesus as an example to the *sans-culottes*. In collaboration with Roux-Lavergne, who later became a priest, he wrote an immense *Histoire parlementaire de la Révolution française* in four volumes which has come in for a good deal of criticism but has also been used extensively by several generations of historians—Michelet's and our own—without much acknowledgment.

The Assembly elected six vice presidents. Recurt has already been mentioned and something has been said about Corbon. Corbon, the ornament worker, was also an occasional typographer and something of a jack of all trades. The reason was not bohemianism but simply that he suffered from ill-health. During the eighteen-forties he directed *L'Atelier*, and at this time he was a Catholic and a follower of Buchez. He had been elected to the Constituent Assembly by a right-wing vote with which he was not altogether out of sympathy. Hence, no doubt, his somewhat complaisant attitude toward the men who, in the rue de Poitiers, constituted an important part of the regime. I have already mentioned the indignation shown by Joseph Benoît, a textile worker elected for the Rhône, at Corbon's bowing and scraping. Unlike Peupin, however, Corbon did not move steadily to the right. He drew increasingly close to the "formalist" republicans, as they were called in 1848 and 1849, as opposed to the "social democrats." Corbon gradually dropped Catholicism, took up freemasonry, and under the Second Empire was involved with the Voltairean paper *Le Siècle*. During the siege of Paris he defeated Hugo to become mayor of the fifteenth *arrondissement*.

We have also seen something of the third vice president, Sénard, a lawyer and representative of the province of Seine-Inférieure. We found him presiding over the reformist banquet in Rouen in 1847 when Sénard was one of Odilon Barrot's henchmen and an active member of the dynastic opposition. After the events which took place in February, he began to acquire a tinge of republicanism, with a leaning toward the policies of the *National*. As *procureur général* of the court at Rouen, we have already seen him harshly putting down the murmur of rebellion which arose among the working-class population of the Norman capital at the end of April. The Assembly was becoming more and more right-wing, and Sénard was to play an important part in June.

The fourth vice president was General Eugène Cavaignac, and the fifth, Guinard, a veteran of the "Rights of Man" and, like Recurt, an old conspirator. Guinard's father had been one of the Five Hundred during the Directorate and he had absorbed republican principles with his mother's milk. The sixth was the Vicomte de Cormenin, better known under his pseudonym of Timon. Timon had made a name for himself during the bourgeois monarchy by his forthright personal attacks on Louis Philippe in his pamphlets. Cormenin's republican ideals contained a touch of Bonapartism, but if Cormenin loved the Emperor he displayed little of his hero's personal courage. His cowardice during the June rising was particularly noticeable. Cormenin was a hopelessly bad speaker but he played an important part in the Committee on the Constitution.

✂ *The Executive Commission*

After dealing with the matter of internal organization, the Assembly proceeded to subject the various members of the Provisional Government to a kind of examination in which each was called upon to account, with varying degrees of success, for his conduct of public affairs. Lamartine's account was naturally impeccable. The Assembly kindly acquitted the government, although this was a judgment it was very soon to retract.

Before a constitution could be drawn up and made law, the Assembly also had to organize an executive authority, although this too was provisional. Either because it objected on principle to putting too much power in the hands of one man, or more probably out of a little mild cunning—because the Assembly was anxious to avoid giving real power to Lamartine—the solution adopted was similar to that of the Directorate. Just as there had been five Directors in 1795, so now in May 1848 there were five members who constituted the Executive Commission. Hence the title of "Pentarchs" which was irreverently bestowed on the members of the Commission.

The creation of the Pentarchy marks Lamartine's first failure. He had tried, often clumsily but with great persist-

ence, to rally large sections of the population to the suppo::
of a Republic which would be very progressive and peac—
loving, and anxious to work with the masses and to their
advantage. Lamartine's policy was undoubtedly a great success with the electorate, because the poet had carried the
day on April 23 by being elected in ten *départements*. But
the members of the Constituent Assembly were on the
whole very much more right-wing than Lamartine. They
valued Lamartine as the man who had done away with the
red flag and had taught the workers a sharp lesson on March
17 and April 16. They accepted him as the siren whose
songs should lull Caliban to sleep, but they did not want to
have the siren himself disturbed by the very one he was supposed to render calm and docile. They wanted Lamartine to
be surrounded by moderates, solid members of the establishment. Lamartine holding out his hand to Ledru-Rollin
was not at all to their liking.

Even in the face of an Assembly veering dangerously to
the right, Lamartine stuck obstinately to his policy of maintaining the balance between the center and the far left. He
had not forgotten Ledru-Rollin's services to the Provisional
Government on April 16, and he considered that it was only
with Ledru-Rollin's aid that the regime had been saved on
February 24 and April 16. With characteristic high-handedness, Lamartine in May was determined that Ledru-Rollin
should still have a place in the government, while Ledru-
Rollin himself asked nothing better than to lay down the
burden of power. Lamartine made an eloquent appeal to
the Assembly not to destroy an association which had given
such strength to the Provisional Government and had ensured the survival of the nation. In any case, the tenets of
February were already dead by May, since there was no
longer any question of Louis Blanc and Albert remaining in

the government. Lamartine kept up the association with Ledru-Rollin, who was the mainstay of radicalism and socialism, but the break with Louis Blanc was irrevocable. Louis Blanc had pleaded in vain with a hostile Assembly for the creation of a Ministry of Labor and Progress, and both Louis Blanc and Albert had recently resigned their posts as president and vice president of the Luxembourg Commission. They had done so regretfully, and with a good deal of resentment, in a manner that was almost secretive, but their action had unfortunate repercussions in plenty of workshops in Paris. Consequently Lamartine exerted all his authority to make the Assembly give Ledru-Rollin a place in the Executive Commission. He had his way, but there were a good many deputies who resented the kind of ultimatum he had delivered and refrained from voting either for Ledru-Rollin or for Lamartine himself. As a result the three moderate *National* men were elected in the secret ballot with very strong majorities. François Arago had 725 votes, Garnier-Pagès 705, and Marie 702, whereas Lamartine gained only 645 votes and Ledru-Rollin 458. They were already in something of a false position with regard to both the Executive Commission and the Assembly.

The post of secretary to the Executive Commission was filled by the publisher Pagnerre, a member of Garnier-Pagè's clan and an opponent of Ledru-Rollin. The Commission tactlessly decided to hold its meetings at the Luxembourg and by so doing upset the *petits bourgeois*, respectable people who saw the Pentarchs as the descendants of the upstart Directors who had inhabited the Luxembourg fifty years earlier and wasted the nation's money on irresponsible luxury. On the other hand, the Pentarchs also offended the workers by installing themselves in the Luxembourg on the ruins of the workers' parliament and giving the impression that the establishment party were taking their first revenge on the common people of Paris.

🖎 *The New Government*

The new government was formed by the Pentarchs. Recurt took over the Ministry of the Interior, and Ledru-Rollin give him in addition two undersecretaries of state: Carteret, whose part in affairs was unimportant, and Jules Favre, who already enjoyed a considerable reputation as a lawyer thanks to his spectacular defense of the rebels at Lyons. It was Ledru-Rollin's idea that Favre would counteract Recurt's tendency to be too weak and easygoing, but Jules Favre proved notoriously unreliable. (He was privately known in the corridors of the Assembly as *la jatte de lait empoisonné*.) Even today, as one of the spiritual fathers of the Third Republic, Jules Favre is still given the benefit of that reputation for republican integrity which had favorably impressed Ledru-Rollin. But behind his grave, austere appearance, his character was devious and disingenuous.

In 1848 his eloquence and authority were employed in the service of the reactionaries' vicious persecution of Louis Blanc, Albert, and Caussidière, and the first proscriptions directed against the republicans were the work of the very man whose picture was so lavishly displayed in the schools of the Third Republic.

Marie's place at the Ministry of Public Works was taken by Ulysse Trélat, a doctor and, like Buchez and Recurt, a conspirator, who had had his hour of glory in the republican party after the July Revolution. He had preceded Raspail as president of the Société des Amis du Peuple and age had not diminished his appetite for conspiracy, although, as we shall see, it was directed rather against the spirit of February and exercised on behalf of the supporters of the *régime à poigne*, the establishment men in the rue du Poitiers, rather than of the social republic. Moreover he possessed none of the qualities which go to make a good statesman.[1] Compared with Trélat, Flocon, who replaced Bethmont at the Ministry of Trade, seems an imposing figure, although Flocon himself was no very remarkable person. He had been one of the leaders of the *Réforme*, but on becoming a member of the Provisional Government he had gradually moved toward the *National* party. So much so, in fact, as to arouse Caussidière's anxiety; I know that Caussidière himself was beginning to be regarded with suspicion by Albert. More reactionary or more revolutionary elements were constantly seen at his side. But Flocon does not seem to have treated his former comrades of the *Réforme* very fairly, and in June 1848 he stood up in the house and solemnly repeated the most ridiculous gossip.

The lawyer Bethmont went from Trade to Culture, and Duclerc replaced Garnier-Pagès at the Treasury. Duclerc was a member of the *National* party but he still had a good deal of energy and did not share the complacent feebleness of Garnier-Pagès. Furthermore he had a bold, practical, and coherent approach to financial reorganization which, unfortunately, he had neither the time nor the means to put into practice.

---

[1] It is, however, worth noting that Proudhon speaks of Trélat with affection and admiration. Louis Blanc, on the other hand, regarded Trélat as a nonentity, and his arguments seem to be well founded.

Jules Bastide, formerly a wood merchant and an old Carbonarist who, like Buchez, had become a convert to Catholicism, took charge of the Ministry for Foreign Affairs. Solemn, inhibited Bastide has been the butt of a good deal of sarcasm. People wondered how the Pentarchs could have chosen this awkward, obscure person, lacking in social graces and the ability to deal with people, to take care of relations with foreign powers at a time when either France or Europe was always in the throes of some serious crisis. Jules Bastide was a man of greater strength and stature than is generally supposed. Historians have abused him without knowing him. The articles he wrote for *La Revue nationale* are not without interest, and Proudhon always showed the greatest regard for Bastide. Bastide's appointment to the Ministry for Foreign Affairs was Lamartine's doing and it is easy to understand when one realizes that Bastide was one of the very few men in the republican party with a genuine desire for peace. Bastide believed firmly that France should not set herself up as the armed missionary of republican ideas in Europe. He wanted to spread these ideas by peaceful means and his conviction was the stronger because he considered that the country had been exhausted by the campaigns of the Revolution and the Empire and that any repetition of these would be lunatic. Since Bastide's republican sentiments were beyond reproach and he had retained strong links with the people and the working classes in particular, Lamartine felt that his intervention would help the Parisian population to resign itself more or less gracefully to the prospect of peace.

Carnot retained the Ministry of Education, but he was on bad terms with the Assembly and his plan for educational reform never came under serious discussion. Although Carnot was a moderate, he had irreparably alienated the notables of the Assembly because he had been responsible for the unfortunate circular suggesting that the people should elect "uneducated representatives." Crémieux stayed at the Ministry of Justice; Admiral Cazy took over the Ministry of the Navy and Cavaignac the War Ministry. Cavaignac was still in Algeria at the time of his nomination and his department was handled meanwhile by Lieutenant Colonel Charras. Armand Marrast remained Mayor of Paris, despite all Ledru-Rollin's efforts to oust him from this key position, but Ledru-Rollin gained a hold over Marrast in keeping Caussidière in the prefecture of police.

The progressive section of the Parisian working-class population had been bitterly disappointed by the elections of April 23. The Luxembourg delegates had carefully compiled a list of democrats and socialists and they had counted on a resounding success. It never occurred to them that their list would not win over 200,000 votes, but in the event churchmen like Corbon and Peupin had won an easy victory over their candidates. Louis Blanc and Albert had been elected because of the reflected glory of the Provisional Government, not because they were socialists. A considerable number of moderate votes had actually been cast for Albert, and many electors were under the impression that he had been one of those associated with *L'Atelier* like Corbon, while others regarded him as a former companion, a comrade of Perdiguier. Agricol Perdiguier, known as "Avignonnais la Vertu," was a joiner and a popular character who was elected nineteenth for the district of the Seine. He was a staunch republican but extremely cautious and conservative in social matters. Perdiguier was a placid, amenable person, fond of a joke and always ready to make up a song and without the fly-by-night side to his character which Albert possessed.

From the first debates of the new Assembly, the extremists became increasingly discontented. Peupin indulged in digs at Louis Blanc, the Pentarchs sat in the Luxembourg and buried the workers' demands in the very place where they had just been heard, and at all this our mechanic from La Chapelle raged inwardly. In the clubs of Raspail, Barbès, and Blanqui, tempers were rising hourly. Many workers remembered George Sand's article in the *Bulletin de la République* on the eve of the sixteenth of April, foretelling that the elections would be rendered null and void by one all-powerful caste and picturing popular resentment swiftly nullifying the elections. Nevertheless the clubbists, disciples of Barbès and Blanqui, had sufficient political sense to realize that they were only a minority and that they could not attack the Assembly directly by pointing to their own failure and the lack of education among the people. Instead they looked for another excuse to demonstrate against the Assembly and bring about its ultimate dissolution, and it seemed to the clubbists that the Polish question would provide the excuse they wanted. The people of Paris were still dreaming with undiminished ardor of the resurgence of that unhappy nation.

The Fifteenth of May

The terrific success of the Feast of Fraternity on April 20 had given great encouragement to all those with a fondness for public celebrations, and the government planned a second festival for which the date fixed was Sunday, May 14. On April 20 the government had presented colors to the

Parisian National Guard. On May 14 the National Guards from the provinces were to receive theirs.

On May 11 the delegates to the Luxembourg, in their present sulky frame of mind, had let it be known that they would take no part in the ceremony, which was consequently postponed. This put the government in a particularly embarrassing position, because a large number of delegates from the provinces, consisting of National Guardsmen, firemen, and choir members, had already begun to arrive in Paris from the twelfth onward. When they discovered that they had made a useless journey they were extremely annoyed and refused to go home again without taking part in the promised celebration. They laid siege to the ministries, and Flocon attempted to get rid of them by handing out free tickets for the shows at the Odéon, the Théâtre Historique, and the Vaudeville, but they regarded Flocon's offer as slender compensation. Recurt was more generous and handed out twice as many tickets as Flocon, but the provincials were still roaming the streets of Paris with no intention of setting out for home. When it came to the point they were more impressed by the harsh words of Raspail or Blanqui than by the elegant badinage of Musset or Rachel's Oriental graces. Musset, thought the fireman from Montargis confusedly, was too clever by half and Rachel too exotic: he preferred the tragic accents of Blanqui. Socially he was a revolutionary, but in the arts he was profoundly conservative and loathed romanticism and literary innovations.

There were others besides the fireman from Montargis, the ophicleidist from Le Mans, and the National Guardsman from Amiens wandering disconsolately up and down the boulevard de Gand and the boulevard de la Madeleine on the fifteenth of May. The Polish envoys were there too, even more pathetic figures. If the fireman from Montargis had met with an unenthusiastic welcome from Flocon and Recurt, this was nothing to the reception given to the delegates from Posen and Lemberg by Lamartine. One anger set off the other. "People were saying," wrote Caussidière, "that the government were going to allow the Polish and Italian patriots to be slaughtered just as they had in 1830. These rumors, joined to the cannonade from Rouen, roused the populace against the authorities."

When the Poles could get nothing out of Lamartine they turned instead to the Assembly, where they had not only friends but also a fellow countryman, Wolowski, a liberal economist and a professor at the Conservatoire des Arts et Métiers. Wolowski, whom we have already encountered as a member of the Luxembourg Commission, was Polish by birth and had been elected for the district of the Seine on April 23 with an overwhelming majority. On May 10 Wolowski presented to the Constituent Assembly a petition from the three Committees of Posnan, Cracow, and Galicia. The Assembly arranged to discuss Polish affairs on Monday, May 15. The clubs, for their part, had also arranged a demonstration for the same day. The scene was set for another Day, a repetition of the seventeenth of March and the sixteenth of April.

Raspail, comparatively moderate, envisaged no more than a large-scale demonstration on behalf of Poland. Blanqui asked nothing better than to make an end of an Assembly which he loathed. However, he felt with some justice that the business had begun badly , and far from issuing a call to arms he preached calm to the more excitable members of his club. Barbès, for his part, was sullen. There was no secret about his fierce hatred of Blanqui and he was reluctant to lend himself to a demonstration which had been inspired by the Blanquists.

Nevertheless, whatever the reservations and grim forebodings growing up in the minds of their leaders, the people were determined to have their demonstration, determined to show their love for Poland and for all oppressed peoples. It was a formidable procession which formed up at the Bastille on May 15 and moved off in the direction of the Grands Boulevards and the Place de la Concorde. "A crowd of onlookers," wrote Daniel Stern, "displayed for one another's inspection the Polish eagle, the harp of Ireland, and the Italian tricolor."

Old General de Courtais appeared on horseback in the Place de la Madeleine and was received with cries of "Long live the people's general!" Courtais was optimistic: a deputation would be allowed into the Assembly to present the petition and, as on the fourth of May, the people would file past the porch of the Palais Bourbon. But the reassuring picture which General de Courtais was comfortably drawing for the crowd bore no relation to the real facts of the situation. The Assembly was frightened by the huge crowds, and furthermore, there were elements in the Assembly itself which were not averse to the mounting excitement. In Courtais's eyes all the Days of 1848 had something idyllic about them, but in fact both sides were more on edge than he believed. Blanqui, amazed at the number and unanimity of the demonstrators, wondered whether the moment for the *Putsch* had not come at last. "Forward!" he shrieked, and the mob forced its way into the Palais Bourbon.

Wolowski was speaking. His voice rose and he gestured wildly: the role he was called upon to play was clearly beyond him. No, he proclaimed, Poland was not dead, only sleeping . . .

"*Vive la Pologne!*" Wolowski's paltry eloquence was drowned suddenly in the great shout. The people poured into the chamber. Lamartine argued fiercely with some of the demonstrators at the entrance to the Palais, but he was overruled. Even so, he did not lose his self-possession, and he and Ledru-Rollin busied themselves assembling those legions of the National Guard which remained loyal to the Pentarchy. In the presidential seat, however, Doctor Buchez was behaving in a thoroughly undignified way. At one moment he was too overcome to do or say anything at all; at the next, he seemed to agree to whatever the clubbists wanted, like a small boy. Later on the reactionaries criticized Buchez bitterly for submitting to the rioters and signing an order forbidding the declaration of martial law.

Raspail read the petition. He did so in a slow, dismal voice and seems to have adopted this singsong tone deliberately, hoping it would have some calming effect on the demonstrators. Defending himself to the High Court judges afterward, Raspail said, "I could see people reeling all around me and I hoped that my monotonous delivery would make them less excited."

Barbès spoke more hysterically than Raspail. It was in the midst of this uproar on the fifteenth of May that he uttered the words which were later to have such broad repercussions: "We must give a thousand millions to the people." Barbès concluded his brief speech with an unsuccessful appeal for silence, but then Blanqui's harsh, piercing voice was raised, and at that time Blanqui was the only man capable of reducing the crowd to spellbound silence.

"The National Assembly," said Blanqui, "must decree

that France shall not sheathe her sword until all Poland has been restored to her former boundaries." Then he went on to demand justice for the massacres at Rouen and finished by a lengthy disquisition on the causes of poverty and the organization of labor.

A voice broke in; it belonged to Sobrier: "No. This is not what matters. Poland! Tell us about Poland!"

The interruption was significant. On the fifteenth of May neither the mechanic from La Chapelle nor the cabinet-maker from the faubourg Saint-Antoine was thinking of the problems which directly affected himself. The mechanic was earning starvation wages and the cabinetmaker was having enough difficulty hawking a few pieces of furniture covertly in the streets as if he were ashamed of it. But today they were not wallowing in dreams of a better life. What they wanted was to sweep oppressive kings and oppressed peoples from the face of Europe. They wanted Ireland, Italy, and Poland to be free. "Poland, Blanqui, tell us about Poland!"

Lamartine had not pacified the workshops of Paris by appointing Bastide to the Foreign Office. Bastide actually mounted the rostrum during that chaotic session on May 15 and recited in his mournful tones all the arguments in favor of a policy of extreme caution, but these arguments cut no ice when set against the passionate dreams of the workers of Paris. "These Prussians and Austrians and Russians all need to be educated with gunfire: then perhaps when we are in arms they will stop their martyrdom of the Poles." Behind the dream the towering image of Napoleon rose again.

Inevitably there were some disturbances at the Palais Bourbon on May 15, in the course of which Ledru-Rollin's erstwhile commissioner at Valence, Napoléon Chancel—

whose misfortunes I have dealt with in an earlier chapter—assaulted the representative Froussard who had replaced him in the Drôme district. However, the demonstrators as a whole did not share Blanqui's bitterness and were more like naughty schoolboys playing truant than rioters getting their first whiff of powder. A great many witnesses, and chief among them the British ambassador in Paris, Lord Normanby, who can scarcely be accused of sympathizing with the Second Republic, have stressed the good humor of the demonstrators. (Lord Normanby's account of 1848 is one long diatribe against Louis Blanc and socialism in general.) Lord Normanby was struck by the good manners shown by the crowd which invaded the Palais Bourbon. "One of their number," he wrote, "on being informed that the bayonet he was carrying was frightening the ladies, immediately placed it beneath a bench. Another inquired very politely whether someone would point out to him MM. de Lamartine, Louis Blanc, and others, while yet another, on reading the name Georges Lafayette upon one member's seat, said, 'And are you, sir, the son of General Lafayette?' On receiving an affirmative answer from the representative he continued, 'Ah, sir, what a pity that your poor father is dead! How he would have liked to be here.'"

The real heroes of the fifteenth of May were not Barbès or Blanqui or Raspail but our fireman from Montargis and the blacksmith Huber. The fireman had somehow managed to hoist himself up into the press box in order to get a better view of the splendid show and was jostling the cynical, worldly Parisian journalist Philibert Audebrand. In the end the fireman tumbled off the box, but being used to precarious situations because of his job, he managed to cling to a beam, dangling in mid-air, and swing himself onto the hemicycle where he perched, red-faced and sweating, waving to the crowd, which roared approval at the fireman's comic figure in his splendid new uniform.[2] But before long another figure took the stage. This was the fair, slender, and dashing individual known as Aloysius Huber. There is still some disagreement about the real sincerity of Huber's motives. Proudhon, somewhat surprisingly, felt a certain sympathy for him. If Blanqui was the classic example of a particular kind of ferocity, Huber, on the contrary, was an out-and-out romantic. (His book, *Nuits de veille d'un prisonnier d'état*, written in a fake biblical style and containing reminiscences of Lamennais, is for all its muddled thinking not without interest.) Pushing Blanqui aside, Huber announced in a manner at once solemn and offhand that the Assembly was dissolved. Huber's way of telling the Assembly it was dismissed was reminiscent of Girardin's suggesting to Louis Philippe that he had better abdicate. The people cheered Huber, and in accordance with what had already become a traditional ritual, were all prepared to go straight to the Hôtel de Ville to set up a provisional government. In the same passionate but pessimistic frame of mind, Barbès and Blanqui trod the path which Lamartine and Ledru-Rollin had taken on the twenty-fourth of February.

Later Huber was accused with some justification of having been a police spy. That he was in touch with the police is certain, and if he was not consciously abetting the establishment it has been suggested that he acted as an *agent provocateur* on the fifteenth of May. The whole wretched business of the fifteenth of May put Louis Blanc increasingly in the wrong and brought about a swing to the right on the part of the peaceable element in the population.

[2] The fireman's name was Paul Segré and he was a painter from Montargis. Like Raspail and Blanqui he was up before the High Court at Bourges in March 1849, where he delivered himself of some peculiarly artless statements.

There can be no doubt that the fifteenth of May served to further the interests of the reactionaries, but that Huber was merely a puppet in their hands still remains to be proved.

The events which took place at the Hôtel de Ville were even more farcical than those which had occurred at the Palais Bourbon. The municipal buildings were being guarded by a Colonel Rey who was an old comrade of Barbès's. When he saw the demonstrators approaching the Hôtel de Ville, Rey smiled and felt no inclination to order his troops to open fire. What Barbès was attempting to do seemed to him more comic than truly serious.

"I'm going to let you pass," he told Barbès. "After all, you are only following the example set you by Dupont de l'Eure and Lamartine on the twenty-fourth of February. If you want to set up a government, go ahead, but it's a funny idea . . ."

Barbès and the clubbists found their way unopposed. Once inside they hurried straight up the main staircase and turned right at the first floor. For the next two hours the Hôtel de Ville led a double life. In one part of the building, on the side overlooking the Seine, the mayor, Armand Marrast, and his assistant Edmond Adam continued to deal with matters in hand and things went on with every appearance of law and order. Meanwhile, in the side of the building which faced the northeast corner of the Place de Grève, a revolution was in full swing. In accordance with the rules laid down by tradition, the people crowded into the square while Barbès, Blanqui, and Albert stood at the windows and waved. Names were flung at the crowd and it was not long before a revolutionary government had been set up. The list agreed on was as follows: Albert, Louis Blanc, Ledru-Rollin, Huber, Thoré, Raspail, Cabet, and Pierre Le-

roux. (Only Thoré's name may be unfamiliar. Théophile
Thoré ran a progressive newspaper called *La Vraie République*. He was an art critic as well as a politician and his
Salons, which appeared under the pen name of Burger,
show that he was a fairly talented one. Baudelaire regarded
them very highly. It was Thoré who assisted Caussidière in
writing the *Mémoires* from which I have borrowed so heavily.)

Marrast, who like Rey had not taken the situation too
seriously, generously told his secretary to go and find Barbès. "Tell Barbès to stop this farce at once," he said, "he'll
be arrested at any moment."

Barbès, who rather fancied himself as a martyr, ignored
Marrast's advice, but Blanqui took the more prudent course
of slipping out of the Hôtel de Ville unobserved. He was
only just in time. Up came the National Guard, and once
again the hosier from the faubourg Saint-Denis saved the
situation. Lamartine and Ledru-Rollin, both on horseback,
harangued the loyal forces of the civic militia. The Pentarchs had matters under control again.

There was the same relaxation of tension at the Palais
Bourbon. The representatives swaggered all the more when
they heard that the rebels had been defeated, because they
had been so craven a few hours earlier. The people had just
behaved with considerable restraint, but the legal authorities gave their rage full rein. Louis Blanc emerged with his
clothes awry and hair plastered over a sweating forehead,
while some of the representatives formed a living shield
around him to protect him from the threats of the National
Guards. Much the same thing happened to General de
Courtais, because the National Guards resented the fact
that the general had made no serious attempt to safeguard
the Assembly and were convinced that Courtais was hand

in glove with the invaders. They abused him, tore off his epaulets, and broke his sword. Courtais was later thrown into prison and spent the following year facing the High Court at Bourges in the company of his presumed accomplices.

❧ The Feast of Concord

The festival which had brought the fireman all the way from Montargis took place after all on Sunday, May 21. It was called the Feast of Concord, but it aroused more satirical comment than admiration. "People laughed at the float representing agriculture, which was described on the program as being drawn by oxen with gilded horns but was in fact pulled by twenty carthorses, and hooted at the five hundred maidens crowned with oak leaves who followed the car. They jeered at the statue of the Republic with four lions crouched at her feet, and altogether persisted in regarding the Feast of Concord as nothing more than a bad imitation of the Feast of the Supreme Being." (Daniel Stern)

These unkind comments came chiefly from the middle classes, but if the members of the establishment boycotted the celebrations laid on by the Pentarchs—and the absence of the clergy was particularly significant in view of the prominent part it had taken in the festival on the twentieth of April—the common people gave it a still wider berth. There is a telling paragraph to be found in a socialist newspaper called *Le Travailleur de la mère Duchêne* which runs: "Mère Duchêne did not attend the celebrations. . . .

What would she be doing among the bayonets and triumphal cars, to say nothing of the nine hundred satisfied pluralists [in other words, the nine hundred representatives] displaying their pedantic impotence? It would have made her blood boil to see our young girls throwing flowers to these . . . bagmen. Celebrations may have some attractions for people with a full belly and twenty-five francs a day and more to nibble at, but for anyone existing in poverty, for anyone who weeps for the fate of Poland, for anyone in fact who has a heart in his body, this was a day of mourning."

🏴 Reaction

The result of the fifteenth of May was an immediate advantage to the reactionaries. Caussidière and his Montagnards had to leave the prefecture of police and Caussidière also resigned, with great eloquence and panache, from his office as a representative. His place at the prefecture of police was taken by Trouvé-Chanel, a banker from Le Mans who had begun his political career in Ledru-Rollin's orbit but was now revolving around Marrast.

Since General de Courtais was in prison, a successor had to be found for him, and Clément Thomas took command of the National Guard. "Clément Thomas," writes Maxime Du Camp, "was famous in the republican party because he had been one of the leaders of the Lunéville conspiracy. On April 16, 1834, when he was a cavalry NCO, he had acted in concert with the Committee of the Society of the Rights of Man which was agitating in Paris in an attempt to incite his comrades to mutiny and to get the fourth, ninth, and tenth regiments of cuirassiers to horse." By May 1848 Clément Thomas, like Recurt and like Guinard, was a conspirator tamed, more concerned with maintaining the status quo than with steering the chariot of the Republic onto the path of socialism. He displayed extreme savagery toward the rebels in June, and this explains his execution at Montmartre twenty-three years later on March 18, 1871, at the dawn of the Commune.

The Assembly set up a committee under the chairmanship of Jules Favre to decide whether legal proceedings should be instituted against Louis Blanc; but although Jules Favre obtained a majority in the committee he was outvoted in the Assembly as a whole. Louis Blanc's innocence was obvious. Marrast, with remarkable disingenuousness, asserted that he had seen Louis Blanc at the Hôtel de Ville. This was a serious charge, since it meant that Louis Blanc had been acting in collusion with Barbès. In fact Louis Blanc had never left the precincts of the Palais Bourbon, and Marrast had to withdraw his testimony.

Even so, this was only a temporary respite for Louis Blanc, and Jules Favre returned to the attack after the events which took place in June, and this time he was successful.

Buchez was written off as incompetent and replaced as President of the Assembly by Sénard, who had become one of the oracles of the Palais National (formerly the Palais Royal). About two hundred middle-of-the-road deputies had formed the habit of meeting at the Palais National. Old Dupont de l'Eure attended the meetings of this group which was already beginning to find the *National* shade of opinion too strong. It was not as fiercely reactionary as the group which was soon to collect in the rue de Poitiers, but even so it was beginning to undermine the authority of the Executive Commission and indulged in acid criticism of Ledru-Rollin and Lamartine.

In the Labor Committee, the Count of Falloux was insisting on the need to modify the National Workshops, or even to suppress them altogether. The new Minister of Public Works, Ulysse Trélat, in association with Garnier-Pagès, was temporarily recovering his taste for conspiracy and going about it with a singular lack of tact. He summoned the director of the National Workshops, Émile Thomas, and suggested that he should go to Bordeaux immediately, adding that he would go to prison if he disobeyed. Thomas was stunned by this strange command. He was replaced by another engineer named Lalanne and it was obvious that the Assembly and the government were getting ready to take action against the National Workshops. These more or less underhand proceedings were answered by vague stirrings on the part of the masses. "The general inactivity left the workers time to indulge in political argument. There was great poverty among the people and this brought them out into the boulevards and public squares every night, where they formed what have been justly called the 'Clubs of Despair.' " (Caussidière)

Louis Bonaparte

It was at this moment that someone who had been neglected by the Assembly but whose name cropped up frequently in the Clubs of Despair reappeared on the political scene. On June 4 and 5, by-elections were held in the Seine and in a number of other *départements*.[3] On the whole there was a much smaller poll than on the twenty-third of April. First of the newly elected representatives in the Seine district, with 146,000 votes, was Caussidière, who had conducted a masterly campaign and succeeded in making a favorable impression on even the most aristocratic audiences. Also elected were General Changarnier, with 105,000 votes; Thiers, 97,000; Pierre Leroux, 91,000; Victor Hugo, 87,000; Lagrange, 78,000, and Proudhon, 77,000. But however great the luster surrounding these names, this was not the most important thing about the elections. Among those successful at the polls was Prince Louis Napoleon Bonaparte, the son of Queen Hortense and nephew of the great Emperor: he obtained 85,000 votes and was moreover elected for three *départements*. Proudhon, writing in *Le Représentant du Peuple* on June 8, commented on this return to the scene: "The people have just indulged in a princely whim: pray God it be the last! A week ago, citizen Bonaparte was still only a black dot in a fiery sky; the day before yesterday he was only a smoke-filled balloon; today he is a cloud bearing storms and lightning in its midst."

Spanning the gulf which had formed between the Assembly and the people came the chariot of Louis Napoleon Bonaparte. On the one hand, the people were growing increasingly restive against the "nine hundred pluralists," the representatives who had declared war on the social republic. On the other, they had no more leaders, since Barbès, Blanqui, Albert, and Raspail were all in prison or in flight, and so turned naturally to Louis Napoleon. Two facts are significant: (1) Some workers from La Villette presented a peti-

[3] At that time one citizen could stand and be elected for several different *départements*. He was then asked to select one, and this led to vacant seats in the other districts for which he had been elected. Hence the constant spate of elections during the Second Republic.

tion to the Assembly to have Louis Napoleon proclaimed consul. (2) The seventh legion (Panthéon, Saint-Victor, Saint-Martin) intended to nominate Louis Napoleon Bonaparte as their colonel in place of Barbès.

Prince Louis's election caused something of a stir in the Assembly. Lamartine, very clearsightedly, had always thought that the greatest danger to the Republic lay in nostalgia for Napoleon and believed that only his own prestige was great enough to overcome that enjoyed by Prince Louis. In this, Lamartine was simplifying the problem he meant to solve, for if Louis Napoleon's star was in the ascendant with the nation, it was on the contrary Cavaignac's which was rising in the Assembly. At the very moment when Lamartine was trying to put all his weight in the balance of fate against Prince Louis, he had no suspicion that Cavaignac had already weighted the scales. It was just this disguised duel that broke out between Cavaignac and Lamartine which was to prove Louis Napoleon's trump card, and which was to destroy first the poet and then the dictator general.

On June 12 Lamartine delivered a determined attack on Prince Louis. (Buchez had demanded that the prince should not be allowed to take his seat.) Lamartine's speech was terse and bitter. It was the more ill-advised in that the orator could feel that he had not got the sympathy of the Assembly. The speech was delivered in two parts. Lamartine asked for the session to be adjourned, pleading fatigue, then he made a moving return to the rostrum. "Citizen representatives," he said, "a number of shots have been fired, one of them at the commander of the Parisian National Guard, another at an officer in the army, and yet a third at the breast of an officer of the National Guard. . . . These shots were fired to cries of 'Long live the Emperor!' This is the first drop of blood to stain the eternally pure and glorious Revolution of the Twenty-fourth of February." And Lamartine went on to advocate maintaining the sentence of exile which had been imposed on the Bonaparte family in 1816 and 1832. It was a pathetic speech, and all the bloodshed and shots fired with which Lamartine hoped to rouse the Assembly to a surge of anger bore no relation to the truth.

The Assembly, rightly considering that an attempt was being made to manipulate it, jibbed. The right wing preferred Louis Bonaparte to Lamartine, and the extreme left espoused the same feelings out of resentment at the poet's dubious conduct in the Provisional Government. Meanwhile the center, those representatives whose activities at their meetings in the Palais National I have already described, congratulated themselves on a coalition between the right and the far left which could bring about the downfall of the Executive Commission—the Pentarchy.

Lamartine's proposal was rejected by the Assembly, but Louis Napoleon very astutely pleaded the conflicts which his presence might arouse and resigned. He wrote a dignified letter to the President of the Assembly which was read out on June 15: "My name is a symbol of order, of national pride and glory, and it would be with the keenest distress that I would see it used to augment the troubles rending our country. Rather than contribute to such a misfortune, I would remain in exile. I am ready to sacrifice everything to the good of France."

♨ The Dissolution of the National Workshops

At this point the question of the National Workshops arose once more. All through the month of June the members of the middle classes were continually saying, "This can't go on." This was a vague formula covering the popular disturbances and the political uncertainty which produced a slump in business and a complete paralysis of the nation's activity. Even the prospect of a revolution no longer terrified the bourgeoisie very much, since they told themselves that this time it would surely mean an end once and for all and that if matters had come to a reckoning between themselves and the workers then it was as well to settle it as soon as possible. Taking a stand against the workers over the matter of the National Workshops meant making the trial of strength which would clarify the situation.

The fatal edict was published on June 21. Workers between the ages of eighteen and twenty-five who were registered with the National Workshops were to be conscripted into the army; the rest would be sent into the provinces, notably to Sologne or the Landes, where they would be employed in land clearance.

Recurt, the Minister of the Interior, had no illusions. "Tomorrow it will be revolution." Of course the faubourgs were up in arms at once. "We know what this means," the cabinetmaker from the faubourg Saint-Antoine told himself. "The government is out for our blood. Dying of fever in the marshes or getting ourselves killed by the Bedouin in Algeria is what we can expect. We might as well die decently on the barricades." On the morning of the twenty-second, fifteen hundred workers assembled in the Place du

Panthéon where they were addressed by a lieutenant of the National Workshops named Louis Pujol. After the fifteenth of May, Pujol had written a "Prophecy of the days of blood" in the same apocalyptic biblical style as that favored by Huber. (Pujol led an adventurous life but politically he was blameless and was not, like Huber, in any way involved with the police. He fought with the Yankees in the War of Secession and perished in a shipwreck in 1866.) Next Pujol and some of his associates went to the Luxembourg and asked to see Marie. Marie, it will be remembered, had played the demagogue to the brigades of the National Workshops. Two months earlier, on March 26, he was saying:

"Ah, you are indeed worthy of the liberty you have won, worthy to live under the Republic which you have founded, and this time you shall not be cheated of your Republic!"

On June 22 it was: "So you don't want to go into the provinces? Well, we'll send you there by force, do you understand, by force . . ."

⚑ The June Days

THE FIRST DAY On the morning of Friday, June 23, Pujol was back in the Place du Panthéon. People were singing the Ça ira to the words of: "Oh! ça ira, ça ira, Lamartine à la lanterne, Lamartine on le pendra." The procession straggled off in the direction of the Bastille where Pujol recalled the victors of the Fourteenth of July. The crowd was growing all the time and there were shouts of "Liberty or death." The first barricade went up at midday near the Porte Saint-Denis, cutting across the rue de Cléry, the boulevard Bonne-Nouvelle, and the rue Mazagran. It is worth while pausing to examine it, because it holds an important place both in social history and in the history of literature. On top of this barricade appeared "a young woman, beautiful, disheveled, and terrible. The girl, who was a woman of the streets"—here I am quoting from Victor Hugo and must leave with the author responsibility for an assertion for which there seems to be no evidence—"hoisted her skirts up to her waist and yelled at the National Guards, 'Cowards, fire, if you dare, at the belly of a woman.' A volley of fire hurled the unfortunate creature down. She gave a loud scream and fell. Immediately a second woman appeared. This one was younger and lovelier still, little more than a child, seventeen at most. She too was a woman of the streets. Like the other she showed her stomach and screamed, 'Fire, brigands!' They fired and she fell, riddled with bullets, on the body of the first." (Victor Hugo, *Choses vues*)

Who were the men engaged in the assault on the barricade? They were National Guards belonging to the first and second legions. In their ranks we should find a great many local shopkeepers, notably our hosier and one of his friends and neighbors, a draper named Leclerc. Leclerc "saw his eldest son fall, mortally wounded, at his side. Assisted by some of his comrades, he carried him home and then returned immediately to take his place in the ranks of the legion, bringing with him his second son to take the place of the one who had fallen." (Pierre de La Gorce) Leclerc afterwards played a symbolic role in the history of the Second Republic. In April 1850, there was a clash between social democrats and the supporters of the regime in a by-election which also became something of a symbol. The social-democrat candidate was the novelist Eugène Sue. Whom would the conservative Union Électorale, which had its headquarters in the rue de Poitiers, put forward to oppose him? The man they nominated was Leclerc, a hero of the establishment, and a hero who was simultaneously humble and a shining example. At the polls Eugène Sue won an easy victory over Leclerc. But to return to the Porte Saint-Denis. Just as the two women who had made such an impression on Victor Hugo fell—and I can add a few supplementary details to the picture by saying that they wore lace caps on their heads and carried a banner in their hands —a strong column of *gardes mobiles*, light infantry, lancers, and artillery emerged into the boulevard. It was commanded by Lamoricière. He was anxious to put down the rising swiftly, and moved into the boulevard Saint-Martin and set up his headquarters in the rue de Bondy, near the Château d'Eau. A little later, however, encountering formidable resistance, he was obliged to retire and transfer his headquarters to the Porte Saint-Denis.

From Friday onward the whole eastern sector of the capital was in the hands of the insurgents. This is the moment to delineate the line of battle, although this can of course be only a brief sketch giving approximate indications of the boundary dividing working-class from bourgeois Paris. This was a line running through the faubourg Poissonnière, the church of Saint-Vincent-de-Paul, work on the construction of which was barely finished, the faubourgs Saint-Denis, Saint-Martin, and Saint-Antoine, the Île de la Cité and the rue Saint-Jacques. It must be remembered that the boulevard de Strasbourg, the boulevard Magenta, the boulevard Sébastopol, and the boulevard Saint-Michel had not yet been built. The old streets of the faubourg

Saint-Antoine and the Quartier Saint-Merri were a traditional nest of rebellion and effectively protected the insurgents. After Friday there were more than fourteen barricades between the Hôtel de Ville and the Bastille and
twenty-nine from the faubourg Saint-Antoine to the Place
du Trône. One vital point was that the rebels failed, in spite
of all their efforts, to gain control of the Hôtel de Ville
where Armand Marrast was still in possession. A few troops
from La Courtille and Reuilly managed somehow to penetrate the barricades and reach the municipal buildings, and
they provided adequate protection. But although the rebels
had been held in check outside the Hôtel de Ville, they did
possess excellent defensive positions. The barriers behind
them—Rochechouart, Les Vertus, La Villette, La Chopi-
nette etc.—through which the reinforcements supplied by
the villages contained between the city bounds and the fortifications could reach them, provided a solid basis for their
entrenchments.

Who exactly were the workers who took part in the uprising? In the faubourg Poissonnière we should find a great
many mechanics, some from La Chapelle, which was at
that time a village housing five thousand workers most of
whom were socialists, while others worked in the establish-
ments of Jean François Cail in the rue de Chabrol. The
mechanics had thrown up particularly effective barricades
in the rue de Bellefond, between the rue Rochechouart and
the rue du faubourg Poissonnière, and they had also dug
themselves in on the site of the Lariboisière hospital. (Here
we are treading the actual ground covered in Zola's novel
L'Assommoir, which opens in the last months of the Second Republic. The heroine, Gervaise, lives in a house in the
boulevard de La Chapelle, not far from the Poissonnière
barrier, and every morning she gazes mournfully at the

scaffolding of Lariboisière.) The barracks of La Villette were occupied by carters, coal merchants, and longshoremen.

The barricades in the Quartier Popincourt had been constructed with an efficiency and method which commanded the admiration even of the attacking generals. They were defended by men who worked in the small metal shops, and in this connection it is worth while commenting on the prominent part played by a number of workers in the decorative trades, and in particular by the workers in bronze, of whom there were a great many in the district of the Filles-du-Calvaire and in the faubourg du Temple. Fifteen years later some of these bronze workers were among the pioneers of the First International.

In the faubourg Saint-Antoine, where the insurrection fought its last stand, we should find chiefly our carpenters and cabinetmakers. In the Cité the barricades were manned by dockers from the quais and workers from the Orleans railroad. On the left bank, in the twelfth arrondissement (Panthéon), the fighting was especially tough: here were the ragpickers of the rue Mouffetard and quarrymen from Gentilly and Arcueil. The quarrymen defended the Barrière d'Italie with grim courage to the bitter end.

Cavaignac must have realized as early as Wednesday evening that he would have to deal with an insurrection, yet he wasted a great deal of time, one and a half days to be precise, and took no action until ten o'clock on Friday. The minister Recurt and General Lamoricière reckoned that Cavaignac's weakness in the initial stages of the insurrection had the most disastrous consequences. What is the explanation? Cavaignac had many more troops at his disposal than Louis Philippe and in June the National Guard behaved with exemplary valor. Indeed, at times their valor was almost excessive and showed signs of a social vindictiveness which had its origins in the basest instincts. The idea that his strongbox was at stake turned the mildest shop-keeper into a lion. The young soldiers of the *gardes mobiles* were equally keen. The impetuous conduct of these Parisian lads surprised even the generals and representatives who had been wondering right up to the last moment on which side of the scales they would throw their weight. "I *committed* them in the fight immediately," Lamoricière remarked jovially, "and now I am sure of them."

In June it was the regular army which showed the least enthusiasm: the troops of the line acted with passive resignation rather than eagerness. In the Place des Vosges, a large detachment of the eighteenth light infantry suffered itself to be disarmed by the workers without any resistance.

All the same, Cavaignac had considerable forces in hand to deal with the rising, and he failed to use them sensibly. The National Guard ought to have been standing to since Wednesday evening, patrolling the streets where rebellion was brewing. Preventive action would have kept this terrible civil war within bounds. As it was, the faubourg Saint-Denis was able to spend the whole of Thursday organizing its defense at leisure without the slightest interference from the forces of law and order.

The same inefficiency was apparent in the twelfth *arrondissement*, where the mayor and his colleagues were convinced that a demonstration by the National Guard in the narrow alleys around the Panthéon would swiftly have discouraged the builders of the barricades. Cavaignac reacted with bland indifference to the suggestions put forward by the authorities in the twelfth *arrondissement*. He was a man of narrow views whose whole outlook was constantly bounded by the memory of the twenty-fourth of February. He failed to see the situation as a whole in both its political and its strategic aspects and was guided solely by considerations of military honor. He could not bear the idea of regular troops being broken and disarmed and never forgot General Bedeau's unfortunate predicament on the morning of the twenty-fourth of February. He was prepared to see the entire capital given over to fire and slaughter rather than submit to the loss of unity and discipline by a single regiment. This was the reason why Cavaignac was reluctant to take the offensive unless he had a large, well-organized force with which to engage an enemy whose strength and resources could be precisely calculated. By his rigid mentality, Cavaignac made it possible for the insurgents to gain their first foothold and so turn the rising into a full-scale war. Having said that Cavaignac did not make up his mind to take action until late on Friday morning, what, when he finally did so, was his plan?

He arranged his forces in three major bodies. The first and by far the largest—comprising about five thousand men —was placed under the command of Lamoricière, and it is this column which we have already encountered early in the afternoon in the boulevard Bonne-Nouvelle. Lamoricière was entrusted with the considerable task of getting the rising under control between the faubourg Poissonnière and the faubourg Saint-Antoine. The second column, under Bedeau, was to attempt to relieve the Hôtel de Ville, while the third, under General Damesme, was to move up toward the Panthéon and clean up the twelfth arrondissement.

The activities of Lamoricière's column fell into three parts. First, in the faubourg Poissonnière, a detachment attempted, not without difficulty, to force the barricades erected by the mechanics in the rue Lafayette and the rue de Bellefond. They advanced by slow degrees but without managing to reach the Clos Saint-Lazare and the Lariboisière hospital, and only penetrated the hospital two days later after stubborn fighting. Second, in the faubourg Saint-Denis, detachments under General Rapatel were also engaged in heavy fighting. The fiercest action was that fought by a battalion of the *gardes mobiles* around the Church of Saint-Laurent. Third, as we have seen, Lamoricière was also trying to advance into the faubourg du Temple but suffered severe setbacks in the attempt. Some of his staff officers informed Cavaignac of the difficulties their commander was encountering. It was then four o'clock and the minister immediately left the Presidency and personally assumed command of a number of battalions. On joining Lamoricière he told him, "You hold the faubourg Saint-Denis at all costs. I'll take care of the Temple."

There was some lively fighting in the rue d'Angoulême, nowadays called after the metalworker and trade unionist Timbaud, who was shot by the Germans. (The union of metalworkers has its headquarters in the rue d'Angoulême.) In June 1848 a particularly large barricade had been erected at the kind of fork formed by the angle of the rue Saint-Maur with the rue d'Angoulême and the rue des Trois-Bornes. It was defended by the members of a club known as the "Montagnards de Belleville." The insurgents had access to the barricade from the rue des Trois-Couronnes and so were easily able to obtain supplies and relief. They inflicted heavy casualties on their assailants, who had two generals and three hundred men dead or wounded. Furiously angry, Cavaignac was compelled to withdraw from the barricade. By this time it was nine o'clock and he returned to the presidential quarters in the Palais Bourbon.

A lively interview took place between Cavaignac and Ledru-Rollin, who was the only representative of the executive powers present there during the rising. Admittedly

Ledru-Rollin had Marie with him, but the slender support provided by a man like Marie on such a day can be imagined. (Lamartine had accompanied Cavaignac to the Temple, Arago was at the Luxembourg, and Garnier-Pagès was going the rounds of the mairies stiffening resistance. Since Garnier-Pagès went only to those districts where law and order was already established, his excursion was as useless as it was uneventful.) This left Ledru-Rollin on his own, besieged by constant appeals for help. General Damesme in particular sent one officer after another to ask for troops, even a single battalion. Ledru-Rollin shouldered his responsibilities bravely. He dispatched an order to all prefects in the regions of Seine-et-Oise, the Loire, and the Somme to send all available regiments and National Guards to Paris. He urged Admiral Cazy to send sailors from Brest and Cherbourg to Paris as fast as possible. But Ledru-Rollin was aware that the establishment distrusted him and he was caught in a terrible dilemma. If he sent troops to Damesme without first consulting the Minister of War, without consulting Cavaignac, he ran the risk of upsetting Cavaignac's carefully laid plans. On the other hand, a refusal to help meant appearing to connive at the disturbances. Furthermore the National Guards who were defending the regime made no bones about repeating that the Executive Commission was betraying them. As Minister of War and therefore in charge of operations, Cavaignac's duty was to stay at the Presidency and not to go playing at soldiers in the rue d'Angoulême. However, Ledru-Rollin's arguments cannot have carried much weight with him, since after this vehement discussion he went straight back to the Hôtel de Ville, anxious to know how Bedeau's column was faring.

In addition to Tocqueville's famous comment on Bedeau that "he was as humane as if he had never fought in Africa," I can also recall another more satirical remark about him by the same writer: "I never saw a military leader so fond of the sound of his own voice." Lamoricière in June was wildly angry and determined to avenge the defeat which the people had made him suffer in February. Bedeau had also been the victim of a bitter defeat in the boulevard Bonne-Nouvelle on the morning of February 24, but unlike Lamoricière he was not inclined to bear malice. On June 23 he again attempted to reason with the insurgents. He had a long conference with Marrast and Guinard at the Hôtel de Ville. The Mayor of Paris and the vice president of the Assembly were more in favor of strong action than the general, and Guinard in particular had absolute faith in Cavaignac and believed that by ruthless opposition to the rising he was acting in the best interests of the Republic. Finally, at about five o'clock, Bedeau was obliged to give orders to fight. A detachment under the command of Edmond Adam cleared the square in front of Notre-Dame, carried the Petit-Pont, and advanced up the rue Saint-Jacques. (After the capture of the Petit-Pont a veritable butchery took place in a house containing a draper's shop called the Deux Pierrots.) A second detachment, led by Bedeau himself, cleared the Place Saint-Michel and proceeded up the rue de la Harpe to meet Adam's force. At the corner of the rue Saint-Jacques and the rue des Noyers (not far from the Marché des Carmes, which still exists today), Bedeau was wounded. The barricades in the rue Saint-Jacques numbered thirty-eight altogether and there was no possibility of reaching the Panthéon and effecting a junction with Damesme. Bedeau fell back on the Hôtel de Ville, where Cavaignac found him. Bedeau's wound was a serious one and he was feverish and excited. He talked incessantly. Cavaignac decided to replace him by the commander of the *garde mobile*, Duvivier. At this point Cavaignac went back to the Presidency and left again at about midnight to resume contact with Damesme's column.

Damesme had set up his headquarters in the Musée de Cluny and had gone up to sup in a small restaurant in the rue de la Harpe whose lights winked through the unusually clear and milky evening. In all this street fighting, the various columns were curiously isolated and the barriers dividing them were at the same time very solid and extremely mobile. The rue des Mathurins, the rue de la Harpe, and the Musée de Cluny are all very close to the rue des Noyers where Bedeau had found himself blocked six hours earlier. By midnight, Damesme was in the very spot where Bedeau had tried unsuccessfully to join up with him. The fighting in the afternoon had been chiefly in two sectors: in the rue des Mathurins itself and the maze of streets running between the Quartier Latin and the Seine, and in the rue Saint-André-des-Arts and the Carrefour Buci, and secondly in the streets running down from the Montagne-Sainte-Geneviève and in the rue Mouffetard in particular, where one company had been disarmed by the insurgents. At midnight, therefore, Damesme presented Cavaignac with a somewhat grim picture of the situation. A council of war was held in the open air at the corner of the rue de la Harpe and the rue de l'École-de-Médecine just by the Café Soufflet and the Hôtel des Étrangers. (The Soufflet has disappeared but the Hôtel, familiar to more than one generation of students, has survived the changes which have taken place in the Quartier and still stands on the boulevard Saint-Michel.) "Tomorrow," Cavaignac told Damesme, "we shall dislodge the insurgents at all costs, even if we have to blow up the library and the church to do it." (By this he meant the library of Sainte-Geneviève and the church of Saint-Étienne-du-Mont.)

Friday night was, on the whole, comparatively peaceful. Both sides were recouping their strength for the next day's fighting. Historians may, however, have laid too much stress on this calm. It was the summer solstice and the night was short and bright. Sniping went on all night in a number of streets, especially around the Hôtel de Ville. Madame Charles Garnier wrote for her son a very clear description of what that night was like. (Madame Garnier, then Mademoiselle Bary, had not yet married the architect who later, during the Second Empire, built the Paris Opéra. Mademoiselle Bary belonged to an academic family and was living at the Lycée Charlemagne.)

"On the night of Friday to Saturday the twenty-fourth, the National Guards captured and recaptured two barricades in the narrow rue de la Tixanderie which ran alongside the Hôtel de Ville. The insurgents held all the houses in this dirty little street and were firing from all the windows and ventilators at the National Guard. The oil lanterns, which even at that time were hung on cables down the middle of the small streets to provide illumination, had all been shattered by bullets. But it was the month of June and the nights so bright that there was light enough for fighting. In Arthur's company there were five killed and twenty-six wounded. [This was the writer's brother, Arthur Bary, who as an eighteen-year-old student of rhetoric had insisted on taking his sick father's place in the National Guard. Arthur Bary was as fanatical a supporter of the regime as the draper Leclerc from the faubourg Saint-Denis.] Since the National Guards were divided from the rebels only by the height of the barricades and the thickness of the stones, they were able to hurl insults at them while reloading, and if the weapons of that time had been more accurate and those firing them had had a better eye they would have killed your uncle, for they aimed at him and shouted, 'You there, the little starveling with the pale face! We'll make you a bit paler yet!' They hated him because he was not wearing a uniform and this showed that he was a volunteer. They shouted at Alexandre Maugeret, who was next to him and wore spectacles: 'We'll close all your four eyes for you!' And at M. Berger, the professor of rhetoric who was very big and fat: 'Hey, you, there's enough of you for four bullets!' And at M. Pront, who was very tall and had white hair: 'We'll cut the old one down to size!' "

THE SECOND DAY   Now we come to the morning of Saturday, June 24, the second day of the rising. First let us go to the Palais Bourbon where the session began at eight o'clock and where some very grave events were to take place. It will be remembered that at the time of the February uprising the Chamber had been calmly discussing the statutes of the Bank of Bordeaux. In June the Assembly was engaged in an equally untimely debate on the conduct of the railroads while the mechanic at La Chapelle was busy polishing his weapons. Inevitably, the first murmurs of revolt were not calculated to add to the authority of those representatives, rare at the outset, who were pleading the cause of the state and who wished to see the state taking over from the Companies. Clearly on Friday the twenty-third, the Assembly ought to have postponed enforcing the decree passed two days earlier authorizing the dissolution of the National Workshops. Falloux, however, made a fierce and successful plea for the decree of June 21 to be regarded as operative. Corbon, while he offered no direct opposition to Falloux's harsh treatment of the National Workshops, spoke up for the workers' associations. He asked for these to be authorized and encouraged even before the Labor Committee had passed a resolution on the subject. Corbon thought that a friendly gesture from the Assembly to the workers' associations could appease the insurgents.

Corbon's intervention was quite useless. The cabinetmaker from the faubourg Saint-Antoine had given up listening to anything the Assembly might say, while the overwhelming majority of the Assembly now wanted nothing but the continuation of the civil war, in the hope that once the faubourg Saint-Antoine had been turned into a charnel house the carpenters and cabinetmakers—those of them who survived—might finally lose their appetite for politics.

The government's behavior on Friday was anything but distinguished. Flocon stood up to speak and placed the claimants dramatically on trial. According to him the builders of the barricades were being subsidized by Bonapartist and Bourbon gold. But Flocon's revelations did not stop here. The Minister of Trade also denounced what he referred to as *foreign gold*. This was a senseless attack on "perfidious Albion" and the next day Lord Normanby protested to the Minister for Foreign Affairs, the unfortunate Bastide, who moreover told the ambassador off the cuff that Flocon had no concrete grounds for his assertions and had merely been casting about for something to soothe the representatives.

Carteret, Undersecretary of State for the Interior, proposed quite simply that the leaders of the monarchist and reactionary parties should be thrown into prison. Denouncing a reactionary plot to the Assembly was a waste of time. Carteret might well have talked like this at the Bastille or the Panthéon, but not in the Palais Bourbon. In any case, after Friday the Assembly was listening with only half an ear to Flocon or Carteret. Many representatives were concentrating chiefly on getting rid of the Pentarchs and they carried this to its conclusion on Saturday morning. Opening the session the president, Sénard, painted a gloomy picture of the situation: "A great many barricades have been erected and fortified during the night. . . . There can be no hope of a solution without a vigorous struggle . . ."

The session broke up in chaos. At nine o'clock Sénard had a long interview with Cavaignac and the two men lowered their voices at the entry of Garnier-Pagès and Pagnerre, the one the secretary and the other a member of the Executive Commission. (The Pentarchs would not resign with a good grace.) The session was resumed, and it was now that a representative from the Landes, Pascal Duprat, made a direct move to overthrow the Pentarchy. (Duprat was naturally able to explain his action by the gravity of the situation, but his attitude is none the less surprising because, although not actually a socialist, he belonged to the most advanced section of the republican party. Having dug the grave of the Republic on June 24, Duprat was exiled after the coup d'état of December 2.) The motion Duprat laid before the house was as follows: "Paris is in a state of siege. All power is to be vested in the hands of General Cavaignac." There was a stir in the Assembly. Tocqueville, an incorrigible liberal, refused to vote for the state of siege. (In his memoirs he blames himself for sticking too firmly to his principles.) However, Bastide followed Duprat onto the rostrum:

"I entreat you, in the name of the country, to put an end to your deliberations and vote as soon as possible. In an hour, perhaps, the Hôtel de Ville will have fallen."

Tocqueville describes with feeling how Bastide, as he uttered these words, displayed a simple dignity which had an immediate effect on the vacillating Assembly. It voted in favor of Duprat's motion. Jules Favre, as vicious and vindictive as ever, proposed the following amendment: "That the Executive Commission shall forthwith cease to exist."

Duclerc spoke against the amendment. "We have just voted for a measure for the public safety," he said. "*I ask you not to vote out of rancor.*"

The Pentarchs were shattered. What had they done wrong? How had they paralyzed Cavaignac's action against the rebellion? They resigned without really understanding the reasons for their downfall. Guizot had refused to listen to the National Guards when they shouted, "Down with Guizot! Long live Reform!" Now the same National Guards were crying, "Down with Lamartine! Down with the Executive Commission! Long live Cavaignac!" And Lamartine had not listened to them. Soon they would forget Cavaignac and then their cry would be "Long live Napoleon! Long live the Emperor!" If the representatives thought the cabinetmaker from the faubourg Saint-Antoine was not easy to govern, they could be answered that the hosier of the faubourg Saint-Denis, who in 1848 brought about the downfall of three political systems in one year, was not an easy man to please either. But though the June rising marked the end of the Executive Commission, the government remained in office. Cavaignac did not want a ministerial crisis while the cannons were roaring inside the capital. (Once the rising had been put down, as we shall see, he reshaped the cabinet in such a way as to satisfy the establishment party.) But to return to the barricades.

The second day of the rising was marked by bloody but indecisive fighting. (1) *In the northern sector:* General Lebreton at the head of the National Guards failed to penetrate either the Clos Saint-Lazare or the site of the Lariboisière hospital. Lamoricière had some success in the faubourg Saint-Denis, carrying the barricades thrown up by the Cavé workshops but failing to reduce the faubourg du Temple. (2) *In the sector around the Hôtel de Ville:* Duvivier, like Bedeau, attempted to reason with the insurgents but his arguments had no effect. The rebels were making progress. They took the *mairie* of the eighth and ninth *arrondissements* (near the Place des Vosges and the church of Saint-Gervais respectively) and were thus within a few yards of the Hôtel de Ville. This was the reason for the cry of alarm raised by Bastide in the Assembly. I have already mentioned the disarming of a battalion of the eighteenth light in the Place des Vosges. (3) *In the left bank sector:* Damesme got through to the Panthéon. The *gardes mobiles* had succeeded in occupying the law faculty building and were firing on the Panthéon and Saint-Geneviève, and a few shells actually grazed the church. The *mairie* of the twelfth *arrondissement* was captured early in the afternoon and Damesme went at once to the rue de la Vieille-Estrapade, where he was fatally wounded. To the representative Valette who was with him on his deathbed he declared, "I have done my duty. Tell that to the Assembly." General Bréa took over command of Damesme's forces and late that evening the insurgents were driven back to the Enfer and Fontainebleau barriers.

The evening was a grim one in the Assembly. The representatives belonging to the left wing and the extreme left, who hardly dared leave the Palais Bourbon for fear of being accused of abetting the insurrection, believed in their hearts that the Republic was dead. The right wing lacked faith in Cavaignac's military genius. Thiers had gathered around him nearly three hundred deputies belonging to the right ad right of center. On the twenty-fourth of February he suggested that Louis Philippe should abandon the capital and return to conquer it at the head of sixty thousand troops. Duvergier de Hauranne's shocked reaction to this proposition will be remembered. On the twenty-fourth of June, Thiers put forward a similar plan and urged the representatives to withdraw to Bourges. Cavaignac interrupted him: "If Thiers goes on I shall have him shot." Thiers was still obsessed by the dream of reconquering Paris, but he had to wait until the spring of 1871 to see his dream become a fact.

THE THIRD DAY, SUNDAY, JUNE 25. CORPUS CHRISTI In the northern sector, Lebreton finally stormed the Clos Saint-Lazare and entered La Chapelle. But Lamoricière, by the Saint-Martin Canal, was having very little success; the fighting was indecisive and this made the general literally furious. Lamoricière even sent a note to Cavaignac, which proves that he had completely lost his head: among other things he demanded the arrest of Lalanne, the director of the National Workshops. In the afternoon, however, he succeeded in gaining control of the faubourg du Temple and by evening he had occupied the northeastern approaches to the Bastille.

In the sector around the Hôtel de Ville the workers were still putting up vigorous resistance. A small revolutionary government had been set up at the *mairie* of the eighth *arrondissement*, presided over by Lacollange, the editor of the paper *L'Organisation du travail*. In the faubourg Saint-Antoine, on the other hand, the mechanic Racary and a timber contractor named Desteract were acting with vigor and intelligence.

Could Duvivier's regulars and *gardes mobiles* prevail over

the amateur soldiers of Lacollange, Racary, and Desteract? The general divided his troops into two detachments which were to meet at the Bastille. The first, under the command of General Regnault, was to proceed by Saint-Gervais and the rue Saint-Antoine, while the second, led by Duvivier himself, was to follow the banks of the river Seine and the Saint-Martin Canal. Regnault took the *mairie* of the ninth *arrondissement* (Saint-Gervais) with some difficulty before he was struck down at point-blank range by a rebel he was interrogating. General Perrot took over Regnault's command. At three o'clock that afternoon the *mairie* of the eighth *arrondissement* finally fell to the regular troops, and at four o'clock the detachment reached the western approaches to the Bastille. Duvivier, at the head of the second detachment, was fatally wounded in the Place de Grève, near the Pont Louis-Philippe. As he lay dying Duvivier showed his generous, farsighted character by saying over and over again, "These poor workers should be given employment: the nation's hand should be opened for them." Duvivier's place was taken by General Négrier, and after protracted fighting along the Quai des Ormes and alongside the two barracks of the Ave Maria and the Celestines, Négrier too reached the approaches to the Bastille. "The red flag waved from the July column and an immense barricade shut off the square from the boulevard Bourdon to the rue Jean-Beausire, and connecting up with the line of barricades enclosing the boulevard Beaumarchais, the rue de la Roquette, the rue du Faubourg-Saint-Antoine, and the rue de Charenton." [4]

Négrier, approaching the Bastille from the south, aimed

---

[4] Charles Schmidt, *Les Journées de Juin 1848* (Paris, Hachette, 1926). This little book is as lively as it is concise, and I have relied on it extensively.

to rejoin Perrot, who was following the rue Saint-Antoine and emerging from the west. Then Négrier fell in turn, and collapsed in the arms of the minister Trélat, who had accompanied him. He was killed by the regular army, and murmured to Trélat as he fell, "I am dying at the hands of a soldier." The bullet which struck Négrier did double execution, for it dealt a mortal wound to the representative Charbonnel at the same time. On Sunday a particularly tragic incident occurred in the faubourg Saint-Antoine as a side effect of the military operations, and more will be said of this in the chapter on the barricades. The Archbishop of Paris, Monsignor Affre, unable to bear the slaughter among his flock any longer, had gone out onto the battlefield in an attempt to mediate between the insurgents and the regular army. He was shot down with a bullet in the groin. The archbishop's death was naturally blamed on the insurgents, but in fact he seems to have been hit by a member of the garde mobile. Monsignor Affre was begging the rebels to lay down their arms and was understandably facing the insurgents rather than the forces of law and order. Consequently the fact that he was hit from behind appears proof that Monsignor Affre, like Négrier, was killed by mistake.

In the third sector, on the left bank, General Bréa, although he had two thousand men at his disposal, was relying more on his eloquence than his guns to help him pacify the twelfth arrondissement and occupy Gentilly and Arcueil. He went the rounds of the barriers encircling the twelfth arrondissement, Enfer, Saint-Jacques, and La Santé, delivering soothing speeches which were generally well received. When he came to the Barrière d'Italie the workers invited him to enter, assuring him that no harm would come to him, and with only the slightest hesitation he crossed the barricade. No sooner did Bréa find himself among the angrily muttering crowd, however, than he was violently abused, dragged forcibly to an *estaminet* called the Grand-Salon at Gentilly, and from there to the Grand-Poste, a kind of coaching inn on the road from Paris to Fontainebleau, and finally shot.

The situation on Sunday night was still grave for Cavaignac, but it was clear that the insurgents could no longer hope to win. The National Guards ordered up from the provinces by Ledru-Rollin were still flocking into Paris, though only the National Guard of Amiens, which fought at La Villette, was actually used in action. Some workers undoubtedly attempted to prevent the arrival of these reinforcements and to this end railroad lines were torn up at Essonnes and Corbeil and trains brought to a standstill. But on the whole the government maintained contact with the provinces and it can be imagined that the prosperous farmers of Normandy, for example, were only too willing to administer a sharp lesson to the Parisian insurgents. On Friday and Saturday the cabinetmaker in the faubourg Saint-Antoine could still hope that the great provincial cities would follow the example of Paris and revolt against the caricature of a republic, but Lyons remained quiet and only at Marseilles did any serious incidents occur. Émile Ollivier acted on this occasion with a mixture of great firmness and magnanimity. By Sunday evening, therefore, our cabinetmaker, entrenched in his position at the Bastille, had lost all hope. The army had pushed right up to the barriers and now only the districts between the Bastille and the Place du Trône were still holding out against the government. (Some remnants of the insurrection were still fighting in La Villette and La Chapelle.)

On Monday morning the situation at the Bastille was even more critical, because the insurgents were also threatened from the east. Up till now they had been confronted to the south by the forces commanded first by Duvivier and later by Négrier, by Perrot's column to the west, and Lamoricière's to the north. Now Lebreton's troops had penetrated into the Place du Trône from Vincennes and had taken them in the rear. By the early hours of Monday morning the fighting was much more sporadic and uncoordinated than during the previous two days. On some of the barricades the rebels were certainly killed to a man, but in most cases negotiations took place and the workers who favored a surrender and cease-fire carried the day over their comrades. There was some complicated parleying between General Perrot and a spokesman for the eighth arrondissement, the former editor of the Progressif de l'Aube, Raymond des Ménards. President Sénard also received emissaries from the insurrectionists. A number of representatives, including Larabit, Druet-Desvaux, and Galy-Cazalet, anxious to stop the bloodshed, attempted to find some grounds for compromise, and already a great many rebels were laying down their weapons at the mairie of the eighth arrondissement. In the event, those poor wretches who looked for an honorable surrender were bitterly duped. Sénard, with his talk of clemency, may have been speaking in good faith, but only Cavaignac—the new dictator—knew the fate he had in store for the vanquished.

Cavaignac did not lack a taste for eloquence and on June 24 he addressed a benevolent proclamation to the insurgents: "Lay down your weapons of fratricide. . . . The government knows there are errant brethren in your ranks." On the twenty-sixth came a fresh proclamation: "Let my name be accursed if I see victors and vanquished in the streets of Paris, instead of only victims." Cavaignac's character contained something of the Tartuffe: on the same day he was already acting with utter ruthlessness toward the rebels cornered at the Bastille. "I want complete surrender," he told Larabit in the presence of four spokesmen from the faubourg Saint-Antoine. "I am ready to declare a truce until ten o'clock in the morning." (It had, in fact, been difficult enough to persuade him to agree to ten o'clock. Initially he had announced that he would resume fire at eight, but this would not have given the envoys time to warn their comrades.) "If at ten o'clock you have still not surrendered, the army will move into your district by main force."

Ten o'clock struck. The barricades were in a pitiable state of indecision. Perrot, more humane than Cavaignac, was still hesitating to open fire. He granted the rebels a ten-minute respite, whereupon they hastily retired. The troops had no trouble in carrying the sixty-five barricades which had been erected between the Bastille and the Place du Trône.

At twenty past eleven Sénard rushed panting into the debating chamber of the Palais Bourbon:

"Ushers, go and find all the deputies and summon them here. Go everywhere. Oh, thank God, thank God! I am so happy!"

When the Assembly learned that the faubourg Saint-Antoine had surrendered a great shout went up: "Long live the Republic!"

Few exclamations have ever been less sincere. If a roll of honor were to be drawn up citing all those who chastised the rebellious proletariat in nineteenth-century France, then Cavaignac should have pride of place in it, although I do not claim that his name should come first of all, since Thiers in 1871 behaved even more ruthlessly than Cavaignac. Proudhon christened Cavaignac the "Charles IX of the Republic." Only four or five hundred of the rebels appear to have perished on the barricades, but more than three thousand were massacred by the soldiers of the *garde mobile* and the regular army after the fighting was over. In all 11,671 persons were arrested. A few of these were executed and some were sentenced to forced labor, but by far the most common penalty was deportation. Countless workers became unwilling colonists. "Thousands of families," says Proudhon, "departed for Algeria where they were sent to fatten the soil of Africa for future owners with their own bodies."

Caussidière concludes his memoirs with an account, extremely restrained, in fact, of the June Days, and for the final words of his book he borrows from Pierre Leroux. Faced with the savagery of June 1848, Leroux said simply, "Passions, passions, nothing but passions!"

⚑ *The Real Victor in June*

Our own account ends as the last barricades are still falling at La Villette and the Bastille, and the "Soldiers of Despair" are billeted at Mazas and Vincennes awaiting internment in the neighborhood of Constantine. The first pages of this book echoed to the cry of "*A bas Guizot! Vive la Réforme!*" uttered with one voice by the hosier of the faubourg Saint-Denis, the cabinetmaker of the faubourg Saint-Antoine, and the mechanic from Chaillot or La Chapelle. Four months later the hosier was shouting, "Down with the Executive Commission! Down with Lamartine! Long live Cavaignac!" The cabinetmaker and the mechanic were silent, defeated by the hosier.

When Pascal Duprat mounted the rostrum in the Palais Bourbon on the twenty-fourth of June to proclaim Cavaignac dictator, he was playing a part analogous to that played by Odilon Barrot on the twenty-second of February when he demanded the impeachment of Guizot. Odilon Barrot was a sincere royalist, but he destroyed a throne. Pascal Duprat was a fervent republican, but he destroyed the Republic. As Proudhon remarks, in a metaphor that is at once daring and sententious, Cavaignac's saber appeared on the stage of history on the twenty-fourth of June and the rattle of this saber brought down the curtain on the February Revolution. But although the shopkeepers had made Cavaignac a dictator, could he really regard himself as the victor of 1848? Once the rebellion had been suppressed he formally resigned his powers in the presence of an Assembly which promptly restored them to him, and the state of siege remained nominally in force until October 29.

While he played along the out-and-out republicans, the Washingtons devoid of personal ambitions, Cavaignac gave certain pledges to the right wing in his reshuffling of the ministries. Sénard replaced Recurt at the Ministry of the Interior and Goudchaux took over Duclerc's position at the Treasury. Lamoricière became Minister of War; Marie, Keeper of the Seals; Armand Marrast, President of the Assembly; and Changarnier, Commander of the National Guard. Marie's first concern as Minister of Justice was to hunt down the socialist and democrat leaders. After a noisy debate the Assembly agreed on the prosecution of Louis Blanc and Caussidière, both of whom went into exile. Marie then struck at the poor press, that is, the republican press, by reintroducing caution money for newspapers.

On November 4 the Constitution which had been worked out and discussed in the Assembly during the summer and autumn became law. The Assembly had decided that national sovereignty was to be expressed in two ways. On the one hand, a single Legislative Assembly was to be elected by the people. (I am by no means a champion of the Senate, but it is possible that in 1848 a second Assembly would have introduced a certain amount of stability into political life. The Constituent Assembly had been simultaneously omnipotent and helpless. And the Legislative Assembly elected in 1849 never really knew what attitude to adopt toward the executive powers or the President of the Republic. At one moment it was stupidly arrogant, at the next sickeningly humble. Twenty-five years later, Gambetta remembered the sad lesson which had been taught by this single Chamber: hence his acceptance of two Chambers and hence too his efforts to create an instrument of republican education in the Senate to which he gave the name of Grand Conseil des Communes de France.) On the other hand, the people were also to appoint a President of the Republic. When both the president and the Assembly held office by virtue of universal suffrage, the problem arose of how to regulate any disputes which might occur between them.

Cavaignac put himself forward as President of the Republic. Administrative power was in his hands and he had no scruples about using or abusing it. He tried to win over the people by representing himself as fundamentally a republican, and even gave a left-of-center air to his government by appointing Dufaure to the Ministry of the Interior and Vivien to the Ministry of Public Works (the former replacing Recurt, the latter Sénard). But all his endeavors were to no purpose. Towering over Cavaignac was the figure of Louis Napoleon Bonaparte, himself enveloped by the gigantic shadow of the Emperor. Louis Napoleon had been re-elected to the Assembly in September and at once found himself in an extremely strong position in parliament, since although the establishment party had been terrified into a leaning toward Cavaignac in June, by the autumn of 1848 they were breaking away from the general, who was too much a republican for their liking. The Committee of the rue de Poitiers, led by Thiers, voted for Louis Bonaparte against Cavaignac. But the Emperor's nephew did not even need the Orleanist vote. He had the confidence of the people. On December 10 he was elected with a vote of five and a half million. Cavaignac had 1,500,000, Ledru-Rollin 370,000, Raspail 37,000, and Lamartine 17,000.

Cavaignac had a majority in only four départements— the royalist areas of the Var, Bouches-du-Rhône, Morbihan, and Finistère. The strongest majorities for Louis Bonaparte were in the four socialist départements of Saône-et-Loire, Creuse, Haute-Vienne, and Drôme. Of the 191,000 votes cast for Louis Bonaparte in Paris and its environs "more than 30,000," wrote Proudhon, "came from socialists who had deserted Raspail because of their hatred for Cavaignac." The latter was, first and foremost, the shopkeepers' candidate. Opinions in the faubourg Saint-Denis were divided. After a good deal of hesitation, our hosier voted for Louis Napoleon Bonaparte, but a great many of his colleagues remained faithful to the general. In one sector of the faubourg Saint-Antoine a ballot paper was found with the words "Cavaignac, prince of blood." It was the signature of one of the "Soldiers of Despair" who had not forgotten the twenty-sixth of June.

All the same, we should not end on this note of hatred and despair. When the carpenter from Saint-Antoine or the mechanic from La Chapelle reached his factory or workshop in that cruel and disillusioned autumn of 1848, he had a new and comforting song by Pierre Dupont on his lips, though he sang it under his breath for fear of police spies and informers.

> La République dure encore
> Malgré nos fautes et nos crimes;
> Comme un reflet de pourpre et d'or
> Son nom rayonne sur nos cimes.[5]

[5] "The Republic lives on, despite all our errors and offenses. Her name shines high above us like a reflected glow of purple and gold."

The Barricades

La barricade était livide dans l'aurore.

This line by Victor Hugo can be said without exaggeration to have ushered in the dawn of the Third Republic. The words have a heavy, funereal ring: Hugo is describing the barricade erected on the morning of December 3, 1851, in the rue du Faubourg-Saint-Antoine, at the intersection with the rue de Cotte and the rue Sainte-Marguerite. The rue Sainte-Marguerite is now the rue Trousseau and the rue Lenoir, next to the rue de Cotte, has become the rue d'Aligre. The statue of the representative Baudin has been removed from its pedestal. But the small street market lying between the rue de Cotte and the rue d'Aligre still preserves the form and the living atmosphere of the period we are describing, and the name Lenoir can still be seen on an old iron shop-sign above a laundry.

In the Place du Marché Lenoir (which is also called the Marché Beauvau), we are in the heart of the Paris of the insurrection. After the coup d'état of December 2 a handful of representatives, Hugo, Schoelcher, Dr. Baudin, and Charamaule among them, attempted to rouse the old revolutionary district against Louis Napoleon. But Saint-Antoine had not forgotten the shots which had been fired in June 1848 with the consent of the very representatives who were now calling them to arms. Hugo wrote sadly that the faubourg was "apathetic." All the same a few workers, with more boredom than conviction, did put up a barricade. Made of a cart, an omnibus, and two small carriages, this seemed a flimsy affair compared with those which had been thrown up in the same area in June 1848. It was more symbolic than practical. The corpulent Schoelcher harangued the workers to no effect. There was a second speech by Charamaule, a royalist representing the district of Hérault in the Assembly. He was not in favor of the Republic, but he was against the coup d'état and the Empire. He was fond of good living, and even his name made him a popular target for satirists, who played on the syllables *Chat–rat–miaule*. He did his best to shake the people out of their apathy: "Aren't you the children of Paris any longer? Do you want to be treated like Prussians or Austrians?" But the people remained silent. They were thinking that three years previously they had demonstrated with simple warmth to induce the government to make an end of the Prussians and Austrians who were dismembering Poland. What answer had they received then from the Palais Bourbon and the Hôtel de Ville? Marrast or Lamartine had told them in no uncertain terms to keep quiet. They were requested not to disturb the kings' peace. Yet now these people who had been duped, guarded, and shot down were expected to come to the rescue of middle-class law and order and restore a constitution which had not so much as given them the right to work. They reacted sullenly. They were already sullen at the Feast of Concord on May 20, 1848, when the representatives, the *cumulards* "with their full bellies," had twenty-five francs a day to spend. And on December 3 the rue Saint-Antoine had some things to say about those twenty-five francs.

"Do you think we're going to get ourselves killed to save your twenty-five francs?"

And then Baudin stepped forward to the barricade and said, "Stay there a minute longer, my friend, and you'll see how a man dies for twenty-five francs."

A column of soldiers approached from the Bastille and rushed the barricade. Baudin was killed and a bullet pierced Schoelcher's overcoat.

Baudin's death went almost unnoticed in the grim December skirmish, and yet Baudin had been president of the Club de l'Avenir and was a popular figure in the faubourg Poissonnière and in the faubourg Saint-Denis. The printers and papermakers who lived in the rue du Caire liked his lectures and his honest, schoolmasterish manner. Alphonse Baudin had even been arrested during the pro-Polish demonstrations on May 15, 1848. But this does not mean that his death on December 3, 1851, was useless. Seventeen years later Gambetta revived the memory of Baudin in his famous speech in the action brought against Delezcluse, and the Empire tottered.

La barricade était livide dans l'aurore.

The veterans of 1848 muttered Victor Hugo's words to themselves, while younger men learned them. The fighters of the Commune, the pioneers of the International and of trade unionism, showed in 1871 that the art of building a barricade had not been forgotten. And even today . . . the revolutionary tide in France may subside from time to time until it is almost imperceptible—even the most turbulent oceans are sometimes calm—but the calm does not last, and from the Hôtel de Ville to La Villette the barricades are, so to speak, always there in the background.

It is a curious fact that the barricades suddenly reappeared in the region of the Hôtel de Ville on December 19, 1827, after an absence from the Parisian scene of nearly two centuries. They had played no part at all in the great French Revolution. The last time the barricades went up under the *ancien régime* was when they were erected in the narrow streets of the capital on August 5 and 6, 1648, announcing the commencement of the minor civil war known by the charming name of the Fronde. The people had not yet started overturning vehicles in the roadway, and contented themselves with placing a few hurdles (*barriques*) to block the way and provide a reasonable degree of shelter: it was from this that the name "barricades" originated. When, 180 years later, in November 1827, Paris once again resorted to building barricades, it was in a spirit more of gaiety than anger. They were hailing the downfall of Villèle.

M. de Villèle was a great financier, but by the creation of annual new *rentes* he alienated a great many of the middle classes and small tradesmen, the readers of the *Constitutionnel* described so vividly by Balzac. Moreover, rightly or wrongly, Villèle stood for all that was most inflexible and unpleasant in the reactionary party. He dissolved the Chamber which was beginning to oppose him, but the 1827 elections were a triumph for the liberals. Charles X was obliged to part with Villèle and call in Martignac instead. Paris was highly satisfied with this, but it was a satisfaction that held a touch of menace. There were a number of clashes between the demonstrators and the regular troops, and several streets were quickly denuded of their pavements.

On the barricades we can find one familiar figure in the person of Auguste Blanqui. This fanatical devotee of violence received his baptism of revolutionary fire on November 19, 1827, and was actually wounded in the affray. 1827 was like a rehearsal for the play enacted in 1830. During the "Three Glorious Days" of July 1830, the two headquarters of the revolution were the faubourg Saint-Antoine and the faubourg Saint-Marcel. Marmont's soldiers certainly succeeded in cutting their way through the barricades between the Hôtel de Ville and the Bastille, but these closed up again after the soldiers had passed and the troops were soon overpowered. Blanqui, Guinard, and Raspail were all among the leaders of the people. Raspail was wounded in the attack on the barracks in the rue de Babylone; at his side fell Vaneau, the Polytechnician who gave his name to the street where Marx lived fifteen years later. Guinard took command of a column which set out from the Panthéon to the Tuileries. In July 1830 Guinard, who from the Hôtel de Ville in 1848 made persistent demands for a determined attack on the faubourg Saint-Antoine, had been the first to enter the Tuileries at the head of the workers from the faubourg Saint-Michel. On June 5 and 6, 1832, Louis Philippe, king by the grace of the barricades, came up against the first barricades to be built during his reign.

Within a few hours a third of Paris was in the hands of the insurgents. The rising of June 1832 deserves special attention because it offers a direct parallel to that of June 1848. It was certainly not as grievous or as fiercely proletarian in character, but even so it was not a middle-class revolution, while in July 1830, just as in February 1848, the tone was distinctly bourgeois. On June 5, 1832, old Lafayette, who was still adored by the people of Paris, might have got the rising under control, but he suddenly panicked and slipped away to shut himself up at home. As for Odilon Barrot, Lafitte, and François Arago, they wasted a great deal of breath in talk but did not act. On the other hand, in June 1832, just as in June 1848, the disposition of the barricades and organization of the rising as a whole give the impression of being well thought out and seem to have been the result of a mysterious kind of clockwork. (The men behind it in June 1832 were the militant members of the society "The Friends of the People"; in June 1848, the ranks of the National Workshops.) The rising was triggered off on June 5, 1832, by the funeral of General Lamarque. The moral roots, if they can be so called, of the demonstration were the same as those which led to the demonstration of May 15, 1848, which had as its object the liberation of Poland. Victor Hugo wrote that the treaties of 1815 acted on Lamarque like a personal affront. He loathed Wellington with an unequivocal hatred which appealed to the multitude, and he had magnificently preserved the gloom of Waterloo for seventeen years, paying little attention to anything which happened in the meantime. As he lay dying even, he clasped to his breast the sword which had been presented to him by the officers of the Hundred Days. Lamarque had subjected Marshal Sébastiani, who was at that time the French Minister for Foreign Affairs, to a passionate interpellation on the subject of Polish affairs, and at the same time as he was shedding tears over Poland, Lamarque was also inveighing against England, making speeches full of references to the Hundred Years War, and concluding that the peace of 1815 was merely what he described as "a pause in the mud." Lamarque's house was close to the rue Castiglioni, not far from the Place de la Concorde. On the fifth of June,[1] a dull, rainy day, the hearse, attended by quite a large crowd of people, traveled via the Place de la Madeleine, the Grands Boulevards, and the Pont d'Austerlitz (with a great many incidents on the way) until the cortege finally came to a halt at the Place Valhubert, where the funeral orations were delivered. (Lamarque's body was to be taken by road to the Landes.) As the orators were speaking, two flags made their first appearance in Paris. The first was the flag of the young Germany, the red, black, and yellow of Weimar which so moved Michelet, and the second, the red flag. This banner was carried by a mysterious horseman dressed in black with waxen face and a huge mustache with the points curled upward in the Spanish fashion. A great deal of ink has been spilled on the subject of the man in black bearing the red flag.[2]

Feelings ran high and it was not long before the barricades were springing up all over the *quartiers* of the Marais, Les Arcis, Les Halles, and the faubourgs Saint-Denis and Saint-Martin. The *mairie* of the eighth *arrondissement* was taken over by the republicans. It is amusing to note that the young Minister of the Interior, Thiers, was dining with a few friends in the famous restaurant called Le Rocher de Cancale in the rue Montorgueil while the people were beginning to tear up the streets fifty yards away.

Guinard also played a considerable part in this insurrection, and another old acquaintance, Bastide, who was a tim-

---

[1] A lively description of the events of the fifth and sixth of June can be found in *La Grande Peur de 1832* by J. Lucas-Dubreton (Paris, Gallimard, 1932).

[2] Cf. Gabriel Perreux, *Les Origines du drapeau rouge en France* (Paris, Presses Universitaires, 1930).

ber merchant before becoming Minister for Foreign Affairs, was building barricades in his timber yard in the rue de Ménilmontant.

The insurrection of 1832 plays a large part in Victor Hugo's novel *Les Misérables* and Hugo gives a lengthy description of a barricade erected in the faubourg Saint-Denis. In fact it is in the June Days of 1832 that the character of Gavroche makes his appearance in Hugo's work. According to Raymond Guyot, who has devoted a great deal of research to the identity of Gavroche, the heroic little man from whom Hugo got his inspiration actually fought on the barricades of December 1851. He was killed in the rue Tiquetonne, not far from the rue Montorgueil, during the disturbances following Louis Napoleon's coup d'état. Later, when Hugo was writing *Les Misérables* in exile, he transposed Gavroche's existence and made his hero perish in the June Days of 1832.

Hugo describes in detail the construction of a barricade: "In a few moments, twenty iron bars had been wrenched from the front of a tavern and the paving of the street torn up for ten yards. Gavroche and Bahorel had intercepted a passing dray belonging to a manufacturer of lime named Anceau: the dray was carrying three barrels of lime and these were set underneath the heaped-up stones. Enjolras had lifted up the trapdoor to a cellar and all the Widow Hucheloup's empty casks went to stand beside the barrels of lime. Feuilly, whose nimble fingers were used to coloring the delicate struts of fans, had buttressed the barrels and the dray with two great heaps of rubble. This rubble, like all the rest, was seized on for the occasion and came from none knew where. Some stay beams had been torn from the façade of a neighboring house and these were laid on top of the casks. By the time Bossuet and Courfeyrac turned around, half the street was already blocked by a rampart taller than a man."

It is a fact that there were barricades in the faubourg Saint-Denis and the faubourg Saint-Antoine in June 1832 which were over nine feet high. But to return to Hugo:

"An omnibus drawn by two white horses passed the end of the street. Bossuet, leaping over the paving stones, ran to stop the driver and, giving his hand to the ladies, obliged the passengers to descend. He then sent the conductor about his business and returned leading the horses and the vehicle. A moment later the horses were ambling loose down the rue Mondétour and the omnibus was lying on its side, completing the blockage of the street."

By the evening of June 5 the government already had the situation in hand, but even so it was still on edge, more so than the king, who rode boldly on horseback from the Tuileries to the Bastille. (Inevitably Louis Philippe was given a chilly reception, but all the same the people appear to have appreciated the monarch's courage.) Nevertheless, fighting went on throughout the night, a good many shots were heard, and there was a ruddy glow in the sky. Raspail, imprisoned at Saint-Pélagie, heard the fusillade and saw the unusual glow in the sky, with a surge of gladness:

"The people are victorious, at last the people will have their rights!"

Raspail rejoiced too soon. The battle whose echoes thrilled the prisoners of Sainte-Pélagie was a desperate one. All through the night of June 5 and well into the morning of the sixth, the murderous fusillade crackled around the barricades erected in the rue aux Ours, the rue Jean-Robert, the rue Brisemiche, and the rue de la Verrerie. It is worth while pausing for a moment in the rue de la Verrerie because there we shall witness an incident which had a profound effect on the mind of the people. A few hundred insurgents had taken refuge in the square formed by the rue Saint-Martin, the rue Neuve-Saint-Merri, the rue du Renard, and the rue de la Verrerie. The system of barricades surrounding the cloister of Saint-Merri was extremely well connected and fortified. Its defenders had no hope of victory and they knew it, but all the time the cordon of National Guards and soldiers was drawing tighter about them they did not give up. They were led by a youth—very young and very handsome—named Jeanne who succeeded in making his escape at the last moment but was arrested not long afterward. Epic battles were fought at 30 rue Saint-Martin and in a butcher's shop in the rue Saint-Merri which were long talked of in the neighborhood. The memory of those who had fought in the cloister of Saint-Merri was still vivid in 1848.

The National Guard of the faubourg Saint-Denis and the faubourg Saint-Martin was on the whole strongly against the rising and extremely loyal to Louis Philippe. In 1832 our hosier from the faubourg Saint-Denis performed miracles in the service of the regime. But as the years went by, loyalty to the bourgeois monarch wore thin, and reading his copies of Le National and Le Siècle, the hosier became convinced that Guizot was a crook and that Louis Philippe had betrayed the interests of his country. And so, in February 1848, he found himself on the same side as the cabinetmakers of the faubourg Saint-Antoine on whom he had been firing sixteen years before. But in June 1848 he rediscovered his real mission as the defender of law and order and once again fought valiantly against the builders of the barricades.

APRIL 13, 1834 News of the insurrection at Lyons reached Paris and once again the barricades went up in the rue Beaubourg, the rue Geoffroy-l'Angevin, the rue Aubry-le-Boucher, the rue aux Ours, the rue Maubuée, and the rue Transnonain. I have already mentioned the tragic events which occurred in the rue Transnonain. (There was fighting in the rue Transnonain again in June 1848.) Shots were fired at some soldiers from one of the houses, whereupon they rushed into the building and and killed everyone inside. Bugeaud was in command of the troops at the time, and Paris never forgave Bugeaud.

SUNDAY, MAY 12, 1839 The rising planned by the club known as "The Seasons" broke out in a way which took Paris by surprise. (It was a period of ministerial crisis, but the political and social situation was not particularly tense.) The crowds in the streets were in a mood to watch the fun. However a group of men plundered an armorers' in the rue Bourg-l'Abbé. The insurgents formed into two gangs: one, under the command of Barbès, headed for the Palais de Justice and joined up with the second at the Châtelet. The insurgents gained temporary control of the Hôtel de Ville, but they were quickly surrounded by the Municipal Guards and the army. Barbès was captured, although Blanqui succeeded in making his escape. It was he who had drawn up the detailed plan of the insurrection. (Blanqui had even carried his passion for detail so far as to specify the exact thickness of each barricade.) Georges Weill, in his excellent *Histoire du parti républicain en France*, records the comments of Langlois, a disciple of Proudhon, on the subject of the twelfth of May. He said that Blanqui appeared to be physically ill: when he and his companions reached the armorers' in the rue Bourg-l'Abbé, he was shivering. The firing was less violent than in 1832, but even so it raged for several hours in the rue Saint-Martin. Yet once again, with the bloody picture of the barricades in the background, the foreground was occupied with the peaceful sight of the small traders of Paris going serenely about their business. One feeble old man "pushing a handcart, filled with bottles of some liquid refreshment, to which he had fastened a tricolor scarf, went to and fro between the barricade and the soldiers, handing out glasses of chocolate impartially to the government and the anarchists." (Victor Hugo)

I have already commented on the bourgeois tone of the February Revolution. The first barricade which appeared early in the afternoon of February 22 went up at the corner of the rue Saint-Florentin and the rue de Rivoli, the second in the rue Duphot, and the third in the rue Saint-Honoré. In other words, in the very quartiers where they were least to be expected. Caussidière and Albert were highly intrigued at the sight. Albert, said Caussidière, failed to recognize those digging up the roadway as his own men. (Hence the distrust which prevailed in the circle of the paper La Réforme toward this insurrection.) On the night of the twenty-third, however, after the incident in the boulevard des Capucines, the barricades went back to what might be called their favorite districts and burgeoned forth in the faubourg Saint-Denis and the boulevard Bonne-Nouvelle. Louis Philippe, in fact, was overthrown by a precarious coalition between the middle-class "barricaders" in the rue de Rivoli and the more traditional kind in the faubourg Saint-Denis.

We need no longer be surprised that these people should have shown themselves so expert in building barricades during the rising of June 1848. Either because they themselves had a revolutionary past, or from an inherited talent, the mechanic of La Chapelle and the cabinetmaker of the faubourg Saint-Antoine were quite capable of tearing up pavements and overturning stagecoaches. When Tocqueville visited the district around the Hôtel de Ville on June 23 he was filled with admiration and astonishment at the calmness and efficiency of those engaged in building the barricades. "The people," he exclaimed, "went about the task with the methodical neatness of engineers, taking up only such paving stones as were needed to lay the base, with the help of the squared stones so procured, of a thick, solid wall, very tidy indeed in appearance, in which they were generally careful to leave a small gap close to the houses through which people might pass."

Their coolness was allied to a burning enthusiasm. The people called on passers-by to help them in their work, and this was how one eminently conservative representative, François de Corcelles, anxious not to be on the receiving end of a worker's bullet, hastily took his turn in ripping up a small section of pavement. However, he proved so clumsy that the workers merely shrugged and sent him on his way with good-humored laughter.

Having made this journey in time, from 1827 to 1848, let us end this chapter with a journey in space and travel through Paris from north to south during the bitter days of June, from the church of Saint-Vincent-de-Paul to the Panthéon. We are already familiar with the chief events of the battle but there is still something to be gleaned from further observation.

In the Place Lafayette, close to the still unfinished church of Saint-Vincent-de-Paul, the mechanics of La Chapelle had built a substantial breastwork of water carts, planks, and paving stones. Their leader was a captain in the National Guard named Legénissel who, with his entire company, had gone over to the rebels. The great barricade at the Porte Saint-Denis, where the two beautiful women described by Victor Hugo met their deaths, was made of a heap of every different kind of vehicle: "*coucous*," as the hackney carriages were called, a few water carts, and an aristocratic carriage. The barricade at the Porte Saint-Martin was even larger and more picturesque than that at the Porte Saint-Denis. It will be remembered that Odilon Barrot had shared his carriage on the twenty-fourth of April with a gang of demonstrators who had dressed themselves up in antique armor like characters out of a play. The workers who built the barricade across the boulevard Saint-Martin on the twenty-third of June raided the nearby Théâtre de la Porte-Saint-Martin for their equipment, and the barricade was surmounted by five women, one of them in mourning, all brandishing halberds and weird-looking swords. The workers in the rue Saint-Denis had taken a locomotive from the Cavé works, besides some cauldrons and sheet iron. The sixty-eight barricades in the rue Saint-Antoine were made out of carts filled with paving stones and uprooted tree trunks.

Now let us pause for a moment in the faubourg Saint-Antoine and listen to the battle cries of the insurgents: Caen and Caussidière, the Republic and Caussidière. (It should be added that Caussidière had become involved in the insurrection only with extreme reluctance. Caussidière, like most of the representatives of the extreme left, sat tight in the Palais Bourbon in a state of utter fright. With great courage, he asked to go and make soothing speeches at the barricades in the name of the deputies, since he thought with some justice that his personal popularity might exercise a salutary influence. But the great majority of his colleagues objected to the proposal on the grounds that mad dogs were to be shot and not reasoned with.) If we look for the leaders who gave our cabinetmaker his firing orders, we should find among them, for example, one elegant individual—so elegant that he fought in highly polished boots— the morose and romantic factory worker Barthélemy. A few years later, in London, Barthélemy killed in a duel another revolutionary, Cournet, whose son played a major role under the Commune. The reasons for the duel are a mystery, but it was probably connected with political differences and seems, in fact, to have been one episode in the quarrel which, even in exile, set the supporters of Ledru Rollin and those of Louis Blanc at odds. Another elegant figure, at the same time passionate and contemptuous, was that of the naval officer and revolutionary theorist Paul de Flotte. In 1850 Flotte was elected as a representative for the Seine. Exiled after the coup d'état, he served under Garibaldi and was killed fighting for freedom in Italy. Lastly, we should mention the young bronze worker Abel Davaud, who vowed that the workers' lot must be improved, that there must be no recurrence of the fighting which took place in June, and that practical solutions to the problem of labor must be found. Throughout the eighteen-sixties, Davaud was a tireless and generally successful champion of the cooperative system, and his was the brain behind the formation of many cooperative societies.

I may perhaps have laid a somewhat excessive emphasis on the importance of the part played by the cabinetmakers of Saint-Antoine in the February Revolution and in the June uprising. (Daniel Stern estimates their numbers at eighteen thousand, although personally I believe this figure to be an exaggeration.) Many of these cabinetmakers were

German or of German ancestry, and they became more or less identified with the League of the Just, which during the July Monarchy attracted a good many workers who had been compelled for political reasons to flee from Prussia or from the minor German states. (Marx is known to have been associated with the work of the League of the Just, and the League is also known to have been closely connected with the secret society called "The Seasons," which was run by Blanqui.) This explains the vigor and determination shown by all these small craftsmen of the furniture trade at the barricades. It may also be observed that those cabinet-makers of Saint-Antoine who were of German origin were particularly receptive to Napoleonic propaganda. This is to touch on a subject which makes it necessary to leave the rue Saint-Antoine for a moment and move on to the barriers of l'Enfer and Italie at the further end of the twelfth *arrondissement,* among the workers involved in the killing of General Bréa. Among the most ferocious was a mason named Lahr who was later executed for Bréa's murder. His very name betrays his German origin and he was well known to Martin Nadaud, who also worked in the building trade. (Martin Nadaud represented the district of La Creuse in 1849.) Lahr worked on the same site as Nadaud and the two men met a few days before the June rising. Nadaud was struck by the Napoleonic fervor of Lahr who was going the rounds of the wineshops shouting, "A la santé du Petit Tondu!"

It was in the faubourg Saint-Antoine that a tragic incident occurred on which I have touched only briefly in an earlier chapter. This was the death of the Archbishop of Paris, Monsignor Affre. I do not know whether Daniel Stern's portrait of Monsignor Affre is psychologically accurate. The Countess of Agoult, who wrote under the name of

Daniel Stern, was a confessed freethinker and it is somewhat alarming to find her plunging boldly and dogmatically
into the soul of a priest. Nevertheless, with these reservations, it is still very interesting and indeed convincing how
plausible—beyond commonplace, emotional hagiography—
a picture of Monsignor Affre she draws. According to Daniel Stern, the archbishop was a chronic worrier, an unambi-
tious man who suffered quite genuinely when faced with
the crowds and tumult of the streets. On the twenty-third
of June he had attended a children's confirmation service at
Saint-Étienne-du-Mont, and when he saw the barricades going up in the Place du Panthéon he displayed a terror out of
all proportion to his actual danger. He was reluctant to return to the archbishop's palace, which was situated at that
time close by Notre-Dame, and instead had spent the night
at the Lycée Henri IV.

On Saturday the twenty-fourth he showed the same lack
of spirit. Although the environs of the Panthéon are known
to have been clear by the evening of the twenty-fourth,
there was still some difficulty in persuading Monsignor
Affre that it was safe for him to return to the archbishop's
palace. By the time he said mass on Sunday morning, however, he appeared completely transformed. He had passed
the night in prayer and having commended his soul to God
had decided to intervene as a mediator in the civil war.
Some of those who were with him attempted to dissuade
him from a course of action the risks of which were obvious.
Frédéric Ozanam, the fervent Catholic teacher who was the
moving spirit of the Society of Saint Vincent de Paul, urged
the archbishop, on the contrary, to carry out his plan, and
when Monsignor Affre, who detested all ostentation, proposed to go out to meet the crowd dressed simply in his
soutane, Ozanam objected that in order to be effective the

proceedings should have a certain solemnity and urged the prelate to wear his purple robes with the pastoral cross on his breast.

Monsignor Affre went to see Cavaignac during the afternoon, after which he returned to the archbishop's palace and left again almost immediately, this time to go to the Bastille. He had some difficulty in obtaining a cease-fire because of the great confusion reigning at the time. General Négrier had just been killed and his body was being carried away, as also was the dying representative Charbonnel. Négrier's column, which was approaching the Bastille from the south, was in a highly nervous state and was for some time without a leader until its command was finally taken over by General Perrot, who from his position at the entrance to the rue Saint-Antoine was already in command of the western sector. However, Monsignor Affre succeeded—though, as I have already said, not without difficulty—in obtaining an hour's truce on both sides. There was a certain relaxation of tension as he walked into the center of the square, accompanied by his old servant Albert.

An examination of the documents relating to the events of June 1848 appears to leave no doubt that this relaxation was genuine, yet historians have on the whole paid little attention to it, although Pierre de La Gorce alludes to it discreetly. However, I should like to stress it particularly and to comment in this connection on the ambiguous nature of man. In the same individual, the average man in the street —I might even call him man eternal—it is possible for two attitudes to coexist: a fundamental kindness and goodwill and a rigidity conditioned by history. Historians, for what are largely professional reasons, are particularly concerned with this second aspect and are apt to gloss over the first. In the Place de la Bastille on the evening of the twenty-fifth of February men's hearts were moved, despite all their grudges and grievances, by the prelate's appeal for peace. Quite a number of workers climbed over the barricades and went to greet Monsignor Affre cordially, and there were signs of a similar move among the soldiers. For a few moments, soldiers and workers fraternized. The coldest and least forthcoming were the National Guards. The archbishop was encouraged to penetrate more deeply into the maze of fortifications set up by the rebels.

The truce did not last long. Firing soon broke out again, owing to a pitiful misunderstanding. While the archbishop was speaking, the representative Beslay, in a neighboring sector, was also striving to reach some kind of armistice. Beslay, who came from Brittany, is another noble and characteristic figure of 1848. He was an engineer, possessed of considerable private means and devoted heart and soul to the cause of the workers. He gave his advice and money unsparingly to further the prosperity of workers' cooperatives. Beslay's ideas were those of Proudhon, and in 1871 he was the *doyen* of the Commune. On June 25, 1848, he was endeavoring to use his influence in the factories of the rue Basfroi and the Quartier Sainte-Marguerite to bring about an agreement between the government and the workers. Unable to make himself heard above the din, he made a gesture of impatience, whereupon one of the rebels seized a drum and beat it to obtain silence so that the representative could go on with his speech. In the Place de la Bastille, the drumbeats were taken to mean the end of the truce and led to the burst of fire which struck the prelate. I have said earlier that Monsignor Affre appears definitely to have been hit by a bullet fired by a member of the *garde mobile* and I would quote one important witness in support of this:

"I, the undersigned, Jaquemet, vicar general to the archbishop of Paris, who had the honor of accompanying him on the mission of peace and charity he had undertaken, hereby testify that, insofar as it was possible to judge in the great confusion, he was not struck down by those defending the barricades. June 26, 1848."

The insurgents saw Monsignor Affre fall with horror and immediately made a stretcher out of crossed rifles on which to lay the wounded man.

"We did not harm you, Monsignor, it was those traitors in the *garde mobile*. We will avenge you . . ."

The rebels carried the archbishop to the house of the priest of the Quinze-Vingts. (Daniel Stern is guilty of a slight error in stating that he was taken to the presbytery of Sainte-Marguerite.) At four o'clock in the morning his own doctor, Dr. Cayol, arrived and after ascertaining that the wound was a mortal one, insisted that Monsignor Affre should be taken back to the archbishop's palace and his last moments made as comfortable as possible. The workers asked with tears that he should be left among them. "He brings us luck," they said. Nevertheless they did as the doctor told them, brought a stretcher, and argued as to who should have the honor of carrying the archbishop. Many people fell on their knees as the prelate was borne past. Soldiers of the twenty-eighth regiment of the line received the archbishop from the hands of the insurgents and all was done with the most touching correctness and respect. On Monday afternoon, Monsignor Affre breathed his last.

Not far from the archbishop's palace stands the Hôtel-Dieu. I have already touched, in the early part of this book, on the fighting which took place on the evening of June 23 at the capture of the Petit-Pont. In order to overcome the insurgents who were holding the left bank of the river Seine and preventing General Bedeau's soldiers from advancing up the rue Saint-Jacques, Guinard decided to lodge a battery of artillery inside the Hôtel-Dieu. The guns were installed in between the beds of the sick and their fire raked the barricade which had been built across the end of the rue Saint-Jacques. I stress this particular incident because it is a dramatic illustration of the horrors of civil war. The barricade under fire from the windows of the Hôtel-Dieu was actually under the command of a number of officers belonging to the twelfth legion of the National Guard, who had gone over to the rebels. These officers were militant republicans of long standing, well known to Guinard because they had been his companions in prison during the monarchy.

After the capture of the Petit-Pont, the fighting continued in the building already mentioned, the draper's shop called the Deux Pierrots. (The shop sign depicted two dandies dressed in Pierrot costume for a ball.) Ferocious hand-to-hand fighting went on under the counters and in among the bales of merchandise. The *gardes mobiles* fired on the rebels who had succeeded in gaining the roof of the building and bodies crashed down into the street below, while a little further on, in the rue des Mathurins, the *gardes mobiles* set up trestles at which to hold an impromptu council of war. Death sentences were pronounced in rapid succession and carried out on the spot.

The Men of the Provisional Government

What kind of men were the leaders of the Provisional Government? To examine the thoughts of the men in power in France at a time when the entire social structure of Europe hung in the balance, and to see what was in their minds, is no easy matter. In describing the events of 1848, I have raised questions which are, properly speaking, psychological and in this way the eleven members of the Provisional Government are already familiar to us. Yet it is only a comparative familiarity, and all the time I have been drawing the portraits of men like Ledru-Rollin or Lamartine with the information and means at my disposal, I have been conscious that the question of what the men of the Provisional Government were really like will, in fact, remain unanswered for many years to come. Indeed, it is bound up with a whole series of almost inextricable problems. The strength of public men lies in their representative character, yet at the same time this typicality may be a fragile and precarious thing: talent is a matter of building a comparatively solid edifice on shifting ground. Viewed in a certain light, the men of 1848 were only incidentally and, so to speak, sketchily representative.

I have often referred to them impersonally as the men of the *National* and the men of the *Réforme*. But in February 1848 subscribers to the *National* numbered less than three thousand. The *Réforme* was read by educated workers in Paris, Rouen, Lyons, and Saint-Étienne, but even so had only a limited readership. The needy and illiterate masses of the working class were a long way from Louis Blanc, and consequently there was no one to give life to the Republic. Neither Lamartine nor Cavaignac can be relegated to the ranks of mediocre individuals, but the only man who really stands out during the years under discussion, the one man who left his own mark triumphantly on history, is Louis Napoleon Bonaparte. Yet although the Prince-President was extremely clever at making use of his name and of the memories of the Empire, he was a typically second-rate character, following his destiny but quite incapable of creating a legend of his own. As soon as he became involved in the contradictions of his system, he slid helplessly toward disaster. In the years between 1830 and 1870, events counted for more than men. If the word "events" seems too abstract in this context, then let us say that the different social classes, the masses with their more or less vaguely defined aims, had a more far-reaching effect than the aims on which a particular individual had set the seal of his own personality.

Dupont de l'Eure, the head of the Provisional Government, was a colorless and not particularly intelligent man, but his great age—he was almost in his eighties in 1848—

made him a legend. He stood for political integrity and continuity of republican beliefs. Dupont is the answer to those pessimists who believe that men demand little in the way of symbols. He undoubtedly loved the people and he was an honest man in the broadest meaning of the word. During the early years of the bourgeois monarchy he presided with great devotion over the Association for Popular Education (an association of which Cabet was secretary). This said, it is also true to say that Dupont's ardent republicanism was occasionally tinged with opportunism. I cannot say whether Georges Weill was guilty of deliberate irony in commenting that Dupont de l'Eure and François Arago were "republicans who performed loyal service to the Empire and Royalty," but there was some justice in what he said. Under the Directorate in 1798, Dupont was a deputy among the Five Hundred. In the reign of Napoleon I he presided over the imperial court at Rouen and was a deputy in the Legislative Body. He had his hour of fame in June 1815, after Waterloo, when as vice president of the Chamber he drew up a proclamation on behalf of the people of France to the effect that the country would only accept a government which guaranteed the liberties set down in the Declaration of the Rights of Man and of the Citizen. Dupont and some of his colleagues were to convey this proclamation to the Allies on their return to France. But Wellington and Blücher were bringing Louis XVIII in their train and they were not interested in the parliament's decision. From 1817 to 1848, Dupont sat uninterruptedly in the Chamber as deputy for the Eure and was Minister of Justice during the first months of the July Monarchy until Louis Philippe dismissed him in December 1830 on the grounds that he was too progressive.

Dupont de l'Eure cut a poor figure in the Provisional

Government. He let fall a tender tear over the abolition of the death penalty for political offenses: "This makes me so happy! Now, even when there are disturbances in the city, we shall never again behold the scaffold in our public squares." However, we must not be under any illusions about this tearful sentimentality. When the Provisional Government was replaced by the Pentarchy, Dupont worked against Lamartine. He was one of those whose meetings at the Palais National helped to undermine the authority of the Executive Commission. Although physically incapable of leading the February Government, Dupont de l'Eure may have felt mortified by Lamartine's omnipotence.

Lamartine was, in fact, the real head of the government. He aimed at being representative and genuinely believed that he was so, and there is no doubt that had the country as a whole been in unison with the poet, the Republic would have been a viable and powerful proposition. Unfortunately for the unity and stability of the regime which was set up in February, not all the votes cast for Lamartine were dictated by the same motives. Some, though not the most numerous, urged Lamartine to go forward and take what was almost the path of socialism, but the majority regarded the poet as the savior of the established order. Lamartine was well aware of the reactionary associations often attached to his name and person. During the demonstrations and celebrations which occurred so frequently after the declaration of the Republic, Lamartine repeatedly pointed to the crowd and told Caussidière and Louis Blanc: "Fundamentally, whatever they may say, all these people want law and order and they are relying on me to provide them with both."

Lamartine was not mistaken, but he was trapped in this reactionary mold. And yet at the same time he wanted to find a place for Ledru-Rollin in his republic. Ultimately, Lamartine failed to create a synthesis of all the different elements he represented. In power, he displayed a curious mixture of diffidence and conceit. Elias Regnault has an amusing story to tell in this connection. It will be remembered that in the elections of the twenty-third of April, Lamartine headed the poll in the Seine district with 260,000 votes, was elected for ten different *départements,* and obtained in all a total of two million votes. Learning of his immense success from Armand Marrast, Lamartine got up from his seat and, raising his eyes to heaven and stretching out his arms, cried out, "Behold me a head taller than Caesar or Alexander." Then, under his breath, he added, "So they say, at least."

Lamartine believed that with his two million votes behind him he could stand in the way of Bonaparte. He forgot that the *Boutique* would not forgive him for Ledru-Rollin, and did not consider him sufficiently reactionary. At the time when Lamartine was embarking on his campaign against the future emperor, he had already been beaten by Cavaignac. It is a curious fact that the more arrogantly he treated Louis Napoleon, the more feebly he defended himself against Cavaignac. In June he was literally making Cavaignac's bed for him, a fact on which Daniel Stern goes so far as to congratulate him, regarding it as evidence of the poet's magnanimous and disinterested spirit. I do not share her opinion. Lamartine in June seems already worn out by power, and if he did lay down his hand, it was from weariness. Hugo describes him as "pale and drawn, with a long beard and clothes that were dusty and unbrushed."

HUGO: What is happening to us, Lamartine?
LAMARTINE: We are f——d!

But on the political level his emotional ups and downs
and his fits of melancholy are venial sins. It is a fact that
many statesmen who shared this defeatist attitude have
made great careers by constantly predicting disasters which
never occurred. Lamartine made more serious mistakes in
government. First, he chose his cabinet ministers badly, and
secondly, he adopted a kind of pose which was promising
and easy but not genuine, and because he gave this impression of a lack of spontaneity he aroused a good deal of distrust. He aimed at being the friend of all the world but had
no devoted followers able to fight for him in a tight corner.
Unlike Garnier-Pagès or Ledru-Rollin, Lamartine had no
clan. Moreover, Garnier-Pagès' followers were a great deal
more united and more aggressive, in spite of all appearances, than those of Ledru-Rollin. Garnier-Pagès was a pitiable Minister of Finance, and brought about the death of
the regime with his idiotic forty-five-centime tax, but he remained in an extremely strong position politically for a very
long time.

Lamartine was handsome. Crémieux, the Keeper of the
Seals, on the other hand was reputed to be one of the ugli-
est men in France. It was no mere insult to liken his features to those of a monkey. During the bourgeois monarchy
one deputy in the Chamber nicknamed him "the talking
flea." Crémieux had an extensive legal practice and his experience at the bar had taught him to drown his vacillating
opinions under a flood of eloquence. Crémieux can be
placed among the "republicans of tomorrow." (Lawyers
like Marie and Bethmont wavered almost as much as Cré-

mieux fundamentally, but they made tougher speeches and played the "noble father," although with nothing like the virtuosity of Jules Favre, who was unrivaled in the role of noble father. Crémieux was pliant, and quite obviously so, and he was adored by his voters in Chinon who sang his praises endlessly.) In June 1848, Crémieux's behavior was timid to a degree. Tocqueville records a delightful conversation between Crémieux and Cormenin in which the two men had no difficulty in mutually persuading one another that it was their duty not to expose their precious persons in the districts where firing was going on. It was a small moment of weakness. Crémieux may not have been overfond of the whine of bullets, but at least on the twenty-third of June he was able to make an intelligent speech to the National Guard.

In the words of Tocqueville: "Unless one had seen Crémieux that day, harassed and untidy, dripping with sweat and caked with dust, with a long scarf wound several times around his diminutive body, yet constantly full of new ideas, or rather of new words and turns of phrase, at one moment putting into action what he had just put into words, the next putting into words what he had just put into action, and unflaggingly heated and eloquent, I do not believe one could ever imagine a man more hideous or more talkative."

Maupas, who was one of Louis Napoleon's most intimate associates and who, appointed Prefect of Police in December 1851, played an important part in the coup d'état, has a spicy story to tell of how, on the morning of the second of December, he received a visit from an extremely attractive lady whose husband was a famous lawyer. The gist of what the visitor had to say was this: "Our house is full of suspicious characters. Heaps of unprincipled people are pressing my husband to go to the barricades and organize the resistance. It will be very hard for him to refuse these requests, and he is in danger of being killed to no purpose. You will be doing us both a service if you will arrest him. Then he will be safe."

The lady was Madame Crémieux.

The Keeper of the Seals in the Provisional Government was a Jew who hailed originally from the Midi. (He also played an important part in the universal Jewish alliance.) His colleague at the Ministry of Finance was another Jew, from Alsace, Goudchaux. Proudhon had some grumbles about Crémieux and Goudchaux. Recalling the all-powerful position of Rothschild during the bourgeois monarchy, he remarked in February, "All we have done is to change Jews." It is only fair to add that Proudhon's remark was inspired by a mixture of amused irony and genuine irritation. It was totally unjustifiable for the Vichy regime to incorporate Proudhon in the ranks of militant anti-Semites. Proudhon was one of the first to nominate Goudchaux as a candidate for the Legislative Body in 1852 and he was on very friendly terms with him. Crémieux may not have been the most warlike of men but Goudchaux, on the contrary, was genuinely courageous. On the twenty-third of June, his pale, dumpy little figure did not flinch from the barricades. "Now," he announced in his strong Alsatian accent, "I want to go and do a little fighting." This, writes Tocqueville, was said "in a martial tone so much at variance with his pacific appearance that I could not keep from smiling."

The Provisional Government, it will be recalled, was strictly hierarchical in structure, and although Crémieux was a member of the government, Goudchaux, who was merely Minister of Finance, properly speaking was not.

Goudchaux, who faced up to the rioters so boldly in June, was timid in confronting the Rothschilds. Lamartine and François Arago had pressed Goudchaux to take on the Ministry of Finance because they were aware that he had close ties with Baron Rothschild and feared the latter might prove a bitter opponent of the new regime. One result of the February Days was that the mob had set fire to Rothschild's château at Puteaux. In 1847 Rothschild had underwritten a loan of 250,000,000 francs and the *National* party were terrified at the prospect of a rupture with the great bank. Caussidière, unlike Lamartine, Arago, and Goudchaux, joyously prodded the baron in the ribs and even offered him some of his Montagnards as protection. Goudchaux left the ministry, as I have said, on March 5. He returned to it in answer to Cavaignac's summons, when reaction set in after the June Days.

The personality of Ledru-Rollin, the Minister of the Interior, was characterized by warmth and generosity. Nadaud, in his memoirs written at the end of his life, still mentions Ledru-Rollin with admiration and affection: "His fine presence, tall figure, and handsome and agreeable features made him one of the most remarkable men it is possible to meet with." Even so, although his somewhat coarse and vulgar good looks drew the crowds like a magnet, they aroused a degree of scorn among the aristocracy and middle classes. To follow up the memoirs of the mason Martin Nadaud, it is worth while quoting those of Maxime Du Camp. He saw Ledru-Rollin rather differently: "Handsomish, with a *coup de vent* haircut and carrying his head slightly to one side . . . with big, puffy cheeks and inclined to the sudden pallor which betrays a heart that is none too steady. He was empty and pompous and his speech full of reverberations smacking of rhetoric. . . . He churned out eloquence as a great chest churns out music. . . . He was common, and the grossness of his spirit seemed to have invaded his body."

Ledru-Rollin was something of a magician and a mountebank, and scandalmongers in 1848 recalled gleefully that among his ancestors had been a celebrated conjuror named Comus. In addition, Ledru-Rollin was accused of moral laxity. He had made a wealthy marriage and openly enjoyed the pleasures his fortune could obtain for him, and this made him an easy target for scandal. The shock to the feelings of country people when they heard of the orgiastic and luxurious existence led by the Minister of the Interior has been described often enough. Ledru-Rollin was made out to be a second Barras living in the center of a harem, and contemporary punsters enjoyed themselves at his expense: "It's all right for him to have a mistress," respectable people said, "but the fellow has more than one, *la Marie* and *la Martine.*"

Daniel Stern, who was a sincere republican herself, judged Ledru-Rollin severely. "Neither in his private life, which he was unable to bend to a strict enough pattern, in his patriotic feelings, which were sincere but flamboyant, in his character, which was open and generous but unstable, in his learning, which was more superficial than profound, nor even in his natural rectitude, which was too often swayed by an inordinate desire for popularity, was he truly fit for leadership."

This judgment does not seem to me altogether fair. Historians in general have been too hard on Ledru-Rollin. As a man he was often capable of undertaking crushing responsibilities in spite of the risks and dangers involved. Gambetta's lieutenant, Eugène Spuller, who was himself a minister and president of the Council during the Third Republic and author of an interesting *Histoire de Quarante-Huit*, aimed what seem to me much more well-founded criticisms at Ledru-Rollin than those of Daniel Stern. Ledru-Rollin was overfond of popularity, but *he did not love power for its own sake*. All too often during the eighteen-forties, progressive republicans had no faith in the possibility of achieving power in the near future, and consequently they viewed social and political questions much more as a matter of education than of power. Spuller considers that this is the real flaw in the republican party in 1848. Ledru-Rollin and his friends were comfortably ensconced in their role as leaders of the opposition and enjoyed the elegant and impassioned verbal battles to be fought from the tribune infinitely more than the crude and exhausting exercise of power.

I have already said that Ledru-Rollin became a member of the Executive Commission very much despite himself, but when he was pushed out of power by the events of June he faced the furious pack of reactionaries loosed against him with intelligence as well as courage. In this he behaved incomparably better than Louis Blanc. On December 25, 1848, he actually turned to attack Cavaignac, and this in an Assembly which was predominantly behind the general. He made a speech of such lucid and passionate conviction that many representatives shifted uncomfortably in their seats and applauded the speaker in spite of themselves. At the presidential elections on December 10, he gained 370,000 votes, but five months later, on May 13, 1849, when the people were called upon to elect their representatives to the Legislative Body, Ledru-Rollin was elected in a number of *départements* with a total of two million votes (the number cast for Lamartine on April 23). Ledru-Rollin was in a position to play a major role in the Legislative Assembly, but he tripped up over the matter of Rome.

On June 13, 1849, he issued a call to arms to the people, arguing with some justification that the expedition mounted against the Roman Republic was a flagrant violation of the Constitution of November 4, 1848. Neither the cabinet-maker of the faubourg Saint-Antoine nor the mechanic of La Chapelle answered his call. They could not see why they should show such zeal on behalf of the Roman people when they had abandoned the Poles to their fate. The silent faubourgs were their comment on a bitter anniversary. It was tactless of Ledru-Rollin and Guinard to ask the people to rouse themselves in June 1849 when a year before they had backed up Falloux and Cavaignac against the insurgents. In June 1848 Ledru-Rollin had summoned the National Guard of Rouen and Amiens to bring Paris to its senses, while Guinard was setting up guns in the Hôtel-Dieu and raking the barricades on the left bank with gunfire. It must be added that Paris had suffered an outbreak of cholera in the spring of 1849 and the epidemic had raged most fiercely in the poorer districts. Even so, the idea of revolution was still sufficiently attractive to encourage the raising of a few barricades in those traditional nests of rebellion, the faubourgs of Saint-Denis and Saint-Martin. It is true that in June 1849 these were due more to the power of habit than to any burning enthusiasm. They were small and in no way comparable to the mighty works of June 1848. But for two hours a revolutionary government presided over by Ledru-Rollin held office in the Conservatoire des Arts et Métiers under the protection of a few social-democrat National Guards assembled by Guinard. But Guinard's forces were very weak compared with those of Changarnier. The abortive attempt at the Arts et Métiers was a farce. Ledru-Rollin escaped from the Conservatoire by breaking a window, though not without a good deal of difficulty, for he was distinctly fat. He made his way to London, where he lived for more than twenty years in exile. The affair of the thirteenth of June, ill-conceived and badly carried out, was the ruin of his career. Instead of agitating uselessly in the streets, Ledru-Rollin could and should have been strengthening his position in the Assembly. (This is a point on which Marx and Proudhon are for once in agreement.) The social democrats were certainly in a minority in the Legislative Assembly compared to the massive contingent of conservatives, but the latter were divided among themselves whereas the 180 *Démoc-Soc* representatives—the 180 Montagnards—led by Ledru-Rollin might have constituted an extremely strong and united minority. Basically, the great weakness of Ledru-Rollin in 1848 and in 1849 was a failure to calculate the forces at his disposal in the streets and in the assemblies. In 1848 he tended to overestimate his strength in the Assembly and underestimate it in the streets. Conversely, in 1849 he underestimated his backing in parliament while supposing that he had at his command in the faubourgs of Paris a force he no longer possessed.

Ledru-Rollin's character contained an element of the theatrical hero, the marquis played by a small provincial actor. In saying this, I am repeating almost word for word what the celebrated humorist Xavier de Montépin wrote in his paper *Le Canard* (Issue No. 3, April 16–23, 1848). The epithet of marquis was, however, more frequently applied to Marrast than to Ledru-Rollin. That Marrast was a sensualist, and even that he deliberately cultivated a certain air of Regency decadence, is undoubtedly true, but on the whole he was more of a pawn than a marquis. Marrast owed his success to General Lamarque. He was a teacher of rhetoric at the Collège d'Orthez when Lamarque summoned him to Paris. At one time, before he became a journalist, Marrast was head tutor at the College of Louis-le-Grand. In 1831 he became the moving spirit of *La Tribune* and then, on the death of Carrel, took over control of *Le National*. When, after the June Days, he took over from Sénard as President of the Assembly upon Sénard's becoming Minister of the Interior, his appointment came as a surprise to many representatives who could hardly picture him in the part.

"He won't last long, with his little squeaky voice and scruffy appearance," was the general view.

"That's not so," retorted Hugo, who recalled that Marrast had once been a schoolteacher. "Marrast is used to schoolboys. Controlling schoolboys and controlling men are very much the same thing."

According to Victor Hugo, Marrast was an outstanding president, and it was as Mayor of Paris and not as President of the Constituent Assembly that Marrast was accused of behaving like "a little marquis of the Terror." Many newspapers, socialist as well as reactionary, represented Marrast's receptions at the Hôtel de Ville as veritable orgies. Ladies of fashion were not above accepting Marrast's invitations and were to be found in the salons of the municipal buildings rubbing shoulders with smoking, card-playing National Guardsmen. These, after the June Days, were looked on as the saviors of civilized life, and patrician ladies regarded them with especial affection.

Tocqueville, who encountered Marrast on many occasions when the two men were working side by side on the Constitutional Committee, found him repulsive, and wrote him off as "a mixture of idleness and impudence." Moreover Tocqueville, whose own speeches were sober and restrained, could not listen to Marrast's endless rhapsodies on his good fortune without irritation. Marrast—if we remember the way he slandered Louis Blanc—may have been a devious sensualist, but he was not venal. He lost the 1849 elections, buried himself in retirement, and died a poor man in 1852 when he was barely fifty.

Leaving Ledru-Rollin and Marrast for the company of the extreme left wing of the Provisional Government, for Louis Blanc, Albert, and Flocon, is like leaving a clan of sensualists to join one of Spartans. Caussidière describes Louis Blanc and Albert spending two and a half francs each on dinner, and in his *Pages d'histoire de la Révolution de Février*, Louis Blanc confirms Caussidière's figure. "My lunch and dinner," he says, "cost me five francs in all." This announcement, moreover, did nothing to disarm his enemies. The retort of an Orleanist like Cuvillier-Fleury was, "We would have preferred to see you dining at ten or twenty francs a head and have to deal with a graver, less excited, and less talkative statesman, and one who does not fill the people's heads with dangerous and idiotic ideas."

Louis Blanc was not without talent, either as a writer or as an orator, and his books show that he had a real talent for writing. *L'Organisation du travail* is a small masterpiece of conciseness and elegance. But Louis Blanc had grave defects. He suffered from an inferiority complex about his short stature, since he was literally minute, even smaller than Thiers, and had to climb on a stool whenever he stood up to speak. Béranger always referred to him as "little Blanc," which infuriated him. Louis Blanc's face was agreeable and intelligent, but he looked very young and this youthful face combined with his small body rendered him liable to frequent misapprehensions. In the early days of the revolution the ushers at the Luxembourg mistook him for a schoolboy looking for his teachers. He dressed with great care and rather innocently believed that he was as attractive to women as he was to the crowds. Malvida von Meysenburg, who was a friend of Wagner and of Romain Rolland, met Louis Blanc on many occasions when he was in exile in London and was struck by his childish vanity in the matter of clothes and gallantry.

Louis Blanc had other problems besides his diminutive stature. He was also acutely conscious of his poverty. He was of Corsican origin, a cousin of Pozzo di Borgo, and there was aristocratic blood in his veins, but having lost his father at an early age he was compelled to work hard to provide for the needs of his family. To present himself as a beggar in some ministerial antechamber or a salon in the faubourg Saint-Germain was a torment to him, and hence the "Hannibalic oath" which he mentions in one of his speeches in the Luxembourg:

"Even as a child, I said that this social order was iniquitous. . . . I shall not forget that I was one of the most unfortunate children of the people, and that society was so hard on me. And I swore a Hannibalic oath against this society which makes so many of our brothers wretched."

The wealthy bourgeois listened skeptically to such pronouncements. Louis Blanc a man of the people? they said. But he is one of us. His father was a tax inspector. Their skepticism was only partly justified, for poverty had deprived Louis Blanc of his class status.

Lamartine, during the first week of the revolution at least, was not averse to the sight of an unruly, threatening mob. Making speeches in the face of leveled guns seemed to him a natural and splendid part of the everyday task of a democratic leader. He possessed all the confidence of the great landed gentry, together with an inexhaustible vitality, and so he could look down on Louis Blanc and treat him like a woman with an attack of the vapors and better fitted for the gossip of a boudoir than for the excitement of the streets. More than once in the course of the Days of 1848, Louis Blanc went deathly pale and had to be carried to a window for air. The President of the Luxembourg Commission himself can hardly have felt that his physical weaknesses made him "one of the people," for he protested vigorously, and even to the point of absurdity, that he had not fainted. Plenty of people did faint in 1848, in the Hôtel de Ville as well as in the Chamber. On the fifteenth of May several representatives were so affected by the sight of the people bursting unceremoniously in on their work that they became unwell and had to be made comfortable on the grass outside the Palais Bourbon. Louis Blanc should have forgiven himself for his weaknesses, but it would have taken a cooler, more confident temperament than his to have shown himself so much indulgence. Besides, Louis Blanc could be bold on occasion, and in fact he amply demonstrated his courage on the fifteenth of May when, overwhelmed to the left and pursued by the virulent hatred of the right, he overcame his weakness and, whatever Marrast may have said, did not desert the Palais Bourbon where he was in the gravest danger. Even so, it is an odd fact that neither Louis Blanc's courage nor his eloquence were of much avail in 1848. Louis Blanc, such a typical figure of the February Revolution, was not in step with his time; he was ahead of it. Lamartine's supple flow of words, far too supple for present-day tastes, lulled his contemporaries and prevented them from hearing the creaking of the revolutionary tumbrils. This in itself is shocking to us and makes his eloquence seem often tasteless and obtuse. Lamartine did in fact draw a veil over the revolution in all its nakedness, but men who preferred false securities to a clear diagnosis of the situation were grateful to him for his soothing words. Lamartine detested what he called Louis Blanc's "terse style," yet this terse, breathless tone has its appeal. Without wishing to appear to be stating a paradox, I would say that Louis Blanc was removed from the political scene so promptly just because he stated the problems of his time so clearly. His contemporaries preferred another, more melodious song, more antiquated and less truthful. In the second place, because he was both a realist and a member of the government, Louis Blanc offered an easy target to those who were never anything but theorists and whose work for the social revolution was all done in the study. To Proudhon, Louis Blanc was literally a whipping boy. He attacked the President of the Luxembourg Commission repeatedly, with a viciousness that was clever and amusing but not particularly intelligent. Distrusted by his colleagues because he was a socialist, and distrusted by the socialists and communists because he was a member of the government, Louis Blanc was extremely vulnerable. But his failure did not mean that his ideas were foolish or utopian. In a long and depressing session—it went on for fourteen hours—on August 25, 1848, the Constituent Assembly debated the question of whether Louis Blanc and Caussidière were to be brought to trial. In the view of those who heard him, Louis Blanc seems to have made an eloquent, effective, and moving speech, yet his audience, who became in such dramatic fashion his judges, on both the left and the right, felt that Louis Blanc was speaking as though in a vacuum, that his words reached neither his friends nor his enemies. It is a fact that when a man feels that his words are falling on deaf ears, he has little hope of compelling anyone to listen to him, and Louis Blanc cherished no illusions about the Assembly. While he was speaking, he could see one of his right-wing colleagues standing right underneath the rostrum, rubbing his hands cheerfully and muttering, "Go on, talk as much as you like, you're still done for."

Remarks of this kind are not calculated to reassure any orator. Nevertheless it was noticeable that Caussidière, who during this session was just as much on the carpet as Louis Blanc and who possessed neither his talent nor his authority, made a much stronger impression on the Assembly. Representatives who voted for the prosecution of Louis Blanc were more lenient toward Caussidière. All the same, both the former Prefect of Police and the erstwhile President of the Luxembourg were condemned by a majority of the Constituent Assembly, and rather than await the rigors of their sentence they set out at once for London. On August 25, what might be called the first proscription train departed. The second left on June 19, 1849, carrying Ledru-Rollin; and the third, in December 1851, was the largest of all, including generals like Cavaignac and Bedeau and Orleanists such as Thiers.

It was not only on the platform that Louis Blanc appeared terse and abrupt. Even in government councils his behavior was ungracious. With him, political differences rapidly turned into personal grudges. Louis Blanc behaved especially unpleasantly toward François Arago, who moreover consistently snubbed him and treated him as a child. Arago was a distinguished sexagenarian and was accustomed to having his own way. Louis Blanc knew that the astronomer's white hair was to some extent sacrosanct in the Hôtel de Ville and it was the very fact that he was compelled to treat him with respect that choked him. After the tragic events which occurred in Rouen in April 1848, François Arago marveled at the way in which General Gérard had succeeded in restoring order. It was Louis Blanc's belief that the government ought to hold a stringent enquiry into Gérard's activities, since the bloody reprisals taken seemed to him out of all proportion to the rioting by the workers. After a lively altercation Louis Blanc defeated Arago, but his victory was brief and ineffectual. The workers mown down by the soldiers' bullets in the district of Martainville only served to further the career of General Gérard, who was appointed divisional commander on June 19, 1848.

Now let us take a look at Ferdinand Flocon, who is a less familiar figure than Albert. Flocon is in a way the answer to the question asked at the beginning of this chapter as to how far the men in the Provisional Government were actually representative. In 1848 the conservatives created a legend that the director of La Réforme was a great one for the tavern and an inveterate pipe smoker. With his amiable, slightly puffy features and general air of genial vulgarity, the skinny Flocon made a perfect butt for the caricaturists, who leaped at the chance to turn his face into the bowl of a pipe.There were worse charges to be laid against Flocon than this. He displayed no masterly qualities when he came to power, and said a great deal that was foolish, especially in his hints about the foreign gold which was supposed to have been financing the uprising in June 1848, but this was said to order and not because he really believed it. He made an undistinguished minister but he was not, like Trélat, totally out of his depth in coping with the tasks entrusted to him. Strictly speaking, he was not a man who had risen from the masses but a product of the secret societies and the Freemasons. To this extent he is a sufficiently modern and representative figure. Just as Buchâtel, the wealthy, Malthusian bourgeois devoid of taste, was highly characteristic of the ministers of the July Monarchy, so Flocon was typical of 1848. On the twenty-fourth of February he did not labor as frantically as Raspail or Lagrange, but he followed his orders to the letter and saw them carried out. Under his apparent docility lay a considerable capacity for firmness. Once in power, he developed and, as it were, slid over from the *Réforme* to the *National*. Cavaignac rewarded him for sliding: after the events of June, Flocon became a minister in the dictator general's new cabinet.

There are two faces to 1848, one Catholic and the other Masonic. There were two Catholic officials in the Assembly, Buchez, the president, and the vice president, Corbon, but Buchez retained close links with the old militant members of the secret societies and Corbon later abandoned the Church in favor of Freemasonry. The government itself was largely composed of Masons: Dupont de l'Eure, Crémieux, Ledru-Rollin, Garnier-Pagès, Marie, and Louis Blanc were all Masons. Cavaignac, it should be added, was also a Freemason, and this explains to some extent the swing in his favor of men like Dupont de L'Eure and the ease with which the *National* party were able to get him proclaimed dictator. André Lebey, an influential figure in Freemasonry in France in modern times, who made a significant study of the period of 1848, was convinced that Freemasonry was the thing which really cemented the Provisional Government together. In André Lebey's view, the fact that two such profoundly different parties as those of the *National* and the *Réforme* were able to come together and present a comparatively united front must have been due to the subtle but firm and consistent influence of Freemasonry.

The Ideologies of 1848

The failure of the February Revolution, the rapid disintegration of the Provisional Government, and the errors, prevarications, and general impotence of men like Lamartine and Louis Blanc have combined to discredit the ideas behind 1848. This is understandable but hardly fair, although the prevailing tone of maudlin and hysterical idealism which characterized the period is unfashionable nowadays and, bearing in mind the actual details of events and individual behavior, even actively repugnant. We have seen the craft and disingenuousness resorted to by men such as Jules Favre, Armand Marrast, and Marie, while even those as touchingly straightforward on the surface as Buchez, Bastide, and Trélat could turn Machiavellian in a crisis, although they gained nothing by doing so. Consequently there seems to be some justification for the aspersions cast during the eighteen-sixties and seventies on the veterans of

1848. During the war of 1870–1871, a great many young republicans and socialists, pioneers of the First International, were justifiably angry to see Jules Favre, Garnier-Pagès, and Crémieux making a fresh appearance in the councils of government. By the sixties, the atmosphere had become more serious, more positive, and more scientific than in 1848. Naturally, in this context, we must be careful to define our terms precisely. The belief in science existed in 1848: Renan's famous work *L'Avenir de la Science* was actually written against the background of the February Revolution. But the scientific fervor of 1848 was of a different kind from that of 1860. The scientific assertions of the positivists of the sixties and seventies were more mystical than they cared to admit and their scientific cult might strike us today as childish and perfunctory, but nevertheless they were trying to free themselves from the dreams and illusions of 1848.

At the same time, I would not have my readers under any misapprehensions about the use of the word "serious." Social and political writing in the sixties was more straightforward and contained less cant than that of the forties. It had lost the vernal, biblical flavor it had possessed twenty years earlier and in this sense was more serious and more austere. But by 1860 society itself, and this is true of both middle and working classes, had become more flexible and easygoing and altogether less straitlaced than in 1848. The passionate high seriousness of 1848 had given way to a more astringent, one might even call it a *racier*, frame of mind. If the worker of 1848 can be likened to a conscientious scholar, the worker of 1870 had a mischievous, urchin side to his nature. When Louis Blanc returned to France in 1870 he no longer recognized his old Paris, and at the same time a former typographer named Georges Duchêne, who had been a delegate to the Luxembourg and had contributed to Proudhon's papers during the 1848 crisis, was saying in effect: "When we were young—in the forties, that is—the women whose lessons we listened to were Madame de Staël, George Sand, and even Madame de Saussure, who wrote some admirable educational works. Nowadays—that is, in the sixties—people are interested only in frippery little actresses like Rigolboche or Cora Pearl."

It is also important to note that the doctrine of art for art's sake appears to be closely linked with the failure of 1848. (This is a favorite idea of Jean Cassou's.) At the time that Pierre Dupont's rendering of the *éclairs de Février* was rending the skies of Paris, Flaubert, Baudelaire, and Leconte de Lisle were all aged about twenty-five, and still trailing clouds of romanticism. With all the fervor of youth, they believed in the swift and splendid transformation of society. Three months later, people were shooting each other in Paris, and after four years France was erasing the word "*Republic*" from her coat of arms. (Pierre Dupont himself duly apologized to the Empire.) The proletariat, which had once idolized Lamartine, was now hissing him and elevating Louis Napoleon onto a pedestal, and applauding the police for throwing the republicans into prison. The idols of 1848—the infallibility of the masses, the good sense of the people, and the peace and justice of universal suffrage—were crumbling. It was obvious that an artist could not commit himself to a proletariat which had proved unworthy of freedom, and so the artists went back to their ivory towers. In the same way in literature, the humanitarian novels like those George Sand had been writing in the eighteen-forties: *Spiridion*, *Le Meunier d'Angibault*, *Le Péché de M. Antoine*, and *Le Compagnon du tour de France*, were being replaced by novels which aimed at detachment and were in fact desolate. Flaubert, in *L'Éducation sentimentale*, which appeared in 1869, actually described the failure of 1848. Similarly, on the ruins of utopian socialism, on the ruins of Saint-Simonism, Fourierism, and Icarian communism, rose the so-called "scientific socialism" of Marx.

The *Communist Manifesto* was written by Marx and Engels at the end of 1847 and exercised no influence on the February Revolution. But however, considering the importance achieved by Marxism in our own time, I have no doubt that there are a number of questions arising in the reader's mind concerning the relationship between utopian socialism and Marxist socialism.

An accurate and comprehensive study of this relationship would be long and complicated, and this is not the place for it. But there are a few observations which may throw some light on the problem. Personally, I believe that any attempt to rehabilitate the utopians against Marx is doomed to failure and dictated for the most part by subconscious social reaction. Time and again it has been the staunchest and most rigid defenders of capitalism who have upheld Saint-Simon or Proudhon against Marx. But on the other hand, the rigid Marxism which denies the utopians any capacity for lucid thinking is as ridiculous as it is distasteful. In some things Saint-Simon or Proudhon saw more clearly than Marx. Marx's strength lies in having phrased his thoughts with a firmness and clarity never achieved by Saint-Simon, or by Fourier, Louis Blanc, Pierre Leroux, or Proudhon. At the beginning of the nineteenth century there were plenty of historians and social reformers who thought there was a connection between ethical and economic behavior. Guizot himself showed great insight on this point. But it was Marx who finally taught people that the superstructure, the

Oberbau, of moral and intellectual life was conditioned by the *Überbau*, or infrastructure, provided by the economic organization, the mechanics of productivity, and the distribution of wealth. The exact nature of this connection may and should be a matter of opinion.

Here we are entering an area whose investigation requires a great deal of method, calm, and intellectual discipline. Marx recognized that ideologies can remain extremely powerful even when the material conditions, the infrastructure, which allowed them to grow and develop have disappeared. In studying 1848, Marx was struck by the fact that instead of simply taking into account their own needs and natural desires, people deliberately dug into the past and dressed up in old, cast-off revolutionary garments; they were acting out the old dramas of history once again, instead of thinking seriously about the revolution that was really called for, simply because it was easier. Human beings are held prisoner by certain catchphrases, by certain attitudes and nostalgic leanings which in turn have their effect on economic development. In an earlier chapter, describing the economic crisis of 1848, I have shown that in England the political effects were almost nonexistent, and yet the crisis was as serious or even more serious on the other side of the Channel than it was in France. But Queen Victoria was treading socially on firm ground. The hosiers of London were not as restless as those in the faubourg Saint-Denis, and while the faubourg du Temple could give birth to Gavroche, Bethnal Green and the filthy alleys of Whitechapel could never have produced the bold and heroic *gamins* to topple a throne.

I would go further and state that even the emergence of Marxism onto the stage of history was due to events which it is difficult to reconcile with the concept of history as

Marx saw it. The first wave of Marxism broke in 1871, after France had been defeated by Prussia. This victory actually testified to the superiority of the Germanic to the Latin races, and Marx, whose theories were derived from Hegel and the great Prussian professors, subsequently gained an authority which he had not owned before 1870, at the congress of the First International. The second wave occurred after the Russian Revolution of October 1917, but if the triumph of communism in Russia was made possible by the efforts of Lenin and his comrades this was not, strictly speaking, a product of Marxism, since according to Marx the process of revolution is a function of the proletariat itself, combined with powerful industrial development.

I have made these general remarks for two reasons. First, because I wanted to show the complex nature of the link established between the moral and the economic life of a people. Marx forged an admirable tool, but one which had to be handled with discretion. Second, because I do not want to see the utopians dismissed in two word: *Vae victis!* —Woe to the vanquished! The historical failure of 1848 does not mean that the thinkers of the period were merely dreamers, fantasists, and abstract theorists. They made mistakes but their greatest error, to my way of thinking, was that they mistook the *pace of history*. They revealed and analyzed, with what is frequently admirable penetration and clarity, the contradictions in which capitalist society was struggling. Fascinated by their own discoveries, they foresaw the rapid disintegration of a system which resulted in such fierce and keen competition. But after all, Marx cherished very similar illusions. The things we can see happening today confirm Louis Blanc's prophecies in *L'Organisation du travail*. Louis Blanc's book may have looked like fantasy in 1848, but a century afterward it has a ring of truth.

Idealists burgeoned in 1848 with a quite extraordinary proliferation and exuberance, as can be seen from a story written by Jules Méry in *La Presse*. (Méry was a prolific writer with a large public.) He records a long conversation he had in the boulevard next to the Parc Monceau with a worker from the National Workshops. The conversation began in a cautious, hesitant, and roundabout way. "In these revolutionary times," Méry wrote, "one should sound out most carefully the person to whom one is speaking. One must know if the other is a legitimist, Orleanist, Fourierist, humanitarian, Saint-Simonian, a republican of '89, '92, or '93, a Thermidorean, an absolutist, a Barbésian, a socialist, a federalist, a communist, a Jesuit, or a Gallican." (The remainder of the story is one huge joke; moreover it emerges, aside from the author's easy mockery, that the worker who provided the material for the piece was a supporter of "nongovernment," in fact, a Proudhonian.)

It would be impossible to draw up even a short list of all the systems that were born or fermented in the brains of Frenchmen during the eighteen-forties. I would merely like to give the reader some clues which may ultimately simplify his journey through the labyrinth.

Two quite different trends are discernible. On the one hand were a number of men creating systems, proposing remedies for the ills that afflicted the city, and drawing up more or less detailed plans for a new world which would be a happier place for the masses. Saint-Simon, Prosper Enfantin, Cabet, Pierre Leroux, and Louis Blanc were all among these. On the other was a large section of society, including a great many of the bourgeois but also plenty of educated working men, in which a tradition was beginning to crystallize, its outlines more or less clearly defined but forming a relatively coherent whole to be summed up roughly as follows: the enfranchisement of the people had begun in 1789, but a handful of ruffians, by assassinating Robespierre and the Montagnards on the Ninth Thermidor, had prevented the natural development of the Revolution. The political freedom bestowed on the country by the Constituents of 1798 had its natural complement in social enfranchisement. Men should not be free only in theory, they ought to have the means to enjoy their freedom, and this meant escaping from servitude and poverty. The watchword of the Volunteers of 1792 who emancipated Europe was "War on the castles, peace to the cottages! " Fifty years later the formula was still valid because the castles were still standing. It was true that the old feudal system of land ownership had been largely destroyed, but a new kind of feudalism, based on industry, had grown up on the ruins which was still more formidable. Under the Restoration and the bourgeois monarchy a great many landed proprietors had actually purchased plants as a means of disposing of the wood from their forests and turned themselves into industrialists. (The Rambourgs of Commentry founded their fortunes in this way.) The figure of the fighting Frenchman was of peasant origin. In 1789 a sudden outburst of fury had roused the Jacques' against their lords, and in the thirties and forties the same kind of fury roused the same Jacques', who had by this time become weavers and miners and iron founders, against the men who were their hereditary enemies. For examples we have only to listen to Joigneaux or Curnier (the former representing the Drôme and the latter the Côte-d'Or under the Second Republic). Both men were fond of recounting the struggle waged by Jacques Bonhomme, who also went by the name of Père aux Guêtres, against M. Joseph de Coffrefort. (As I recall, Jean Guêtré is a favorite character of Pierre Dupont's.) M.

de Coffrefort succeeded in making his fortune by plundering convents during the Revolution. In the properties and buildings so acquired he installed machines. . . . Now he is a landowner and manufacturer. Jean Guêtré has to destroy him, and it is no easy task. Joigneaux enumerates for him all the enemies of the Republic: "The fat wealthy moneylender, the squire, the servant at the big house, the lawyer, the justice, the *curé*, the exciseman, the retired officer, and the insurance agent." Pierre Joigneux was an engineer and Jacques Bonhomme and Jean Guêtré were not to take him too literally at his word. A great many lawyers, Garnier-Pagès the elder, Joly père, and Michel de Bourges among them, as well as many officers like Cartel and Courtais, were working for the education and emancipation of the people.

During the bourgeois monarchy, Robespierre and Babeuf reappeared in the republican pantheon as demigods of fraternity. This is somewhat surprising in view of Robespierre's remarks to the Convention on April 24, 1793: "Equality of property is an illusion, and the agrarian law a ghost conjured up by irresponsibles to frighten idiots." Robespierre was more concerned with "making poverty an honorable state than with proscribing wealth." Babeuf, counts on the one hand among the heirs of the Hébertist traditions—and Hébert had been put to death by Robespierre—and on the other, among the Thermidoreans who brought down Robespierre. Babeuf was connected with Tallien and with Fouché. He denounced the Jacobins as "terrorists." However, when in the year IV he hatched his famous Conspiracy for Equality, he was involved with some former friends of Robespierre's. One old conspirator—he was sixty in 1830—Filippo Buonarrotti, in a little book on the Conspiration des Égaux, actually managed to produce a masterly synthesis of Robespierre and Babeuf. His enthusiasm for the men who aimed to overthrow a government easily overcame historical accuracy. When the republicans were being tried before the Chamber of Peers for their part in the disturbances of April 1834, Buonarroti was among their defenders. He died in 1837, and his influence left an indelible mark on Blanqui.

In this way a kind of perfunctory communism was born and grew up which for that very reason was just the thing to spread through the workshops of the Temple, the faubourg Saint-Antoine, and the faubourg Saint-Marcel. It was framed in the imagery of the Jacobin Republic and the Terror, and propagated by the secret societies, by the Charbonnerie, by the society of the "Friends of the People," and above all by the "Rights of Man." Let me say again that it differed profoundly from the great systems constructed by men like Saint-Simon or Fourier in the privacy of their studies. Nevertheless, the two streams of thought do meet and mingle in a more intimate fashion than is generally admitted. Saint-Simon had connections with the lodge of the "Friends of Truth" and one of his most energetic followers, Bazard, was among the founders of the Charbonnerie. Hippolyte Carnot, who was Minister of Education in the February Government, was a former disciple of Saint-Simon. Pierre Leroux was an active member of the "Rights of Man." Proudhon belonged to the Freemasons, and Masonic ideals can often be detected in his work. Louis Blanc, who as I have already observed was a talented writer, undertook a history of the revolution, and Victor Considérant, who became head of the École Sociétaire on the death of Fourier, ran a newspaper called *La Démocratie pacifique* which formed part of the chorus of republicanism. Considérant also took part in the campaign for reformist banks. Eugène Sue, who popularized Fourier's doctrines in his novels, and in particular in *Martin ou l'Enfant trouvé*, was elected social-democrat representative for the Seine in 1850. (He died a few years later in exile.) But in this connection, by far the most interesting and significant case is that of Cabet. Étienne Cabet played a leading part in the Charbonnerie, in which he was a member of the *Vente suprême*.[1] He was also secretary of the Association for Popular Education. Exiled to London during the early years of the July Monarchy, he had to find something to occupy his time and wrote his *Histoire populaire de la Révolution*. Cabet contributed to the deification of Robespierre. Babeuf, however, he deals with somewhat harshly. This is not because his beliefs were so very different from those of Babeuf. Despite himself, Cabet was jealous because he realized that Buonarrotti's little book on *Les Égaux* was read like the gospel by the cabinetmakers and locksmiths of the faubourg Saint-Denis or the faubourg Saint-Martin. He did not attack Babeuf openly because to do so would in any case have been to commit the kind of blasphemy which could wreck his popularity, but he could not resist a passing dig at his precursor. Cabet regarded himself as a modern Socrates, or even a modern Jesus Christ, and he gave his gospel to the world in the form of a novel in imitation of Rousseau's *La Nouvelle Héloïse*.

Cabet's book, *Le Voyage en Icarie*, appeared in 1840, al-

[1] The *Charbonniers*, or Carbonarists, held their meetings under the guise of charcoal sales. Each "sale" was made up of twenty members. First came the *ventes particulières*, above them were the *ventes centrales*, and then a *haute vente*, or *vente suprême*, which usually had seven members and which controlled the society. Buchez, Bazard, and Flotard, founder members of the Charbonnerie in France, all belonged to the Haute Vente. Étienne Cabet was born in Dijon in 1788. His father was a cooper with a small private fortune and Étienne had no difficulty in completing his studies and then becoming a magistrate, *procureur général* for Corsica, and deputy for the Côte-d'Or during the reign of Louis Philippe.

though a few copies were circulating in 1839 under the title *Voyage et Aventures de lord William Carisdall en Icarie*. That admirable historian of Cabet's doctrines, Jules Prud-hommeaux, has stressed the resemblance between *Le Voyage en Icarie* and *La Nouvelle Héloïse*. "The love story of Dinaïse, Valmor, and Lord William is based on that of Julie, Saint-Preux, and milord Édouard. Valmor's sister Corilla is the same devoted confidante as Claire d'Orbe." Moreover Icaria, where Lord William lands, abounds in exactly the kind of "noble savage" so dear to Rousseau. Man is naturally good; it is evil institutions which have soiled him. "Do not all philosophers agree that a natural, primitive, and universal community (all things to all people) endured for centuries until the first division and the creation of property? Are they not agreed that the rights and effects of this primitive community are preserved today in certain conditions, that this division could only come about on the tacit understanding that it should interfere with the existence of no one, and that in what might be called a case of necessity there could be no human law which would prevent a man from taking from the property of another the produce necessary to maintain life?"

How does the Icarian commonwealth function? "The entire territory with the mines beneath it and the buildings above forms one single domain, which is our 'social domain.' All the movable goods of its members, together with all the produce of the land and of industry, form a single 'social capital.' This social domain and capital belong indivisibly to the people, who work and exploit it as a whole; they themselves administer it through their own delegates and then share the produce equally among them." I cannot give a complete synopsis of *Le Voyage en Icarie* here, although it is still worth reading, but I must stress the optimism of Cabet's system: men should be able to govern themselves correctly with the aid of their right reason. Cabet gives an overwhelming importance to education in his system. (He emerges as a remarkably sensible educationalist.) Strong in his conviction of rightness and of his power to convince his fellow men, Cabet was scornful of violence, although he was creating a world in which the individual was bound by very strict controls. The Icarian communist did not believe that problems could be solved with bullets, and a great deal of the nonviolence of the February Revolution was due to Cabet. A serious corrective to this, however, was the fact that Cabet did not cancel out Babeuf and helped to magnify Robespierre. The cabinetmaker from the faubourg Saint-Antoine read Le Voyage en Icarie with uncritical admiration: a handful of his neighbors actually went to America to found an Icarian community at Nauvoo in Illinois. In this connection I have edited some letters written by a tinsmith who actually lived in the faubourg Saint-Antoine and went to Nauvoo in 1849 with an enthusiasm equaled only by his later disillusionment. Thus, in 1848, our cabinetmaker trusted the Provisional Government implicitly because he believed that Lamartine, Marrast, Louis Blanc, and Marie were going to build Icaria overnight. But when he saw his comrades nonchalantly pushing a few barrows about in the Champ de Mars, his dreams took a more cynical turn. He thought, not unreasonably, that there were dark and hostile forces at work in the government and told himself that strong measures would probably be more effective than the guileless confidence he had shown in February. He reread Buonarroti and so paved the way for June. Cabet's crushing defeat in the April elections is already known.

Of all the great builders of social systems, Cabet, at the

period under discussion, was incontestably the one who had the profoundest effect on the working class. Pockets of Icarian workers were to be found in all the major cities, especially in the southwest, even during the Second Empire. The influence of Saint-Simon and his followers was of a quite different order. For reasons which will be gone into later, the workers had been repelled by a school whose vocabulary and formulae—the exploitation of man by man, and the organization of labor—were nonetheless in common use in 1848. The history of Saint-Simonism is an exciting subject, although I shall go into it only briefly here. Saint-Simon was an aristocrat with a touch of the adventurer. During the *ancien régime* he fought at the side of Lafayette in the American War of Independence. During the Revolution he gambled and speculated. Under the Empire he planned his system and dreamed of reorganizing society along positive, scientific lines. Saint-Simon, even more than Auguste Comte, can claim to be the inventor of sociology. He dreamed, too, of a United States of Europe: European federation seemed to him the natural conclusion of the Napoleonic Wars. At the end of his life, a lonely and embittered man, meditating on his failure, he attempted suicide but only succeeded in wounding himself severely. Badly disfigured, he died in 1825. His two closest followers, Bazard and Enfantin, soon disagreed. Bazard, one of the leaders of the Charbonnerie, was a tough, stern, and unimaginatively devoted character. Prosper Enfantin was a former student at the Polytechnic and a man of remarkable beauty who combined a keen business sense with an unshakable mysticism. He believed that the ultimate truth was to be found in the couple, and was waiting to hail the Female Messiah. At one time he thought that George Sand was destined to fill this role, but the author of *Le Meunier*

d'Angibault was the possessor of a sound Berrichon common sense out of place on the Saint-Simonian Olympus.
Enfantin carried out his role of high priest tirelessly and
without fear of ridicule. As a result of the furious arguments
which put him at loggerheads with Bazard, Bazard was laid
low by a heart attack.

"From necessity and inclination I am, almost passionately," Enfantin would say, "a man of power rather than a
man of liberty."

According to the philosophy of Saint-Simon, societies,
after going through the theocratic stage of domination by
priests and then the aristocratic stage—in which they were
governed by nobles, princes, and kings—progressed at a
pace which varied with their degree of maturity toward the
industrial age. In a celebrated and macabre parable, Saint-
Simon pictures a dual railway accident. In the first, the
king, the dauphin, members of the royal family, generals,
princes of the Church, and top civil servants all perish. The
damage done by such an accident would not be extensive
since all these individuals can be automatically replaced by
others who would carry out their routine tasks with the
same distinction, or rather lack of distinction. The victims
of the second accident are engineers, inventors, the great
textile manufacturers and ironmasters, and all the most go-
ahead industrial magnates. After a blow of this kind it
would be a long time before France could occupy anything
but a secondary place in the world. The followers of Saint-
Simon glorified the productive elements and chastised the
leisured classes. They were apostles of the doctrine of
plenty, believing that men must undertake great works in
order to guarantee the general welfare. Enfantin went to
Egypt with a project for driving a canal through the isthmus
of Suez. With great courage and at the cost of immeasura-

ble sacrifice, he began the work which was completed by Ferdinand de Lesseps in the eighteen-sixties. The Saint-Simonians said "glory to the producers," but they did not say "glory to the property owners." They held that "property is a fact of society, dependent like all other facts of society on the belief in progress, and can therefore be understood, defined, and controlled in various ways at different times."

The religious aspect of Saint-Simonism has been the subject of a good deal of amusement. Most followers of Saint-Simon became great industrialists and played a major role in the national economy. Schneider, the owner of Le Creusot, Stéphane Mony, who controlled the Commentry collieries, Dorian, the Unieux ironmaster, Paulin Talabot, owner of the Grande-Combe mines, and Michel Chevalier, who was responsible for negotiating the Franco-British trade agreement of 1860, were all followers of Saint-Simon. Enfantin himself occupied a seat on the board of the P.L.M. That all these sober, comfortably off gentlemen should have gone to a monastery in Ménilmontant and sung peculiar hymns and dressed up in purple aprons buttoned up the back as a symbol of fraternal solidarity has aroused little more than titters. The religious fervor of the Saint-Simonians has been considered merely a youthful extravagance, a preposterous dream to be laid aside with the onset of gray hair. It is not as simple as this. The disciples of Saint-Simon certainly believed in building, in multiplying the number of factories, lighting blast furnaces, drilling mine shafts, and spreading plenty everywhere, but unlike some liberal economists, they did not think that there were any immutable laws for a harmonious distribution of wealth and that the great mass of the people, whether they were workers or employers, tended to behave like animals in the jungle. They believed in plenty, but also in harmony. The Saint-Simonians were greatly concerned, as Fourier was also, with the *problem of vocation*. They believed that certain people were *generous men*, endowed with a *sense of social destiny*. It was these men who ought to control production. In short, over and above the ordinary producer was the *producer possessing the soul of a priest*. It was this sacerdotal caste which would prevent the economy from immolating too many men on the new battlefields. Personally, I consider this a stroke of genius. It is common knowledge that, left to their own devices, the masters of the economy amass nothing but ruins. The idea of limiting and transforming their power through those who possess a broader vision and a purer soul is not necessarily altogether fantastic. It is even possible that one day society may move in the direction of Saint-Simonism.

But I have said enough about this system to demonstrate that it contains certain obvious points which would not appeal to the workers. The society envisaged by the disciples of Saint-Simon was an extremely hierarchical one. It was neither liberal nor egalitarian, and the people, who were still looking back nostalgically to the time of the Revolution, and regarded the Revolution and the Empire as the great leveling factors for the masses, distrusted from the outset those they referred to as the "red Jesuits." In the faubourgs an angry working-class voice answered back the Saint-Simonian speakers: "They are 'classifiers' who take it upon themselves to shepherd us into a fold of subjection from which we shall never escape."

The man who said this was a maker of measuring instruments in a street near the Châtelet. His name was Vinçard. But we must always remember that men are seldom as rigid as their words would have us believe. The very Vinçard who so accurately pointed out the chink in the Saint-Simonian armor was very soon won over. During the eighteen-forties Vinçard ran a small review called *La Ruche populaire*, which propagated the doctrines of Saint-Simon and was edited exclusively by workers. I have quoted in another chapter a passage written by Jean Baptiste Coutant from *La Ruche populaire*. Coutant was a typographer who contributed in the sixties to a paper called *L'Opinion nationale*, the editor of which was actually an old disciple of Saint-Simon named Adolphe Guéroult. The little group which gravitated around Vinçard and *La Ruche* was far from negligible, and it is worth while remembering that although the Parisian man was not as a general rule attached to a school whose basic tenets were complex and aristocratic, he was by no means indifferent to certain aspects of Saint-Simonian propaganda. Listening to the followers of Saint-Simon gave his ideas about the class struggle and the wrongs of the capitalist system a more precise turn. Raymond Bonheur, who preached Saint-Simonism in the Quartier des Archives, declared that although "many workers did not yet feel the sequence of events," they pricked up their ears at the word "competition." This word was "appreciated in all its ugliness by men who were seeing their businesses failing. . . . The sufferings of the unemployed were the key to a better life."

Saint-Simon was an aristocrat. Charles Fourier, on the other hand, was a clerk. He described himself as a "*sergent de boutique*." Setting aside his deeply original genius, he had the character of a Prudhomme or a Gaudissart. He indulged in the kind of furtive dreams associated with commercial travelers eyeing pretty waitresses. He was unmarried and led a narrow, restricted life in his tiny flat near the Palais Royal, regulating his daily life down to the minutest detail, just as he did the Phalanstery which was the product of his imagination. He returned home every day at a set time to wait for the wealthy and generous patron who would enable him to put his system into practice. Like Saint-Simon, he believed at one time that Napoleon I might be the initiator, or rather the guardian angel, of the new society which was coming to birth. The two epithets which Fourier particularly disliked were "moralist" and "republican," and he hated the idea of being regarded as either. Like Saint-Simon, he was indifferent to visions of equality, and although he was passionately devoted to freedom of action and freedom of instincts and believed fervently in the opportunity for men to develop all their faculties, he was not greatly interested in political freedom.

From this it appears that the great shade of Napoleon which brooded over the thought of the two forerunners of socialism must be given its due. Napoleon III, after all, had dreams of being a Saint-Simon on horseback. All the same, neither the Emperor nor any wealthy capitalist appeared at Fourier's door to bring the Phalanstery to life. But before his death in 1837, Fourier had the satisfaction of recruiting a number of disciples. Foremost among them was his compatriot from Franche-Comté, Victor Considérant, a former student at the Polytechnic and a former artillery officer. But however important their place in social history, the Fouricrists made much less impression than the followers of Saint-Simon. In the eighteen-fifties, Considérant made plans for founding a Phalansterian colony in Texas, but the enterprise was stillborn. Considérant's failure was much more complete and devastating than Cabet's at Nauvoo or Enfantin's in Suez.

Fourier has been regarded, with some justification, as the forerunner of Freud. He devoted careful study to the capacities of children and wrote some penetrating chapters on education. (This perspicacity is all the more curious in that Fourier disliked children and never bothered to conceal the fact.) Fourier believed that in a so-called civilized society based on the principle of competition men do not, as a general rule, do the things they want to do. He thought that the reason people wanted money and indulged in the fierce pursuit of wealth was chiefly that they were afraid of looking foolish, but also that they wished to forget the violence they were doing to their unconscious selves. Instinct urged them to take up a particular profession and society; heredity or propriety prevented them. Consequently they engaged all the more fiercely upon the road they had been obliged to tread, just because it was not their proper path. The leaders of the Phalanstery were the men responsible for the "burgeoning of vocations."

On the other hand, Fourier also thought that a great deal of time and effort was wasted in the performance of domestic tasks. These tasks could be carried out by the group, thus releasing the individual. Fourier, in fact, looked forward to the American apartment block with its communal restaurant. He considered that four hundred families should provide all the vocation needed to create a coherent and very nearly self-sufficient social unit. Like Saint-Simon, Fourier wanted people to have plenty, and modern methods of production. At the same time, he feared the morally and physically stifling effect of sprawling, octopuslike cities. He envisaged the Phalanstery existing in the country. There is a great deal of good sense in all these dreams. Even today, given the ease with which electric power can be provided over great distances, industries are being concentrated in small agglomerations functioning with great technical efficiency, and these agglomerations are situated a long way from the inhuman cities. The modern world is moving in the direction of a combination of town and countryside which corresponds very much with Fourier's views. It is revealing to note that Fourier is nowadays being studied very carefully by young sociologists in Soviet Russia.

Fourier was not particularly concerned with political problems. I have mentioned his antagonism toward the Republic. Considérant too, in the early days of his activities, paid little attention to problems of government as such. He even evinced a certain slightly contemptuous loyalty to the July Monarchy. However, as the cracks which were to destroy the system of the Juste-Milieu became increasingly apparent, Considérant went over to the republican camp and joined the social democrats. His paper, *La Démocratie pacifique*, contributed to maintaining the fuss over the banquet of the twelfth *arrondissement* during the winter of 1847.

Cantagrel, who was, after Considérant, Fourier's most energetic and representative disciple, entered the Legislative Assembly, representing the *département* of Loire-et-Cher. During the Second Empire he was an active member of the republican opposition. Sébastien Commissaire, an army NCO of Lyonnais origin who was also a representative of the people during the Second Republic—I have already mentioned his severe strictures on Albert in his memoirs—wrote quite rightly: "The Phalanstery found few supporters among the working class." But many of the same observations can be made about Fourierism as on the school of Saint-Simon. Working-class leaders who did not openly accept the Phalanstery nevertheless pondered Fourier's ideas. A typical example is that of Corbon, who put forward ideas on the subject of education which were very similar to those of Fourier. He said that what was needed was to channel the passions rather than tame them. It is worth noting that the ornamentalist Pottier, who among other things composed the *Internationale*, was a Fourierist.

I shall not return to the case of Louis Blanc, since the mechanics of the Social Workshops which he advocated in *L'Organisation du travail* have already been considered in dealing with the National Workshops. The Saint-Simonians and the Fourierists tended to fight shy of the state. Louis Blanc, on the other hand, believed that the state had a duty to assist the most underprivileged sections of the nation and contribute to the setting up of Social Workshops. But we should not take Proudhon's attacks on Louis Blanc too literally. He was much less of an authoritarian supporter of state control than his too-clever opponent claimed.

One of the most original faces of 1848 is that of Pierre Leroux. He was the *philosophus hirsutus* of the Second Republic. With his unkempt hair and a certain flamboyant untidiness of appearance, he fascinated George Sand and it is through her novels, and in *Spiridion* in particular, that we can most easily form a picture of Pierre Leroux. It is not easy to summarize his ideas, which were as vague and disorganized as the man himself. Moreover, Leroux was concerned as much with metaphysics and high philosophy as with social economy. He demolished that great university theorist of the July Monarchy, Victor Cousin, with great ability and intelligence. Cousin was the man who codified the species of eclecticism on which several generations of *lycée* students were brought up. Pierre Leroux, on the other hand, analyzed the structure of French society, and he was one of the few writers to disturb the comparative stagnation of the French people during the first half of the nineteenth century. Whereas in England and in Prussia industrialization was accompanied by a considerable demographic growth, in France, with its Malthusian government, the birth rate was reduced. Leroux dabbled in Saint-Simonism and himself observed that Saint-Simon and Fourier were his "comrades." His system, if such it can be called, since "vagary" would actually suit it better, was the *circulus*.

Pierre Leroux devoted a great deal of study to the value of human waste products as fertilizer, and waxed indignant at man's heedless neglect of his own excrement. The *circulus* is the methodical utilization of human waste.

When he was in exile after the coup d'état, Pierre Leroux came into frequent contact with Victor Hugo and the two men had long conversations as they walked by the sea. Pierre Leroux has described these meetings in a fine but too little known book called *La Grève de Samarez*. Hugo, at this period, was engaged in writing *Les Misérables*, and I have often wondered whether the long passages about the sewers, which are called the "intestines of Leviathan," in Hugo's book are not also an effect of these meetings. "Do you know what this fetid flow of subterranean filth really is? It is the flowering meadows, the green grass, the thyme and sage, the game, the cattle, it is the contented lowing of great oxen in the evening air, it is the scented hay, the golden corn, it is the bread on your table, the hot blood in your veins, it is health and joy and life."

Pierre Leroux worked as a laborer and as a printer's compositor, but his family, although it suffered many hardships, was not of humble origin. Pierre Joseph Proudhon was closer to the people. His father was a cooper and his mother a servant in a suburb of Besançon. (The region of Franche-Comté breeds many revolutionaries.) Proudhon was able, however, to embark on the study of the classics at the College of Besançon, and was very far from being the self-taught man depicted all too often by his biographers. To be more precise, he was not self-taught in any typical or systematic sense. He tried to make himself "one of the people" but he did not naturally belong among them. He was an incomparable journalist with a brilliant flair for seeing what kind of paper the workers wanted, but his own contacts with the workers were only incidental. He kept himself surrounded by ordinary men, but not by men who worked in factories. In 1840, Proudhon published a *Mémoire sur la propriété*, which created something of a scandal, and it is actually in this memoir that the famous statement "property is robbery" is to be found. In practice, Proudhon was a much more moderate and reasonable person than his vocabulary suggests. He distinguished between several aspects of property. Proudhon had the kind of detached and captious turn of mind which adored legal quibbles. A cousin of his had been a teacher of law and the juridical blood ran in Pierre Joseph's veins. Proudhon's ideas amounted to a proposal to return to the community what the ancient Romans had called the property of the *quirites*, but he was not trying to deprive the peasant smallholder of his cows and his fields. He was the opposite of Saint-Simon and of Fourier in that he did not preach the doctrine of plenty. He was a moralist and he wanted people to lead worthy rather than affluent lives. He was a passionate defender of 1789 because the Revolution had substituted the reign of justice for the reign of grace. He was fiercely antireligious, saying that "when men talk about God it is because they want either my freedom or my purse." The Church, founded as it was on the principles of aristocracy and arbitrary rule, was necessarily monarchical and should vanish in the light of justice. All the same, Proudhon was as frenetically anti-Jacobin as he was anti-Catholic. Robespierre had restored a dictatorial, monarchical system in France. In its healthy period, the Revolution had been destructive, a work of *undoing*.

Proudhon was the apologist of the Gironde. He loathed the Jacobins and the Montagnards because they had compressed the country in a vise of iron and so had done the work of reaction.

Proudhon's great idea during the Second Republic was "free credit." Proudhon was convinced that on the day the community was able to dispose of its surplus without paying a tax to the banks and the capitalists, produce would be bartered justly and the golden age would reign in the world. In the economic field, he looked forward to mutual credit and free exchange. In 1849 he founded a "People's Bank," which was to institute a process of free exchange by lending money to the workers' associations at exceptionally advantageous terms. But the People's Bank was only a spark in the hay and its failure was even more pitiful than that of the Phalansterian colony in Texas.

Proudhon was a champion of anarchy and "nongovernment." This explains both his success and his failure with the masses in 1848. He fulminated against the priest, the officer, and the magistrate, and a great many workers who were acutely conscious of the painful straitjacket imposed on them by society applauded him. At the same time, they were dismayed by Proudhon's constant attacks on the Jacobins and the communists, on Robespierre and Babeuf.

In 1848 there was a kind of continuous two-way traffic between the ideologies of authoritarianism and anarchy. Louis Napoleon Bonaparte reaped the benefit of this movement, and in two ways. Some workers on the authoritarian side said, "He may serve our turn better than those chatterboxes in the Assembly, and he will give us the *milliard* which Barbès demanded in vain from the Constituents." The anarchists said, "Since the problem of government is after all a secondary one, and society is more important than politics, let us not pay too much attention to the actual form of the state: let us not be taken in by words like 'Republic' and 'Empire.' "

After the pronunciamento executed by Louis Bonaparte, Morny, and Maupas, Proudhon wrote a small book entitled *La Révolution sociale démontrée par le coup d'état* in which the Prince-President was partially absolved from his crimes against the Republic. Goudchaux, the former Minister of Finance who had fought boldly against the workers in June 1848, greeted Proudhon's book indignantly. "Luckily," Goudchaux said to comfort himself, "it is not a popular edition, it is fortunately an expensive book; otherwise, what damage might it not do in the workshops of Paris?"

While the Republic was in its decline, in 1850 and 1851, a twofold movement was beginning to emerge. On the one hand, a great many Montagnards were looking increasingly toward a decentralization of power. A curious and highly typical case is that of Ledru-Rollin. In 1848, Ledru-Rollin was deeply involved in the memory of his great forebears and of the Montagnards, but for a time while in exile he adopted a philosophy of nongovernment very similar to Proudhon's. Because he had been incapable of governing he took a stand against all government. I would refer those of my readers interested in such matters to a pamphlet which Ledru-Rollin published in 1851, the purport of which is significant: *No more president, no more representatives.*

At the same time, a former member of the Frankfurt Parliament named Rittinghausen was circulating his ideas on the subject of "direct government" among a few groups of republicans. Rittinghausen dilated on the form of democracy practiced in the Swiss cantons and generally envisaged autonomous communes in which the citizens would gather constantly in the forum and, so to speak, run public affairs without any intermediaries. Proudhon was not impressed by Rittinghausen's theories. He was sufficiently intelligent to see that there was something messy, cumbersome, and even arbitrary about such a way of conducting affairs. "Any Constitution is either a drudge or a nag," he said arrogantly, and his disgust with all forms of government whatever extended even to direct government.

However, Joseph Benoît, for example, the communist textile worker who represented the Rhône in the Legislative Assembly, was seduced by Rittinghausen's theories.

Nevertheless the second stream, which was authoritarian and Babouvist, was still vigorously alive. The Constitution of 1848 provided for two elections to be held in 1852. On the one hand the citizens were to elect the legislators and on the other they were to re-elect a president of the Republic. Owing to the fact that the law of May 31, 1850, laid down very strict residential qualifications for the exercise of the vote, a great many citizens found themselves excluded from the polls. We find secret societies such as the "Marianne" and the "Jeune Montagne" in which the ideas of Robespierre, Babeuf, and the "Rights of Man" flourished, being revived, especially in the valley of the Loire and the southeast. The members of the secret societies had some vague and heated idea of going to the polls in 1852 gun in hand, and that this time, at last, they would not be cheated of their social-democrat revolution. "In February 1848 we were too gentle. In 1852 we shall spare no one. We swear it on our swords! Long live the sword!"

The cry of "Long live the sword!" echoed all too frequently in the ears of the bourgeois of Marseilles during the summer of 1851, until they took fright and became increasingly convinced that only the Empire could save them from drinking the cup of revolution.

I think the very divagations of this study have demonstrated with comparative clarity the manner in which the builders of social systems influenced the leaders of the working class to take a more peaceful line, and how these leaders were afterwards disillusioned and resorted once again to hasty and violent conclusions, so that in the end, through this maze of enthusiasms, certainties, hesitancies, and disappointments, the Napoleonic sword made its triumphant mark. But beyond this dry analysis, does it not seem that there is a curse on the workers who, in their moments of trusting emotional abandon, are defeated by clever manipulation, and who in their hour of violence are defeated by the very fear they have inspired?

Biographical Dictionary

Arago, Dominique François (1786–1853). A distinguished astronomer, he was Minister of War and the Navy in the Provisional Government and a member of the Executive Commission.

Adam, Edmond (1816–1877). A journalist of the moderate left, he was the right-hand man of Armand Marrast on *Le National*. He was married to Juliette Lamber, whose salon was the gathering place of the literati for many years.

Audebrand, Philibert (1815–1906). A journalist who wrote for *Le National* and *La Réforme*.

Babeuf, François Émile (1760–1797). An early theoretician of utopian communism, he led the Conspiration des Égaux to overthrow the Directory in 1796. He is generally considered today to have been the founder of the modern communist tradition.

Barbès, Armand (1809–1870). A radical republican and founder, in the 1830s, of the secret societies of "The Seasons" and of "The Rights of Man," he was a leader of the insurrection of May 12, 1839. Released from prison by the February Revolution of 1848, he was convicted of leading the demonstration of May 15. Imprisoned until 1854, he lived in exile thereafter.

Barrot, Odilon (1791–1873). Leader of the dynastic opposition under the July Monarchy, he was a partisan of moderate, legal reform. Although he rallied to the Republic, his place in the spectrum of 1848 politics is definitely on the right. Prime minister in December 1848.

Barthélemy, Emmanuel (born 1813). A "mechanic," he was active in the June Days. While in exile in London, he fought and killed Cournet in a duel over a personal insult.

Bastide, Jules (1800–1879). An editor of Le National until 1846, he collaborated with Buchez on La Revue nationale. He was briefly Minister for Foreign Affairs under the Second Republic.

Baudin, Jean Baptiste (1811–1851). A partisan of Saint-Simon and Fourier, he was a member of the Mountain in 1848. He organized resistance to the coup d'état of December 2, 1851, and was killed on the barricades. His name became a rallying cry for the left under the Second Empire.

Béranger, Pierre Jean de (1780–1857). Writer of satirical songs and poems, he was particularly prolific during the Restoration. He was a liberal republican whose politics bore a tinge of Bonapartism, but he sat with the Mountain in the Constituent Assembly of 1848.

Berger, Jean Jacques (1790–1859). A right-wing republican, he took part in the February Revolution and was elected to the Constituent Assembly. After the presidential elections, he became Prefect for the Seine and was ever loyal to Louis Napoleon thereafter.

Bethmont, Eugène (1804–1860). A republican and liberal, he made his reputation as a defense lawyer for the left in the 1830s. Minister of Trade under the Provisional Government, he became Minister of Justice in Cavaignac's government of June 1848.

Blanc, Louis (1811–1882). A socialist, he favored the creation of a wide network of producers' cooperatives (ateliers sociaux), of which the National Workshops of 1848 were a parody. He was one of the leaders of the extreme left in 1848 until forced into exile for his part in the June Days.

Blanqui, Louis Auguste (1805–1881). Socialist and revolutionary, he participated in most of the secret societies and revolts of the 1830s. In 1847, he established the Central Republican Society and played a leading part in both the February and June Revolutions of 1848. In exile under the Empire, he returned to become one of the most important leaders of the Paris Commune of 1871. He spent almost forty years of his life in prison, but nonetheless managed to exercise a great influence over his contemporaries and later generations of socialists, particularly in regard to revolutionary tactics.

Bonaparte, Louis Napoleon (1808–1873). Nephew of Napoleon I (Victor Hugo called him Napoleon the Little). He several times conspired to overthrow the July Monarchy and liked to describe himself as a socialist. In reality, an authoritarian who did nothing to disturb and much to help the French bourgeoisie of his era, he was elected president of the Second Republic in 1848 and became emperor after his coup d'état of December 2, 1851.

Bréa, Jean Baptiste (1790–1848). General and commander of government troops in June 1848, he was killed by the insurgents.

Buchez, Philippe (1796–1865). An ardent Catholic, he was also a socialist and republican of a moderate sort. His greatest contribution was the

Histoire parlementaire de la Révolution française (1834–1840) in 46 volumes, an edition of the proceedings of the several revolutionary assemblies that helped to keep the left-wing tradition alive during the hard times of the July Monarchy. He was a deputy mayor of Paris in 1848 but played no great role in that year.

Bugeaud de la Piconnerie, Thomas Robert (1784–1849). Marshal of France, he commanded in the suppression of the revolt of April 1834 in Paris and was in large measure responsible for the massacre of the rue Transnonain. He was named commander of the Paris garrison in February 1848, and was soon dismissed by the Provisional Government. Louis Napoleon made him commander in chief of the Army of the Alps.

Buonarroti, Filippo Michele (1761–1837). Co-conspirator with Babeuf in 1796, he was the organizer and leader of numerous secret societies in Belgium, Italy, and Switzerland from 1802 until his death. His book *La Conspiration pour l'Égalité*, about the events of 1796 (published in 1828), greatly influenced several generations of the European left.

Cabet, Étienne (1788–1856). A republican and utopian socialist, he published his *Voyage en Icarie* in 1840. His principle of communal organization is as follows: "The first right, to live. The first duty, to work. To each according to his needs, from each according to his capacity. The common happiness." He was popular among the Parisian artisans but opposed the seizure of political power by violence. In 1849 he went to Illinois to found a utopian colony.

Carnot, Hippolyte (1801–1888). Son of Lazare Carnot, the "organizer of victory" of the French Revolution, he was a Saint-Simonian. A moderate republican, he was Minister of Education in the Provisional Government and favored free and obligatory universal education. He opposed Napoleon III and became a solid republican senator in the Third Republic.

Caussidière, Louis Marc (1808–1861). A democrat and socialist, he was active in the workers' movements of the 1830s in Lyons and Saint-Étienne. He was a partisan of Ledru-Rollin and Prefect of Police of Paris for a brief time in 1848. He lived in exile in London after the June Days.

Cavaignac, Godefroy (1801–1845). Elder brother of the general, he was a republican and organizer of secret societies in 1830s. He was an important contributor to *La Réforme*.

Cavaignac, Louis Eugène (1802–1857). Governor general of Algeria, he was elected to the Constituent Assembly in 1848. He commanded the troops that quashed the June Revolution and became prime minister immediately thereafter. He was defeated in the presidential elections by Louis Napoleon.

Cazot, Théodore Joseph Jules (1821–1912). An ardent republican of 1848, he was active in his home *département* of the Gard. He went on to become a deputy and senator in the Third Republic.

Chancel, Napoléon (1808–1883). A socialist revolutionary and follower of Blanqui, with whom he worked in the Central Republican Society in 1847 and 1848. He was commissioner of the Provisional Government in the

Drôme, and was later condemned to deportation for his part in the demonstration of May 15.

Changarnier, Nicolas (1793–1877). A general who succeeded Cavaignac as Governor General of Algeria, he resigned to head the Paris National Guard after the June Days. In January and June 1849, he had the entire Paris garrison under his command. He was an Orleanist and a lifelong opponent of the Republic.

Charamaule, Hippolyte (1794–1886). A moderate republican, he was one of the organizers of the banquet campaign. He was commissioner of the Provisional Government in the Hérault. Later he tried to rouse Paris to the barricades against Louis Napoleon. His failure led him to retire from politics.

Charbonnel, Félix (1797–1848). An army officer and moderate republican, he fought against the June Revolution and died on the barricades with Négrier.

Charbonnerie. A secret society on Masonic lines founded in 1821, it appealed especially to young bourgeois, professionals, and army officers. Its younger members were generally republicans, but Bonapartism also had adherents in the organization. The program was in favor of a liberal utilitarianism and political freedom. Following the failure of several military plots to seize power, other forms of politics tended to replace the Charbonnerie after the 1820s.

Colet, Louise (1808–1876). Poet and mistress to Flaubert and Musset.

Compagnonnage. Journeymen's associations organized among the artisans who traveled around France practicing their trade and perfecting their skill before settling down permanently in one place. They had some of the characteristics of a modern union, but also those of secret Masonic societies, employing initiations and passwords, and indulging in rivalries with one another. Although reformed by Perdiguier in the second quarter of the nineteenth century, they tended to disappear with the rise of modern forms of industry.

Considérant, Victor (1808–1893). A disciple of Fourier, he was the editor of a newspaper called *La Réforme industrielle* in the 1840s. A member of the Constituent Assembly in 1848, he supported the June Revolution and planned the insurrection of June 1849 in cooperation with Ledru-Rollin. He later established a Fourierist colony in Texas (1855–1857).

Cormenin, Louis Marie Delahaye, Vicomte de (1788–1868). A member of the parliamentary left under the July Monarchy, he voted conservatively in the Constituent Assembly of 1848 and was the principal author of the Constitution of that year.

Cournet, Frédéric (1808–1852). A republican naval officer, he participated in both Revolutions of 1848. President of the Democratic Socialist Committee of Paris in 1850, he organized resistance to the coup d'état of 1851 before fleeing to London. He was killed in a duel by Barthélemy, a follower of Louis Blanc.

Courtais, Amable Gaspard Henri, Vicomte de (1790–1877). A republican deputy from 1842–1848 and member of the Constituent Assembly, he was made a general and given command of the Paris National Guard by the Provisional Government. He refused to lead the troops against the demonstration of May 15. Although acquitted of complicity in the event, he retired from politics in 1849.

Crémieux, Adolphe (1796–1880). Lawyer and politician. He was a very moderate revolutionary in 1848. Minister of Justice under the Provisional Government, he was a partisan of Louis Napoleon. As a member of the Government of National Defense in 1870, he granted electoral rights to Algerian Jews.

Damesme, Edouard (1807–1848). Appointed a general in 1848, this professional officer took part in the repression and died as a result of wounds.

Delahodde, Lucien (1808–1865). A member of the republican secret societies of the 1830s and close friend of Albert, he was in reality a police spy. He was discovered and imprisoned in 1848. His book *La Naissance de la République* (1850) explains the 1848 Revolutions as a republican conspiracy.

Delezcluze, Charles (1809–1871). A lifelong republican and radical, he was representative of the Provisional Government in the Nord in 1848. Exiled and later imprisoned, he played a leading role in the Paris Commune of 1871 and was killed on the barricades.

Druet-Desvaux, Jacques Louis Mathieu (1793–1868). Right-wing representative in 1848, he tried, along with his colleagues Galy-Cazalat and Larabit, to negotiate with the insurgents on June 25. An attempt was made to force them to declare for the revolution, but when they refused to do so, they were released unharmed.

Du Camp, Maxime (1822–1894). A republican of liberal leanings, he fought in the National Guard in the June Days. He later fought with Garibaldi in 1860, but became viciously antirepublican after the Paris Commune. In later years he was elected to the Académie Française, and some said that this was the reward for his political change of heart.

Duclerc, Charles (1812–1888). A journalist specializing in economic affairs, he became Minister of Finance for a short time in 1848. He was against the repression of the June Revolution. Active in the Third Republic, he was Prime Minister in 1882–83.

Dufaure, Jules Armand Stanislas (1798–1881). Minister of Public Works and deputy during the July Monarchy, he sat on the right of the Constituent Assembly. He was Minister of the Interior under Cavaignac and Louis Napoleon in 1848–49.

Dupont, A. Pierre (1821–1870). Poet and songwriter.

Dupont de l'Eure, Jacques Charles (1767–1855). A remnant of the Great Revolution, his task was to confer a claim to respectability on the Provisional Government. He was a Cavaignac supporter.

Dupont-White, Charles Brook (1807–1878). An economist, he was a vigorous partisan of state intervention as an engine of progress.

Duprat, Pierre Pascal (1815–1885). A member of the moderate left in 1848, he was against both the Mountain and the socialists. On June 23, he called for the imposition of the state of siege upon Paris. Exiled by Louis Napoleon, he was later active in the Third Republic.

Duvergier de Hauranne, Prosper (1798–1881). A deputy from 1831 to 1848, he was a partisan of Thiers and favored the creation of a liberal monarchy. His opposition to Guizot caused him to favor the February Revolution.

Duvivier, Franciade Fleurus (1794–1848). An army officer who had served in Algeria, he was made a general by the Provisional Government. He organized and led the mobile National Guard which served Cavaignac so well in June. He died as a result of wounds acquired in the fighting.

Falloux, Frédéric Alfred Pierre DuCoudray, Comte de (1811–1885). A right-wing Catholic, he preached a theocratic form of government. His name is most closely associated with the Law on Teaching of 1850, which broke the state school monopoly in favor of the clergy.

Favre, Jules (1809–1880). He made his reputation as a defense lawyer in the trials resulting from the abortive revolt of April 1834. A moderate republican, he supported Cavaignac in June 1848. A deputy from 1858 to 1870, he was a senator and minister under the Third Republic.

Flocon, Ferdinand (1800–1866). A Swiss journalist, he was editor in chief of *La Réforme*. A member of the Provisional Government, he supported Ledru-Rollin and was against the June Revolution. In the 1850s he was active in revolutionary movements directed against the ambitions of the Piedmontese monarchy.

Fourier, François Marie Charles (1772–1837). Mathematician and utopian socialist theoretician, he hoped to organize society into communities known as Phalansteries, where work would be apportioned according to the natural inclinations of the participants. His influence on the generation of 1848 in both Europe and the United States (Brook Farm) was great.

Froussard, Jean Baptiste (1792–1849). A republican member of the Constituent Assembly in 1848, he was general commissioner of the Provisional Government in the Isère and neighboring départements with headquarters at Grenoble.

Galy-Cazalat, Antoine (1796–1869). See Druet-Desvaux.

Gambetta, Léon (1838–1882). Republican leader of the Third Republic, he was one of the most influential politicians of the 1870s. He was the founder of the party that came to be known as the Opportunists, signifying its conservative orientation in matters of social policy.

Garnier-Pagès, Louis Antoine (1803–1878). A sponsor of the banquet campaign, he was the most conservative member of the Provisional Government. He became Minister of Finance and Mayor of Paris in 1848. After 1864 he was a member of the parliamentary opposition to Louis Napoleon.

Gavroche. A street urchin in Hugo's *Les Misérables* who is killed while fighting on the barricades. By extension, the Parisian poor.

Genoude (pseudonym of Antoine Eugène Genoud) (1792–1849). A priest, he edited the *Gazette de France*. He was a legitimist and anti-Orleanist, which led him in 1848 to support parliamentary reform and universal suffrage.

Gérard, Étienne Maurice (1773–1852). Marshal and peer of France, he fought with distinction in the revolutionary and Napoleonic wars. Prominent in the July Days of 1830, he was twice Minister of War under Louis Philippe and developed a plan for dealing with insurgency in Paris which proved to be inadequate in 1848. He was relieved of his post as Grand Chancellor of the Legion of Honor by the Provisional Government.

Girardin, Émile de (1806–1881). Bonapartist writer and journalist, he was instrumental in creating a popular press by lowering the price of newspapers and using them as advertising vehicles. Editor of *La Presse* (1836–56, 1862–66).

Goudchaux, Michel (1797–1862). A banker and militant liberal, he collaborated on *Le National*. A moderate republican, he was Minister of Finance both in the Provisional Government and under Cavaignac in 1848.

Guinard, Joseph Augustin (1799–1879). A republican member of secret societies, he was deputy mayor of Paris and chief of staff of the National Guard in 1848. A member of the left, he nonetheless rallied to Cavaignac in June, before cooperating with Ledru Rollin in the attempted coup of a year later.

Guizot, François (1787–1874). Minister and chief representative of the July Monarchy after 1840, he is often remembered for his response to the demand for social legislation: "Get rich!" Less cynical than the remark makes him seem, this Calvinist was a staunch defender of a status quo based on monarchy, economic liberalism, and the reign of bourgeois notables. 1848 spelled his political doom. In retirement he turned to the writing of history, concerning himself particularly with the history of England, a country whose political arrangements he much admired.

Huber, Aloysius (1812–1865). A disciple of Pierre Leroux and members of left-wing republican secret societies, he probably acted as an agent *provocateur*, especially in the demonstration of May 15, 1848.

Lacordaire, Jean Baptiste Henri (1802–1861). A Dominican priest, he made his reputation as a powerful preacher in the 1830s and 1840s. He called for freedom of conscience and of the press and went into voluntary exile rather than support the Second Empire.

Lalanne, Léon (1811–1892). An engineer, he replaced Émile Thomas at the head of the National Workshops but played no other political role.

Lamarque, Maximilien, Comte (1770–1832). A Napoleonic general, he was a member of the opposition in the Chamber of Deputies during the Restoration. He died in the cholera epidemic of 1832, and his funeral was the occasion for the antigovernment riots of June 5–6.

Lamartine, Alphonse Marie Louis de (1790–1869). Great romantic poet, he published a history of the Girondins (1848) that came close to being the bible of the moderate republicans. Briefly at the head of the Provisional Government, his lack of dynamism and decisiveness cost him first his clientele on both left and right and later his reputation. He was defeated for the presidency by Louis Napoleon and retired from politics. When asked what caused the February Revolution, he replied, "France was bored," meaning that the July Monarchy had alienated almost every class in the nation by its lack of imagination and its subservience to other powers, notably Great Britain, in foreign affairs.

Lamennais, Jean Marie Félicité Robert de (1782–1854). A Roman Catholic priest, he started out as an apologist for legitimism and the Church in his celebrated *Essai sur l'Indifférence* (1817). But he moved progressively to the left and became antiroyalist and liberal, especially after 1830. He founded a newspaper, *L'Avenir*, in that year with Lacordaire and Montalembert. But he was the only one of the three to resist the papal condemnation of 1834 and to die excommunicated.

Lamoricière, Louis Christophe Léon Juchault de (1806–1865). A general, he rallied to the Provisional Government in February 1848 and commanded under Cavaignac's orders in June. Banished in 1852 because of his opposition to Napoleon III, he became chief of papal forces in 1861 and lost to the Piedmontese.

Larabit, Marc Denis (1792–1876). See Druet-Desvaux.

La Rochejaquelein, Henri, Marquis de (1805–1867). Leader of the legitimist opposition under the July Monarchy, he favored the February Revolution, because he hated Guizot. He later supported Louis Napoleon.

Lefebvre, Georges (1874–1959). Leading historian of the French Revolution, his major works include *La Grande Peur de 1789* (1932) and *The French Revolution* (last edition, 1957, now available in two-volume translation).

Le Play, Pierre Guillaume Frédéric (1806–1882). A sociologist and economist, he was one of the first to study social and familial institutions in relation to environment. An early user of social survey methods, he was a staunch defender of Christianity and existing institutions who insisted on the merits of custom and tradition.

Leroux, Pierre (1797–1871). Journalist and politician, he believed in an egalitarianism based on Christian principles. He vigorously defended the Revolutions of 1848 and is credited with having coined the word "socialism."

Lessert, Abraham Gabriel Marguerite de (1786–1858). A peer of France, he was Prefect of Police of Paris from 1836 and retired at the February Revolution of 1848.

Marie, Pierre Thomas Alexandre (1795–1870). A member of the dynastic left during the July Monarchy, he became Minister of Public Works in the Provisional Government. It was he who set up the National Workshops, in what many think to have been a deliberate caricature of Blanc's social workshops. He later became President of the Constituent Assembly and Minister of Justice.

Marmont, Auguste Frédéric Louis Viesse de, Duc de Raguse (1774–1852). Napoleonic general and Marshal of France, he rallied to the Restoration and led Bourbon troops during the July Days of 1830.

Marrast, Armand (1801–1852). Editor in chief of *Le National*, he was a moderate republican and antisocialist. He was a member of the Provisional Government and Mayor of Paris in 1848.

Martignac, Jean Batiste, Vicomte de (1778–1832). Prime Minister and Minister of the Interior during the Restoration.

Molé, Louis Mathieu (1781–1855). Peer of France, he was Louis Philippe's prime minister from 1836 to 1839. The sworn enemy of Guizot, he was active in right-wing politics in the Second Republic. He supported Cavaignac against Louis Napoleon.

Montalembert, Charles Forbes, Comte de (1810–1870). Much influenced by Lamennais in his youth, he broke that connection after the papal condemnation of 1834. As a member of the Constituent Assembly of 1848, he sat on the extreme right and showed himself to be violently Catholic and monarchist, although he spoke in favor of (Catholic) nationalist movements in Poland and Ireland.

Nadaud, Martin (1815–1898). A mason by trade, he was elected to the Legislative Assembly in 1849. A supporter of Cabet, he sat with the Mountain. In exile from 1852–70, he was a moderate politician in the Third Republic.

Négrier, François (1788–1848). A general who made his reputation in Algeria, he was a centrist representative in 1848. He died leading a column of troops against the rebels at the Bastille in June.

Nemours, Louis Charles Philippe, Duc de (1814–1896). Second son of Louis Philippe.

Ollivier, Émile (1825–1913). As general commissioner of the Republic in the Bouches-du-Rhône in 1848, he suppressed the June rising in Marseilles. A lawyer and moderate republican, he rallied to the so-called Liberal Empire in 1867, so much so as to become its guiding spirit and prime minister in 1869.

Pagnerre, Laurent Antoine (1805–1854). A moderate republican and liberal, he was the republican publisher and bookseller in Paris during the July Monarchy. He was a friend of Garnier-Pagès, who made him deputy mayor of Paris and later secretary general of the Provisional Government in 1848. He was for the repression of the June Revolution and only moderately opposed Louis Napoleon.

Pecqueur, Constantin (1801–1887). A minor socialist writer of the Saint-Simon and Fourier schools, he was a member of the Luxembourg Commission in 1848. Material progress, he was sure, would lead to the creation of a morally more perfect society.

Perdiguier, Agricol (1805–1875). A journeyman joiner, he undertook, with some success, to reform the *compagnonnages* on the basis of cooperative action and mutual aid. Elected a representative in 1848, he spoke against the repression of the June Revolution. He was one of the last representatives of the artisan-oriented Jacobin tradition.

Perrot, Benjamin Pierre (1791–1865). General and commander of the Paris garrison in 1847, he was relieved of his post by the Provisional Government. After June, he became chief of staff of the National Guard of the Seine and a determined supporter of Louis Napoleon.

Petit, Jean Martin, Baron (1772–1856). A veteran of the Napoleonic Wars, he was created a peer of France under the July Monarchy. In 1848 he was the leader of the Society of the Tenth of December that called for the restoration of the Empire.

Pritchard, George (1796–1883). An English missionary in Tahiti, he tried to stem the development of French control by staging an insurrection in 1844. He was expelled by French forces, but the French government was soon compelled to apologize and to pay him an indemnity, much to the disgust of the nationalistically oriented left.

Proudhon, Pierre Joseph (1809–1865). A foremost anarchist theoretician, he played no role in the February Revolution but was elected a member of the Constituent Assembly. He shunned the June Days and his activity in the Assembly was constantly disruptive. Anything short of the complete and immediate establishment of an anarchist society was repugnant to him.

Pyat, Félix (1810–1889). Playwright and lifelong democrat, he was a member of the Mountain in 1848. He joined with Ledru-Rollin in the abortive coup of June 13, 1849, and spent twenty years in exile as a result.

Rachel (pseudonym of Élisa Félix, 1821–1858). Great French tragedienne, she was appearing at the Comédie Française when the February Revolution took pace. On March 6, she showed her loyalty to the Republic by singing the *Marseillaise* no less than thirty-five times.

Raspail, François Vincent (1794–1878). A republican from his youth, he was a member of the Charbonnerie and fought on the barricades in 1830. He was active in the February Revolution and was sentenced to six years imprisonment for his part in the demonstration of May 15, 1848. He received 36,000 votes in the presidential election of December.

Regnault, Elias (1801–1868). Editor of the *Bulletin de la République*, official organ of the Ministry of the Interior, he became one of the first historians of the revolutions of 1848 by publishing *La Révolution française, histoire de huit ans, 1840–1848* in 1851.

Rémusat, Charles, Comte de (1797–1875). A philosopher and liberal politician, he was moderately opposed to Louis Philippe. In 1848, he sided with Thiers and attempted to prevent the proclamation of the Republic. He was extremely antirepublican, but rallied to the Third Republic in 1871 and served for two years as Minister for Foreign Affairs under Thiers' presidency.

Schoelcher, Victor (1804–1893). A member of the Mountain and representative in 1848–49, he was noted for his abolitionist activities. As Undersecretary of the Navy in 1848, he prepared the decree ending slavery in the French colonies.

Sébastiani, Horace, Comte de la Porte (1772–1851). Napoleonic general, he became Marshal of France in 1840. A friend of Louis Philippe, he was sent to London as ambassador in the 1830s.

Sénard, Antoine (1800–1885). Public prosecutor at Rouen under the Provisional Government, and later President of the Constituent Assembly. He supported Cavaignac but became a strong republican in the 1870s.

Sobrier, Marie Joseph Camille (1812–1854). A republican of socialist leanings, he was briefly Prefect of Police in February 1848. With Lamartine's help, he organized the auxiliary police known as "*les terribles montagnards.*" Active in planning the demonstration of May 15, he was subsequently condemned to seven years imprisonment.

Stern, Daniel (pseudonym of Marie, Comtesse d'Agoult, 1805–1876). An ardent democrat, republican, and feminist, her salon was the gathering place of the left opposition to the Second Empire. She was Liszt's mistress and the mother of Cosima Wagner. She collaborated with George Sand on *La Revue indépendante* and wrote memoirs on 1848.

Sue, Eugène (1804–1857). Novelist whose most famous work is the *Mystères de Paris* (1842). He was a socialist of the Fourierist school and a partisan of the June Revolution. He worked particularly for the inclusion of peasants and urban workers in a common revolutionary movement.

Taschereau, Jules Antoine (1801–1874). A journalist, he was a member of the moderate liberal opposition during the July Monarchy and sat on the right of the Constituent Assembly in 1848.

Thiers, Louis Adolphe (1797–1877). A statesman whose career spanned a good part of the nineteenth century, he first played an important role in the July Days of 1830. He went on to become first a minister and then a liberal opponent of the July Monarchy, and was an antirepublican conservative in 1848. In exile under Louis Napoleon, he returned to become first president of the Third Republic in 1871.

Thomas, Émile (1822–1880). Engineer and director of the National Workshops. He believed in class collaboration, for "the worker of yesterday is the bourgeois of today, and the worker of today is the bourgeois of tomorrow." He was arrested on May 27, 1848, for opposing the closing of the workshops.

Trélat, Ulysse (1795–1879). A republican and liberal, he was one of the founders of the secret society called "Aide-Toi, le Ciel t'Aidera." He was Minister of Public Works in May–June 1848, after which he retired from politics. In 1871, he became a very conservative municipal councilor in Paris.

Trochu, Louis Jules (1815–1896). General and aide to Bugeaud, he later became president of the Government of National Defense in 1870.

Vivien, Alexandre François Auguste (1799–1854). Prefect of Police in Paris in 1831 and Minister of Justice under Thiers in 1840, he was a member of the dynastic opposition. A conservative in 1848, he held the Public Works Ministry under Cavaignac.

Bibliography

The literature on the revolutions of 1848 and the Second Republic is immense, if not always valuable. The following is only a small selection of the more important works.

I. WORKS BY CONTEMPORARIES

Blanc, Louis, *Histoire de la révolution de 1848* (two vols., 1870).

Caussidière, Marc, *Mémoires* (two vols., 1849).

de Falloux, Fréderic, *Mémoires d'un royaliste* (1888).

Garnier-Pagès, Louis, *Histoire de la révolution de 1848* (ten vols., 1860–1871).

Lamartine, Alphonse de, *Histoire de la révolution de 1848* (two vols., 1849).

Marx, Karl, *Class Struggles in France* (1848–1850) (numerous editions available).

Idem., *The Eighteenth Brumaire of Louis Bonaparte* (numerous editions available).

Stern, Daniel, *L'Histoire de la révolution de 1848* (three vols., 1850–1853).

Thomas, Émile, *Histoire des ateliers nationaux* (1848).

de Tocqueville, Alexis, *Recollections* (American edition, 1951).

II. LATER WORKS

Bastide, P., *Doctrines et Institutions politiques de la seconde république* (two vols., 1945).

Bourgin, G., 1848. Naissance et mort d'une révolution (1948).
Chevalier, Louis, Classes laborieuses et classes dangereuses (1958).
Daumard, A., La bourgeoisie parisienne de 1815 à 1848 (1964).
Dautry, J., Histoire de la révolution de 1848 en France (1948).
Dommanget, M., Un drame politique en 1848 (1948).
Idem., Les idées politiques et sociales d'Auguste Blanqui (1957).
Duveau, Georges, La vie ouvrière en France sous le second empire (1946).
Guillemin, Henri, La tragédie de quarante-huit (1948).
Idem., Le coup du deux décembre (1951).
La Gorce, Pierre de, Histoire de la seconde république (two vols., 1886).
McKay, D. M., The National Workshops (1933).
Schmidt, Charles, Les journées de juin 1848 (1926).
Seignobos, Charles, Le révolution de 1848—le second empire (1848–1859),
    Vol. VI of Ernest Lavisse (ed.), Histoire de la France contemporaine
    (1921).
Simpson, F. A., The Rise of Louis Napoleon (1925).
Tchernoff, M., Associations et sociétés secrètes sous la IIe république (1905).
Tudesq, A. J., Les grands notables en France, 1840–1849 (1965).

It is also necessary to refer to the files of the leading periodical in the field, unhappily no longer published: 1848 et les Révolutions du XIXe siècle.

Index

Adam, Edmond, 91, 123, 142

Affre, Monsignor, 95, 152, 176–9

Agoult, Countess of: see Stern, Daniel

Albert, worker, 51, 79, 111, 112, 129, 172; and April elections, 88, 91, 99, 109–10, 114; in Provisional Government, 55–6, 57

Algeria, 33; Governor General of, 54

Ami du Peuple, L', 62, 87, 95

Arago, Emmanuel, 57

Arago, Étienne, 57

Arago, François, 50, 53, 54, 57, 83, 99; in Assembly, 110, 200; and Dupont de l'Eure, 184; in 1832, 166; in June Rev., 141

Army: see National Guard

Association for Popular Education, 184, 213

Assommoir, L', 136

Atelier, L', 54, 55, 64–65, 75, 106, 114

Audebrand, Philibert, 121

Aumale, Duke of, 33, 63

Avenir de la Science, L', 204

Babeuf, François Émile, 46, 71, 211

Balzac, Honoré de, 15, 31, 62, 164

Banquets, 5; reformist, 7–8, 9, 107; of the 12th *arrondissement*, 9–20, arrangements for, 9–13; Barrot and, 13–14, 20; Lamartine and, 14–15; Louis Philippe and, 16–17; people and, 17–19

Barbès, Armand, 115, 117, 127, 129, 171; in May demonstration, 119, 121–2, 123, 124

Barricades, 3, 34; Blanqui in, 165, 171; in February Rev., 31, 35, 45; history of, 161–76; the

Fronde, 164; in 1827, 164–5, in 1830, 165; in 1832, 165–70; in 1834, 171; in 1839, 171–2; in 1842, 172–3, 173–6; in June Rev., 134, 136–7, 151, 156; Raspail in, 165; in Rouen, 97

Barrot, Madame, 14, 43

Barrot, Odilon, 7, 35, 81, 157, 165; in Chamber of Deputies, 48; and February Rev., 9 ff., 13 ff., 17, 20, 29, 37; and Louis Philippe, 39, 42; and National Guard, 25; popularity of, 42–3; at Rouen banquet, 8, 9

Barthélemy, Emmanuel, 175

Bary, Arthur, 144

Bary, Mademoiselle, 144–5

Bastide, Jules, 49, 113, 120, 146–7, 149, 167

Baudin, Dr. Alphonse, 161, 162, 163

Bedeau, General Marie Alphonse, 43, 53, 149; in February Rev., 34, 35, 36–7; in June Rev., 139, 141–2, 143, 180

Benoît, Joseph, 101, 107, 229

Béranger, Pierre Jean de, 196

Berger, Jean Jacques, 145

Bethmont, Eugène, 54, 57, 112

Blanc, Louis, 7, 52, 92, 111, 114, 115; and Assembly, 127, 157; demonstrations and, 83, 84, 91, 122, 123, 124; elections and, 79, 80, 88, 89, 99, 109–10; and February Rev., 9, 50; labor laws and, 66–8; and Luxembourg Commission, 69, 70; Normanby on, 121; personality of, 196–201; in Provisional Government, 51, 53, 54, 56, 86, 101

Blanqui, Auguste, 10, 71–2, 129; as agitator, 83–4, 115, 116, 117, 118, 121, 176; in the barricades, 165, 171; and Huber, 122; in May demonstration, 124; and Guard election, 87, 88–9; and

Poland, 119–20; and Provisional Government, 90

Blücher, General, 184

Bocage, 49

Bonaparte, Louis Napoleon, 39, 60, 70, 86, 183; in politics, 128–31, 158–9, 227

Bonaparte, Napoleon, 120, 158, 184

Bonheur, Raymond, 220

bonnets à poil, 83, 87; see also National Guard

Bord, Muret de, 28

Borgo, Pozzo di, 197

Bourges, Michel de, 211

Bréa, General Jean Baptiste, 149, 152–3, 176

Broglie, Prince Albert de, 11

Buonarroti, Filippo, 46, 79, 212, 215

Buchez, Philippe, 55, 130, 202; in the Assembly, 105–6, 111, 119; replaced, 127

Bugeaud, Thomas Robert, 31, 39, 171; in February Rev., 33–4, 35; and Louis Philippe, 33, 36; and Provisional Government, 63

Bulletin de la République, 89, 115

Cabet, Étienne, 18, 19, 61, 71, 83; in May demonstration, 123; philosophy of, 214–15; in Popular Ed. Assoc., 100, 213

Cabinetmaker of faubourg Saint-Antoine, 5, 6, 18, 19, 79, 159; vs. hosier, 82, 170; in June Rev., 137, 153, 156

Cail, Jean François, 70, 136

Canard, Le, 194

Carbonarists, 14, 57, 106, 113, 212–214

Carnot, Hippolyte, 22, 54, 57, 99, 113–14, 212

Cassou, Jean, 205

Caussidière, Marc, 24, 45, 79, 93, 172; in April elections, 88, 92,

99; in Assembly, 103, 111, 112; exiled, 157, 200; in June elections, 129; on June Rev., 156; memoirs of, 124, 196; on Poland, 117; as Police Prefect, 57–9, 114, 126

Caution money, 157

Cavaignac, General Eugène, 3, 54, 60, 101, 149–50, 178; in Assembly, 107, 130; dictator, 157–195; in June Rev., 137–44, 147, 154–5; and Poland, 117; Proudhon on, 155–6, 157; in War Office, 114

Cavaignac, Godefroy, 51, 54

Cazy, Admiral, 114, 141

Chamber of Deputies, 13, 19, 20, 27–8, 46–9

Chancel, Napoléon, 78, 120

Changarnier, General Nicolas, 63, 90, 129, 157

Charamaule, Hippolyte, 162

Charbonnel, Félix, 152, 178

Charbonnerie: see Carbonarists

Charras, Lieutenant Colonel, 114

Château, the, 16, 38, 41

Château d'Eau, 38, 135

Chevalier de Maison-Rouge, Le, 18

Chevalier, Michel, 218

Choiseul-Praslin, Duchess of, 22

Cholera, 193

Choses vues, 134

Club de l'Avenir, 163

Clubs of Despair, 128

Colet, Louise, 8

Commissaire, Sébastien, 55

Committee on the Constitution, 108

Committee of the rue de Poitiers, 159

Communist Manifesto, 206

Communists, 18, 61, 92, 212

Comte, Auguste, 216

Concord, Feast of, 125, 163

Considérant, Victor, 11, 69, 71, 100, 212, 221

Conspiration pour l'Égalité, dite de Babeuf, La, 79

Constitutionnel, 98, 164

Constituent Assembly, 50, 78, 94, 102; Caussidière in, 103, 111, 112; Cavaignac and, 107, 130; Constitution of, 157–8; Corbon in, 106–7; elections to, 97–101; extremists in, 115, 118; Garnier-Pagès in, 110, 147; in June Rev., 145; Labor Committee of, 101; and Lamartine, 131; leadership of, 105–8, 109–14; Ledru-Rollin in, 109–10; Luxembourg Commission, 110, 116; Marie in, 110; Marrast in, 114, 127, 157; and May demonstration, 127; mechanic and, 115; National party in, 110, 112, 127; and Poland, 117, 118, 119; work of, 102–4

Corbon, 55, 94, 99, 101, 114, 202; in Assembly, 106–7; in June Rev., 145–6

Corcelles, François de, 173

Cormenin, Vicomte de, 107–8

Courant, Lieutenant Colonel, 30

Cournet, Frédéric, 175

Courtais, Vicomte de (also General), 54, 103; imprisoned, 126; and May demonstration, 118, 124–5; as National Guard commander, 87, 88

Cousin, Victor, 224

Coutant, Jean Baptiste, 6, 220

Crémieux, Adolphe, 8, 41, 48, 50, 187–9; as Justice Minister, 114; in Provisional Government, 53, 99, 103

Damesme, General Édouard, 139, 141, 142, 149

Davaud, Abel, 175

Delahodde, Lucien, 59

Delezcluze, Charles, 163

Démocratie pacifique, La, 11, 212

Demonstrations, 81–2, 88, 89, 90–1; May, 118–21, 122, 123, 124–5, 127, 129

Deputies, Chamber of: see Chamber of Deputies

Deschamps, Frédéric, 65, 78, 97

Dommanget, Maurice, 87

Druet-Desvaux, Jacques, 154

Du Camp, Maxime, 25, 30, 62, 126

Duchâtel, Count, 12, 13, 17, 22, 86; resigns, 27, 28

Duchêne, Georges, 204

Duclerc, Charles, 112, 148, 157

Dufaure, Jules, 158

Dumas, Alexandre, 18, 49, 99

Dupont, Pierre, 160, 205, 210

Dupont de l'Eure, Jacques Charles, 51, 53, 99, 127, 184–5

Dupont-White, Charles Brook, 69

Duprat, Pascal, 147–8, 157

Duvergier de Hauranne, Prosper, 7, 8, 17, 38, 81, 150

Duvivier, General Franciade Fleurus, 90, 99, 143, 149, 150–1

Dynastics (party), 20, 29, 45, 48

École Polytechnique, 37

Education, 77–9, 100

Education, Minister of, 54, 99, 113

Éducation sentimentale, L', 62, 75, 206

Elections, 79–81, 87, 95; April, 96–100; Caussidière in, 88, 92, 99; Garnier-Pagès in, 99; Lamartine and, 80, 89, 99, 159; Marie in, 89, 99; National party in, 88, 89, 98–100; June, 129; September, 159

Enfantin, Prosper, 216–17

Engels, Frederic, 206

Executive Commission, 108–11, 115, 128, 131, 147–8

Falloux, Count of, 128, 145–6

Families, the, 46

Fauvelle-Delabarre, 35–7

Favre, Jules, 111, 127, 148

Feast of Fraternity, the, 93–4, 115

February Revolution, 5–52; barricades in, 31, 35, 45; Barrot in, 9 ff., 13 ff., 17, 20, 29, 37; Bedeau in, 34, 35, 36–7; Blanc in, 9, 50; Bugeaud in, 33–4, 35; Chamber of Deputies in, 27–8, 46–9; First Day of, 17–23; Guizot and, 20, 27, 28, 29; hosier in, 53, 81–2, 92; Hôtel de Ville in, 50, 53; Louis Philippe in, 16, 17, 21, 22, 25, 29; Le National in, 30, 44–5, 48; Municipal Guard in, 26–7, 37, 38; National Guard in, 11, 12, 22, 24–6, 27; Second Day of, 24–32; Thiers in, 31–2, 35, 38–9; Third Day of, 33–52; workers in, 46

Feudalism, 210–12

Finance, 72–4

Finance, Minister of, 54, 61, 72; Duclerc as, 112; Garnier-Pagès as, 73–4; Goudchaux as, 157

Five Hundred, the, 107, 184

Flaubert, Gustave, 8, 9, 62, 75, 205, 206

Flocon, Ferdinand, 7, 45, 201–2, in June Rev., 146; and National Guard, 116; in Provisional Government, 51, 53, 99; in Trade Ministry, 112

Flotte, Paul de, 175

Foreign Affairs, Minister of, 19, 22, 29; Bastide as, 113, 120, 146; Lamartine as, 53, 74–7

Forty-five-centime tax, 74

Fould, Achille, 72, 73

Fourier, Charles, 11, 206, 212, 220–224

Frederick William IV, King of Prussia, 77

Freedom of the press, 77

Friant, General, 25

Friends of the People, The, 166, 212

Froussard, Jean Baptiste, 121

Galy-Cazalet, Antoine, 154
Gambetta, Léon, 158, 163
Garde mobile, 59; in April demonstration, 90–1; in June Rev., 135, 140, 152, 180, 181
Garnier-Pagès, Louis Antoine, 31, 43, 45, 54; in Assembly, 110, 147; and Caussidière, 59; and elections, 99; in June Rev., 141; as Finance Minister, 73–4; and National Workshops, 66, 126; in Provisional Government, 51, 53, 84, 92
Gazette de France, 7
Genoude, Abbé de, 7
Gérard, Marshall, 16, 21, 42, 97, 200; Plan, 21–2
Girardin, Émile, 39–40, 60
Girondins, 18
Goudchaux, Michel, 54, 57, 61, 189–90; and Bank of France, 72, 73; as Finance Minister, 157
Grand Conseil des Communes de France, 158
Guéroult, Adolphe, 220
Guinard, Joseph, 107, 127, 142, 165, 167
Guizot, François, 6, 7, 12, 40, 74, 81; and February Rev., 20, 27, 28, 29; and National Guard, 16, 25–6; and reformist banquet, 10, 17
Guyot, Raymond, 168

Hélène, Princess: see Orleans, Duchess of
Histoire de la Seconde République française, 66, 93
Histoire de Quarante-Huit, 192
Histoire des Girondins, 84
Histoire du parti républicain en France, 171

Histoire parlementaire de la Révolution française, 106
Histoire populaire de la Révolution, 213
Hortense, Queen of France, 129
Hosier of faubourg Saint-Denis, 5, 6; after February Rev., 53, 81–2, 92; in June Rev., 156; in National Guard, 17, 124, 134, 170
Hôtel de Ville, 34, 37, 122; in February Rev., 50, 53; in June Rev., 136, 139
Huber, Aloysius, 121, 122–3, 133
Hugo, Victor, 30, 40, 102, 107, 166, 195; on the barricades, 134, 135, 151, 163, 168–9, 172; in June elections, 129; in politics, 162

Icaria, 19, 214–15
Ideologies, 203–30; art for art's sake, 205; communism, 212; feudalism, 210–12; Fourier, 220–4; Icaria, 214–15; Leroux, 224–5; Marx, 206–8; Proudhon, 225–9; Saint-Simon, 216–20
Interior, Minister of, 12, 22, 43, 87, 89; Dufaure as, 158; Ledru-Rollin as, 53; Recurt as, 111, 132; Sénard as, 157
Italie, Barrière d', 137, 152
Italy, 74, 76

Jacobins, 46, 71
Jacqueminot, General, 22, 24–5, 31
Jaquemet, 179
Jeanne, 170
Joigneaux, Pierre, 210, 211
Joinville, Prince of, 63
Journal des Débats, 98
June Revolution, 133–56; aftermath, 156–60; barricades in, 136–

137, 151, 156; Bedeau in, 139, 141–2, 143, 180; cabinetmaker in, 137, 153, 156; Caussidière in, 156; Cavaignac in, 137–44, 147, 154–5; Constituent Assembly and, 145; Corbon in, 145–6; First Day of, 133–45; Flocon, 146; garde mobile, 135, 140, 152, 180, 181; Garnier-Pagès, 141; hosier, 156; Hôtel de Ville, 136, 139; Lamartine, 141; Lamoricière, 137–8; 139, 140, 142, 149, 150, 154; Ledru-Rollin, 140–1, 153; Marrast, 136, 142; mechanic, 156; National Guard, 134, 137, 138, 144, 153; Second Day, 145–150; Sénard, 147, 154, 155; Thiers, 149; Third Day, 150–6; workers in, 133, 136, 137, 139, 153

Justice, Ministry of, 114, 184

Keeper of the Seals, 12, 157

Labor Committee, 128
Labor Laws, 64–6
Lacordaire, Jean, 102, 103
La Gorce, Pierre de, 66, 93, 134, 178
Lagrange, Charles, 30, 46, 57, 129
Lalanne, Léon, 128, 150
Lamarque, General Jean Maximin, 166–7, 194
Lamartine, Alphonse de, 14, 15, 30, 46, 52, 87; in Assembly, 108, 113, 120, 131; and elections, 80, 89, 99, 159; as Foreign Affairs Minister, 53, 74–7; in June Rev., 141; and Louis Napoleon, 130–1; and May demonstrations, 124; and National Guard, 90; National Work-Shops, 68; and the people, 84–6, 119, 121; personality of, 185–7; in Provisional Govern-
ment, 47–8, 49, 53, 55, 56, 61; resigns, 148

Lamennais, Jean, 99, 102, 122
Lamoricière, General Louis de, 39, 41–2, 135; in June Rev., 137–8, 139, 140, 142, 149, 150, 154; as War Minister, 157
Larabit, Marc, 154, 155
La Rochejaquelein, Henri de, 7, 48, 63
Lafayette, General, 121, 166
Lafayette, Georges, 121
League of the Just, 176
Lebey, André, 202
Lebreton, General, 148, 150, 154
Leclerc, 134, 135, 144
Ledru-Rollin, Alexandre Auguste, 7, 11, 45, 126, 128, 190–4; in Assembly, 109–10; and demonstrators, 91–2, 119; and elections, 79, 80, 88–9, 99, 100; in Executive Commission, 111; in June Rev., 140–1, 153; in May demonstrations, 123, 124; in Provisional Government, 48, 49, 50, 78, 84
Lefebvre, Georges, 73
Le Play, Pierre, 69
Legitimists, 7, 63, 99
Legislative Assembly, 98, 158
Leopold I, King of Belgium, 76
Léotade, Brother, 18
Leroux, Pierre, 71, 100, 123, 129, 156, 224–5
Lesseps, Ferdinand de, 218
Lhuys, Drouyn de, 20
Lieven, Princess of, 12
Lireux, Auguste, 47
Lisle, Leconte de, 205
Louis Philippe, 6, 12, 74, 86, 169, 170; abdication of, 38–44; and Barrot, 39, 42; and Bugeaud, 33, 36; in February Rev., 16, 17, 21, 22, 25, 29; asked to resign, 27–8; and Thiers, 31–2, 35
Luxembourg Commission, 69, 70–1, 87, 101; and Assembly, 110, 116

Lyons, 30, 57, 153, 171

Malthusians, 12
Marcus: see Caussidière, Marc
Marie Amélie, Queen of France, 17, 27, 41
Marie, Pierre, 44, 45, 86, 87, 141; in April elections, 89, 99; and Assembly, 110; Keeper of Seals, 157; in Provisional Government, 47–8, 53; as Public Works Minister, 54, 66, 68; and Pujol, 133
Marmont, General Auguste, 165
Marrast, Armand, 11, 12, 13, 14, 17, 45; in Assembly, 114, 127, 157; and elections, 99; in June Rev., 136, 142; as mayor, 123, 124; and National Guard, 82; and the people, 86, 87; personality of, 194–6; in Provisional Government, 49, 53, 55, 68, 73, 85; and Trouvé-Chanel, 126
Martignac, Jean de, 164
Martin, Alexandre: see Albert
Martin ou l'Enfant trouvé, 213
Marx, Karl, 165, 176, 206–8
Maugeret, Alexandre, 145
Mechanic of La Chapelle, 5, 19, 79, 82, 159; and Assembly, 115; and Blanqui, 83–4; in June Rev., 156
Mémoire sur la propriété, 226
Ménards, Raymond des, 154
Méry, Jules, 209
Meunier d'Angibault, Le, 205, 217
Michelet, Jules, 106, 167
Misérables, Les, 168–9
Molé, Count, 28, 31
Moniteur, Le, 55, 70
Montagnards, 58–8, 99, 126
Montagnards de Belleville, 140
Montalembert, Charles de, 102
Montépin, Xavier de, 194
Montpensier, Duke of, 39, 41
Mony, Stéphane, 218
Mourir pour la patrie, 18

Municipal Guard, 20, 21, 26–7, 37, 38

Nadaud, Martin, 176
National Guards, 3, 16, 31, 37, 104, 170; Barrot and, 25; Bugeaud and, 34, 39; Courtais in, 87, 88; election, 87, 88–9; in February Rev., 11, 12, 22, 24–6, 27; Flocon and, 116; in Gérard Plan, 21; hosier in, 17, 124, 134, 170; in June Rev., 134, 137, 138, 144, 153, 157; Lamartine and, 90; Marrast and, 82; in Polish demonstrations, 119, 124; provincial, 116–17, 153; and Provisional Government, 81–3, 87, 90, 93; Recourt and, 116
National, Le, 7, 11, 17, 18, 54, 170; in February Rev., 30, 44–5, 48, 53; party of, 44–5, 50, 51, 107; in April election, 88, 89, 98–100; in Assembly, 110, 112, 127; in Provisional Government, 55–7, 68
National Workshops, 66–8, 86, 128, 145; creation of, 72; dissolution of, 132–3; Garnier-Pagès and, 66, 126; "Les Amis" in, 166; Recurt and, 132; Réforme and, 68
Navy, Minister of, 54
Ne criez pas à bas les communistes, 92
Négrier, General François, 151, 152, 178
Nemours, Duke of, 22, 39, 40, 47
Nitot, Père, 5, 10
Normanby, Lord, 121, 146
Nouvelle Héloïse, La, 214
Nuits de veille d'un prisonnier d'état, 122

Ollivier, Démosthène, 103
Ollivier, Émile, 65, 78, 153
Opinion nationale, L', 220

Organisation du travail, L', 67, 150, 196, 224

Orleanists, 7, 13, 93, 99, 159

Orleans, Duchess of, 40–1, 47, 48

Ozanam, Frédéric, 177

Pages d'histoire de la Révolution de Février, 196

Pagnerre, Laurent, 44, 45, 93, 110, 147

Paris, Count of, 40, 41, 42, 47–8

Pascal, typographer, 54

Patrie, La, 72

Pecqueur, Constantin, 69, 70

Pentarchs: see Executive Commission

Perdiguier, Agricol, 114

Perrot, General Benjamin Pierre, 151, 152, 154, 155, 178

Petit, General, 60

Peupin, 101, 107, 114

Poland, 74, 76, 77, 166; demonstration for, 118–19, 120; envoys from, 117

Police, Prefect of, 13, 16, 24; Caussidière as, 57–9, 114, 126

Pompières, Labbey de, 14

Presse, La, 39, 40

Progressif de l'Aube, 154

Proudhon, Pierre, 65, 66, 69, 71, 102, 113; on Cavaignac, 155–6, 157; on Huber, 122; in June elections, 129; on Louis Napoleon, 159; philosophy of, 225–9

Provisional Government, 4, 53; Blanc in, 51, 53, 54, 56, 86, 101; Blanqui and, 90; Bugeaud and, 63; Crémieux in, 53, 99, 103, 187–9; education, 77–8; elections, 79–81, 87, 95, 96–100; finance, 72–4; Flocon in, 51, 53, 99; Garnier-Pagès in, 51, 53, 84, 92; labor, 63–72; Lamartine in, 47–8, 49, 53, 55, 56, 61; Ledru-Rollin

in, 48, 49, 50, 78, 89; Marie in, 47–8, 53; Marrast in, 49, 53, 55, 68, 73, 85; and National Guard, 81–3, 87, 90, 93; National party in, 55–7, 68; problems of, 63–101; *Réforme* in, 45, 56, 58; workers and, 71, 91

Prudhommeaux, Jules, 214

Public Works, Minister of, 54, 66, 68, 111, 128, 158

Pujol, Louis, 133

Railroads, 145

Rambuteau, 22–3, 26, 27

Rapatel, General, 140

Raspail, François, 46, 57, 100, 112, 115, 129; as agitator, 115, 116, 117, 119, 121; in the barricades, 165; as editor, 62, 87–8; on the Feast of Fraternity, 93–4; in May demonstration, 123; in September elections, 159

Recurt, 105, 117, 126, 137, 157; in Assembly, 106, 111; and National Guard, 116; and National Workshops, 132

Red flag, 61, 109, 151, 167

Réforme, La, 7, 9, 11, 15, 16, 18; in Provisional Government, 45, 56, 58; and National Workshops, 68; party, 45, 56

Regnault, Elias, 89, 186

Regnault, General, 151

Rémusat, Charles, 35

Repartition des richesses, La, 69

Représentant du Peuple, Le, 129

Republicans, 98–9

Révolution sociale démontrée par le coup d'état, La, 228

Revue nationale, La, 113

Revue retrospective, La, 87

Rey, Colonel, 123, 124

Right of Assembly, 77

Rights of Man, The, 19, 46, 126, 229

Rittinghausen, 228–9
Robespierre, Maximilian, 18, 210, 211
Rochechouart, 136
Rolland, Romain, 197
Rothschild, 60, 189
Rouen, 8, 9, 97, 107
Ruche populaire, La, 6, 220

Saint-Simon, 106, 206, 216–20
Salic Law, 41
Sallandrouze, 16
Sand, George, 89, 115, 205, 217
Saussure, Madame de, 205
Schoelcher, Victor, 162, 163
Seasons, the, 19, 55, 58, 171, 176
Sébastiani, General Tiburce, 22, 31, 34, 37, 38
Second Republic, 10, 44, 49–50; feelings about, 62, proclaimed, 52; Provisional Government of, 63–101
Secret societies, 19, 46, 57
Sénard, Antoine, 8, 97, 107, 127; as Interior Minister, 157; in June Rev., 147, 154, 155
Siècle, Le, 15, 16, 18, 21, 107, 170
Slavery, 77
Sobrier, M. J. C., 58, 83–4, 120
Soccas, 31
Socialists, 7, 206; of La Réforme, 56; of Limoges, 96–7; mechanics, 136
Société des Amis du Peuple, 112
Soult, Marshal Nicolas, 42
Spiridion, 205, 227
Spuller, Eugène, 191, 192
Staël, Madame de, 205
Stamp tax, 77
Stern, Daniel, 29, 51, 61, 104, 175; on Affre, 176–9, 180; on Feast of Concord, 125; on Ledru-Rollin, 191; on Polish demonstration, 118
Strasbourg, Martin de, 45, 50

Subervie, Baron, 53
Sue, Eugène, 135, 213
Suffrage, 7, 8; and education, 77–8; elections, 79–81; 87, 95, 96–100

Talabot, Paulin, 218
Taschereau, Jules, 10, 87, 88
Thiers, Louis, 20, 28, 29, 102, 155, 167; Barrot and, 35; in February Rev., 31–2, 35, 38–9; in June elections, 129; in June Rev., 149; and Louis Napoleon, 159; and Louis Philippe, 31–2, 35
Thomas, Clément, 126, 127
Thomas, Émile, 66–7, 68, 128
Thoré, Théophile, 123–4
Timon: see Cormenin, Vicomte de
Tocqueville, Alexis de, 35, 173; on the Assembly, 147–8; on Barrot, 43; on Bedeau, 141–2; on Marrast, 195
Trade, Ministry of, 112, 146
Trade unions, 64
Traité de la charité dan ses rapports avec l'économie sociale, 12
Travailleur de la mère Duchêne, Le, 125–6
Treasury: see Finance, Minister of
Trélat, Ulysse, 111–12, 128, 152
Trochu, Louis Jules, 33–4

Union Électorale, 135

Vivien, Alexandre, 158
Voyage en Icarie, Le, 18, 213, 214
Voyage et Aventures de lord William Carisdall, 214
Vraie République, La, 124

War, Minister of, 53, 114, 141, 157
Waterloo, Battle of, 166

Wellington, Duke of, 166, 184

Weill, Georges, 171, 184

Wolowski, L. F. M., 69, 117, 118–119

Workers, 7, 8, 9; Albert, 55; and the Executive Commission, 115; in February Rev., 46; vs. industrialists, 60–1; in June Rev., 133, 136, 137, 139, 153; and labor laws, 64–9; of Limoges, 96–7; and Provisional Government, 71, 91

Zola, Émile, 136

VINTAGE CRITICISM,
LITERATURE, MUSIC, AND ART

V-418 AUDEN, W. H. *The Dyer's Hand*
V-398 AUDEN, W. H. *The Enchàfed Flood*
V-269 BLOTNER, JOSEPH and FREDERICK GWYNN (eds.) *Faulkner at the University*
V-259 BUCKLEY, JEROME H. *The Victorian Temper*
V-51   BURKE, KENNETH *The Philosophy of Literary Form*
V-643 CARLISLE, OLGA *Poets on Streetcorners: Portraits of Fifteen Russian Poets*
V-569 CARTEY, WILFRED *Whispers from a Continent: The Literature of Contemporary Black Africa*
V-75   CAMUS, ALBERT *The Myth of Sisyphus and other Essays*
V-626 CAMUS, ALBERT *Lyrical and Critical Essays*
V-535 EISEN, JONATHAN *The Age of Rock: Sounds of the American Cultural Revolution*
V-655 EISEN, JONATHAN *The Age of Rock 2*
V-4   EINSTEIN, ALFRED *A Short History of Music*
V-632 ELLMAN, RICHARD (ed.) *The Artist as Critic: Critical Writings of Oscar Wilde*
V-13   GILBERT, STUART *James Joyce's Ulysses*
V-646 GILMAN, RICHARD *The Confusion of Realms*
V-363 GOLDWATER, ROBERT *Primitivism in Modern Art*, Revised Edition
V-114 HAUSER, ARNOLD *Social History of Art*, Vol. I
V-115 HAUSER, ARNOLD *Social History of Art*, Vol. II
V-116 HAUSER, ARNOLD *Social History of Art*, Vol. III
V-117 HAUSER, ARNOLD *Social History of Art*, Vol. IV
V-438 HELLER, ERICH *The Artist's Journey into the Interior and Other Essays*
V-213 HOWE, IRVING *William Faulkner: A Critical Study*
V-20   HYMAN, S. E. *The Armed Vision*
V-12   JARRELL, RANDALL *Poetry and the Age*
V-88   KERMAN, JOSEPH *Opera as Drama*
V-260 KERMODE, FRANK *The Romantic Image*
V-581 KRAMER, JANE *Allen Ginsberg in America*
V-452 KESSLE, GUN, photographs by, and JAN MYRDAL *Angkor*
V-83   KRONENBERGER, LOUIS *Kings and Desperate Men*
V-677 LESTER, JULIUS *The Seventh Son*, Vol. I
V-678 LESTER, JULIUS *The Seventh Son*, Vol. II
V-90   LEVIN, HARRY *The Power of Blackness: Hawthorne, Poe, Melville*
V-296 MACDONALD, DWIGHT *Against the American Grain*
V-55   MANN, THOMAS *Essays*
V-720 MIRSKY, D. S. *A History of Russian Literature*
V-344 MUCHNIC, HELEN *From Gorky to Pasternak*
V-452 MYRDAL, JAN and photographs by GUN KESSLE *Angkor*
V-118 NEWMAN, ERNEST *Great Operas*, Vol. I
V-119 NEWMAN, ERNEST *Great Operas*, Vol. II
V-24   RANSOM, JOHN CROWE *Poems and Essays*
V-108 SHAHN, BEN *The Shape of Content*
V-415 SHATTUCK, ROGER *The Banquet Years*, Revised
V-186 STEINER, GEORGE *Tolstoy or Dostoevsky*
V-278 STEVENS, WALLACE *The Necessary Angel*
V-39   STRAVINSKY, IGOR *The Poetics of Music*

V-100   SULLIVAN, J. W. N.   *Beethoven: His Spiritual Development*

V-243   SYPHER, WYLIE (ed.)   *Art History: An Anthology of Modern Criticism*

V-266   SYPHER, WYLIE   *Loss of the Self*

V-229   SYPHER, WYLIE   *Rococo to Cubism*

V-458   SYPHER, WYLIE   *Literature and Technology*

V-166   SZE, MAI-MAI   *The Way of Chinese Painting*

V-162   TILLYARD, E. M. W.   *The Elizabethan World Picture*

V-35   TINDALL, WILLIAM YORK   *Forces in Modern British Literature*

V-194   VALERY, PAUL   *The Art of Poetry*

V-347   WARREN, ROBERT PENN   *Selected Essays*

V-218   WILSON, EDMUND   *Classics & Commercials*

V-360   WIMSATT, W. and C. BROOKS   *Literary Criticism*

V-500   WIND, EDGAR   *Art and Anarchy*

V-546   YATES, FRANCES A.   *Giordano Bruno and the Hermetic Tradition*